Building Web Services with Microsoft Azure

Quickly develop scalable, REST-based applications or services and learn how to manage them using Microsoft Azure

Alex Belotserkovskiy

Stephen Kaufman

Nikhil Sachdeva

BIRMINGHAM - MUMBAI

Building Web Services with Microsoft Azure

First published: May 2015

Production reference: 1220515

Published by Packt Publishing Ltd.
Livery Place
35 Livery Street
Birmingham B3 2PB, UK.

ISBN 978-1-78439-837-8

www.packtpub.com

Credits

Authors
Alex Belotserkovskiy
Stephen Kaufman
Nikhil Sachdeva

Reviewers
Harsh
Alon Fliess
Harshwardhan Joshi

Commissioning Editor
Kunal Parikh

Acquisition Editors
James Jones
Greg Wild

Content Development Editor
Akashdeep Kundu

Technical Editor
Mrunmayee Patil

Copy Editors
Pranjali Chury
Brandt D'Mello

Project Coordinator
Milton Dsouza

Proofreaders
Stephen Copestake
Safis Editing

Indexer
Monica Ajmera Mehta

Production Coordinator
Arvindkumar Gupta

Cover Work
Arvindkumar Gupta

About the Authors

Alex Belotserkovskiy is a technical evangelist for Microsoft Russia and lives in Moscow. He specializes in cloud, Internet of Things, and high performance computing topics. Alex is actively engaged in both local and international speaking activities, and works with top customers and partners to provide professional technical and technological support for their cloud projects.

Alex was the first Russian Windows Azure Most Valuable Professional, in 2012, and is a Microsoft certified developer and enterprise administrator. He is an experienced Microsoft technologies instructor.

I would like to thank my fiancee, Olga Vilkhivskaya, for putting up with my late night writing sessions and ideas. I would also like to express deep gratitude to Andrey Ivashentsev, Technical Evangelism Unit Lead for Microsoft Russia, without whose efforts this book would not have happened. Alexey Bokov, Technical Evangelist in Microsoft, has my gratitude for continuing to give me valuable experience and advice on how to do things in a better manner.

Stephen Kaufman works for Microsoft as a solution architect in the Americas Office of the CTO and is the lead architect for the US Azure PaaS Center of Expertise (CoE).

He is a public speaker and has appeared at a variety of industry conferences nationally and internationally at events, such as TechEd North America, TechEd EMEA, Microsoft SOA and BPM conference, as well as many internal Microsoft conferences over the years discussing application development, integration, and cloud computing, as well as a variety of other related topics.

Stephen is also a published author with two books—*Pro BizTalk 2009* (`http://www.apress.com/book/view/1430219815`) and *Pro Windows Server AppFabric* (`http://www.apress.com/book/view/1430228172`), both by *Apress Publishing*—as well as a number of whitepapers and other published content, including a blog at `http://blogs.msdn.com/skaufman`.

In addition, he is a board certified architect (CITA-P-IASA Global) and continues to work mentoring and sitting on architecture certification review boards.

Lastly, Stephen was a contributing author for the Azure Architecture Certification Exam 70-534, Architecting Azure Solutions.

Nikhil Sachdeva is a senior consultant at Microsoft. He has over 11 years of experience in architecting and implementing scalable web applications and services using Microsoft technologies. He has been involved with Microsoft Azure since its early days and currently works as a subject matter expert in building custom Platform as a Service (PaaS) solutions on the Azure platform. He has a passion for writing and is a contributing writer for *Introducing Windows Azure for IT Professionals*, *Microsoft Press*, and has contributed to several other Microsoft articles and blogs on Microsoft Azure and related technologies. His recent passion is building highly scalable and available solutions for the Internet of Things (IoT) and frequently rants his experiences at `http://connectedstuff.net`.

I would like to thank my beautiful wife, Pratibha, for encouraging me to pursue my passion for writing and supporting me throughout the process. Thanks for being my support system, my buddy, my critic, and for giving me the best gift of life, our newborn son, Ayansh. A special thanks to the team at Packt Publishing for their continuous support and patience.

About the Reviewers

Harsh works as a software engineer for Microsoft. He has worked on quite a few things and he feels that it still hasn't been enough for his exploration and he should keep trying new technologies and keep learning.

Besides his interest in cloud computing (read Azure) and programming in general, he likes reading and fiddling with CTF questions and ciphers. He started the HackCon (Build the Shield) event in Microsoft, which is Microsoft's version of Capture the Flag events. He is also a moody blogger and tries to keep his portfolio up to date. You can find him at `http://hars.in`.

I would like to thank my friends and colleagues from whom I learn every day.

Alon Fliess is the chief architect and founder of CodeValue. He got his BSc degree in electrical and computer engineering from Technion, the Israel Institute of Technology. He is also recognized as a Microsoft Regional Director (MRD). He is an expert in many technologies, be it Windows internals, C++ Windows programming (Win32/WinRT), .NET with C#, Windows Azure Cloud Computing, or Internet of Things (hardware and software).

Alon spends his time doing many interesting tasks such as software architecting, designing, mentoring, and programming. He is the author and technical reviewer of several computing books. Alon is an active member of several Patterns & Practices councils, among them is project Hilo—a Windows Store Application in C++/CX and XAML.

He is one of the experts in the Microsoft Israel community. He helps Microsoft clients in many technological aspects. He gives lectures at Israeli and international conferences, such as NDC, CVCon, TechEd, and more.

To Deepti Thore, who gave me the chance to review this book, and to Milton Dsouza, who had the patience to wait for me to complete the review—thank you both.

To my beloved wife, Liat, and my three children, Yarden, Saar, and Adva, thank you for all your understanding and support.

Harshwardhan Joshi lives and works in Pune and loves spending time with his wife, and pet cat named "Hulk". He calls himself "a Cloud engineer who writes APIs for a living". He has been passionately working on several Microsoft technologies from .NET Framework, Microsoft Silverlight, WF, and WCF to Microsoft Azure for the last 7 years and has worked on creating several exciting products. He has been working on Microsoft Azure since its inception. He currently works with RapidCircle as a Cloud Consultant. In his previous stint with Icertis, he was one of the core members responsible for building highly scalable, always available, and high performance APIs on Microsoft Azure.

You can meet him at events organized by the Pune User Group, a group for avid developers in Microsoft Technologies in Pune. He stays updated on the latest cars and engines hitting the market. He is a regular contributor to the Team-BHP forum. He can also be found on Twitter at `@hjoshi`.

Thanks to Packt Publishing for this amazing opportunity to review this book on Microsoft Azure. I hope you all enjoy reading this book as much as I enjoyed working on it. I would also like to thank my family and friends for being extremely supportive.

www.PacktPub.com

Support files, eBooks, discount offers, and more

For support files and downloads related to your book, please visit `www.PacktPub.com`.

Did you know that Packt offers eBook versions of every book published, with PDF and ePub files available? You can upgrade to the eBook version at `www.PacktPub.com` and as a print book customer, you are entitled to a discount on the eBook copy. Get in touch with us at `service@packtpub.com` for more details.

At `www.PacktPub.com`, you can also read a collection of free technical articles, sign up for a range of free newsletters and receive exclusive discounts and offers on Packt books and eBooks.

`https://www2.packtpub.com/books/subscription/packtlib`

Do you need instant solutions to your IT questions? PacktLib is Packt's online digital book library. Here, you can search, access, and read Packt's entire library of books.

Why subscribe?

- Fully searchable across every book published by Packt
- Copy and paste, print, and bookmark content
- On demand and accessible via a web browser

Free access for Packt account holders

If you have an account with Packt at `www.PacktPub.com`, you can use this to access PacktLib today and view 9 entirely free books. Simply use your login credentials for immediate access.

Table of Contents

Preface

With multiple cloud platforms out there, it is easy to get confused when making a technology decision for your projects. This gets further complicated with the plethora of development tools and frameworks available today. Microsoft Azure simplifies this problem by providing a scalable and manageable platform for customers to easily deploy, monitor, and troubleshoot their cloud-based applications. Its seamless integration with new and existing Microsoft tools and inherent support for open source software makes it an obvious choice for building cloud-based applications and services.

Whether you are new to Microsoft Azure cloud development or you have been creating cloud applications, there will be something new for you in this book. We will cover the full application development architecture and cover all tiers of an application. We will also cover a number of patterns that you will encounter, from solutions that are completely hosted in the cloud to hybrid solutions where applications are split between the cloud and on-premises networks.

What this book covers

Chapter 1, Getting Started with the ASP.NET Web API, introduces the ASP.NET Web API framework and provides an overview of its application and internals. It will guide you through the stages of creating a Web API and deploying it in Microsoft Azure.

Chapter 2, Extending the ASP.NET Web API, discusses various extensibility and customization options available in the ASP.NET Web API framework. It guides the reader through various extension points, such as custom routing, message formatters, content negotiation, and securing a Web API. It also discusses various hosting options for deploying Web APIs.

Chapter 3, API Management, provides a set of tools that assist API developers in managing and monitoring Web APIs. We will discuss various options of publishing, marketing, monitoring, and managing a Web API using API management.

Chapter 4, Developing a Web API for Mobile Apps, provides an overview of Mobile Services and walks through a scenario of creating a Web API using Mobile Services. Mobile Services provides an easy-to-use environment to rapidly build cross-platform apps for Windows, iOS, Android, and other platforms. Its rich built-in capabilities for managing backend login, data, authentication, and notifications makes it a compelling option for developing mobile applications.

Chapter 5, Connecting Applications with Microsoft Azure Service Bus, discusses Windows Azure Service Bus, which allows for related and brokered messaging using a range of different features (such as Topics and Queues).

Chapter 6, Creating Hybrid Services, demonstrates how to create Hybrid Services to connect on-premises Large Object (LOB) / database to cloud-based applications. Essentially, this chapter builds on the previous chapter, demonstrating how you can use the elements of the Service Bus to create Hybrid applications. It will also demonstrate how to effectively maintain these applications.

Chapter 7, Data Services in the Cloud – an Overview of ADO.NET and Entity Framework, explores how to create data services in the cloud using Entity Framework and ADO.NET.

Chapter 8, Data Services in the Cloud – Microsoft Azure Storage, explores how you can use cloud-based Azure Storage technologies.

Chapter 9, Data Services in the Cloud – NoSQL in Microsoft Azure, explores how to use DocumentDB, a fully managed, highly scalable NoSQL data management service based on Azure, as well as ways to start using other open source Azure options such as MongoDB.

What you need for this book

The hardware requirements are as follows:

- 1.6 GHz or faster processor
- 1 GB of RAM (1.5 GB if running on a virtual machine)
- 10 GB (NTFS) of available hard disk space
- 5400 RPM hard drive
- DirectX 9 capable video card running at 1024 x 768 or higher display resolution

The software requirements and their download or purchase sources are mentioned in the following list:

- Windows 8.1 or greater at `http://www.microsoftstore.com/store/msusa/en_US/pdp/Windows-8.1/productID.288401200?tduid=e43fc220a3cc8877116cc4a027cb6456`
- You can also use your MSDN license to download a copy
- Visual Studio 2013 Community Edition or greater at `https://www.visualstudio.com/en-us/products/visual-studio-community-vs.aspx`

Note that the samples have only been tested on Visual Studio 2013 and not on Visual Studio 2015 preview.

- Azure SDK 2.5 at `https://www.microsoft.com/en-us/download/details.aspx?id=44938`
- Entity Framework at `https://www.nuget.org/packages/EntityFramework/6.1.1`
- Other helpful tools:
    - **Resharper**: `https://www.jetbrains.com/resharper/`
    - **Chrome Postman**: `https://chrome.google.com/webstore/detail/postman-rest-client-packa/fhbjgbiflinjbdggehcddcbncdddomop?hl=en`
    - **Fiddler**: `http://www.telerik.com/download/fiddler/fiddler4`
    - **Azure Storage Explorer**: `https://azurestorageexplorer.codeplex.com/`
    - **Service Bus Explorer**: `https://code.msdn.microsoft.com/windowsazure/service-bus-explorer-f2abca5a`

Who this book is for

If you are a developer or an architect who wants to develop end-to-end RESTful applications in the cloud, then this book is for you. You will need professional knowledge of C# to work through the projects in this book.

Conventions

In this book, you will find a number of text styles that distinguish between different kinds of information. Here are some examples of these styles and an explanation of their meaning.

Code words in text, database table names, folder names, filenames, file extensions, pathnames, dummy URLs, user input, and Twitter handles are shown as follows: " By default, the domain name is set to `azurewebsites.net`."

A block of code is set as follows:

```
async Task<int> GetContentLengthAsync(string uri)
{
    int contentLength;
    using (var client = new HttpClient())
    {
        var content = await client.GetStringAsync(uri);
        contentLength = content.Length;
    }

    return contentLength;
}
```

When we wish to draw your attention to a particular part of a code block, the relevant lines or items are set in bold:

```
public static void Register(HttpConfiguration config)
{
// Web API configuration and services
// Web API routes
config.MapHttpAttributeRoutes();
config.Routes.MapHttpRoute(
name: "DefaultApi",
routeTemplate: "api/{controller}/{id}",
defaults: new { id = RouteParameter.Optional }
);
}
```

Any command-line input or output is written as follows:

```
PM> Install-Package Microsoft.AspNet.WebApi
```

New terms and **important words** are shown in bold. Words that you see on the screen, for example, in menus or dialog boxes, appear in the text like this: "Click on **Publish** to open the Publish wizard, and select **Microsoft Azure Websites** as the publish target."

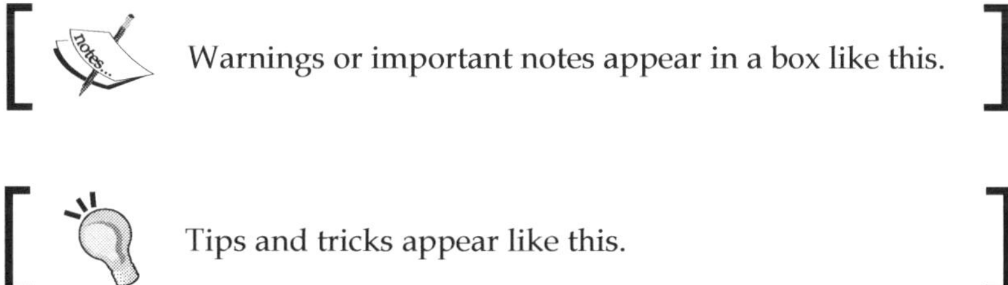

Warnings or important notes appear in a box like this.

Tips and tricks appear like this.

Reader feedback

Feedback from our readers is always welcome. Let us know what you think about this book—what you liked or disliked. Reader feedback is important for us as it helps us develop titles that you will really get the most out of.

To send us general feedback, simply e-mail `feedback@packtpub.com`, and mention the book's title in the subject of your message.

If there is a topic that you have expertise in and you are interested in either writing or contributing to a book, see our author guide at `www.packtpub.com/authors`.

Customer support

Now that you are the proud owner of a Packt book, we have a number of things to help you to get the most from your purchase.

Downloading the example code

You can download the example code files from your account at `http://www.packtpub.com` for all the Packt Publishing books you have purchased. If you purchased this book elsewhere, you can visit `http://www.packtpub.com/support` and register to have the files e-mailed directly to you.

Errata

Although we have taken every care to ensure the accuracy of our content, mistakes do happen. If you find a mistake in one of our books—maybe a mistake in the text or the code—we would be grateful if you could report this to us. By doing so, you can save other readers from frustration and help us improve subsequent versions of this book. If you find any errata, please report them by visiting `http://www.packtpub.com/submit-errata`, selecting your book, clicking on the **Errata Submission Form** link, and entering the details of your errata. Once your errata are verified, your submission will be accepted and the errata will be uploaded to our website or added to any list of existing errata under the Errata section of that title.

To view the previously submitted errata, go to `https://www.packtpub.com/books/content/support` and enter the name of the book in the search field. The required information will appear under the **Errata** section.

Piracy

Piracy of copyrighted material on the Internet is an ongoing problem across all media. At Packt, we take the protection of our copyright and licenses very seriously. If you come across any illegal copies of our works in any form on the Internet, please provide us with the location address or website name immediately so that we can pursue a remedy.

Please contact us at `copyright@packtpub.com` with a link to the suspected pirated material.

We appreciate your help in protecting our authors and our ability to bring you valuable content.

Questions

If you have a problem with any aspect of this book, you can contact us at `questions@packtpub.com`, and we will do our best to address the problem.

Introduction

Application Programming Interface (API) is not a new buzz word in the programming world. If we take a history tour of all programming languages ever developed, we will notice that any language that allowed software components to communicate and exchange information supports the notion of an API. An API can be as simple as defining a function in the procedural language such as C, or can be as complex as defining a protocol standard; while the structure and complexity of an API may be varied, the intent of an API mostly remains the same. Simply put, an API is a composition of a set of behaviors that perform some specific and deterministic tasks. Clients can then consume this API placing requests on any of the behaviors and expect appropriately formatted responses.

For example, consider the following code snippet that leverages the `System.IO.File` type in the .NET framework to read from a text file and print its contents in a console window:

```
static void Main(string[] args)
{
    string text = System.IO.File.ReadAllText
      (@"C:\MySample.txt");
    System.Console.WriteLine("Contents of MySample.txt =
      {0}", text);
}
```

In the preceding example, the `System.IO.File` type exposes a set of specific behaviors that a client can consume. The client invokes a request by providing the required input and gets back an expected response. The `System.IO.File` type acts like a third-party system that takes input and provides the desired response. Primarily, it relieves the client from writing the same logic and also relieves the client from worrying about the management of the `System.IO.File` source code. On the other hand, the developers of `System.IO.File` can protect their source from manipulations or access; well, not in this case because the .NET Framework source code is available under **Microsoft Reference Source License**. The bits for the .NET Framework source can be accessed at `https://github.com/Microsoft/dotnet`.

If we now take the preceding API definition and stitch it with a Web standard-like HTTP, we can say that:

A Web API is a composition of a set of behaviors that perform concrete and deterministic tasks in a stateless and distributed environment.

If this feels like a philosophical statement, we will look at a more technical definition when we delve in the ASP.NET Web API in the coming sections.

[Note that the semantics of a Web API do not necessarily require it to leverage HTTP as a protocol. However, since HTTP is the most widely used protocol for Web communication and unless some brilliant mind is working on a garage project to come up with an alternative, it is safe to assume that Web APIs are based on HTTP standards. In fact, Web APIs are also referred as **HTTP Services**.]

Before we get into the details of writing our own Web APIs, let's try consuming one; we will use the Bing Map API for our example:

Bing Maps provide a simple trial version of their **Map Web API** (`http://msdn.microsoft.com/en-us/library/ff701713.aspx`) that can be used for scenarios such as getting real-time traffic incident data, location, routes, and elevations. To access the API, we need a key that can be obtained by registering at the **Bing Maps Portal** (`https://www.bingmapsportal.com/`). We can then access information such as location details based on geo coordinates, address, and other parameters.

In the following example, we fetch the address location for the Microsoft headquarters in Redmond:

The response should look as follows:


```
{
    "authenticationResultCode":"ValidCredentials","brandLogoUri":
      "http:\/\/dev.virtualearth.net\/Branding\/
      logo_powered_by.png","copyright":"Copyright
      © 2015 Microsoft and its suppliers.
      All rights reserved. This API cannot be accessed
      and the content and any results may not be used,
      reproduced or transmitted in any manner without
      express written permission from Microsoft
      Corporation.","resourceSets":[{"estimatedTotal":1,
      "resources":[{"__type":"Location:http:\/\/
      schemas.microsoft.com\/search\/local\/ws\/rest\
      /v1","bbox":[47.636677282429325,
      -122.13698331308882,47.644402717570678,-
      122.12169668691118],"name":"Microsoft Way,
      Redmond, WA 98052","point":{"type":"Point",
      "coordinates":[47.64054,-122.12934]},
      "address":{"addressLine":"Microsoft Way",
      "adminDistrict":"WA","adminDistrict2":"King Co.",
      "countryRegion":"United States","formattedAddress":
      "Microsoft Way, Redmond, WA 98052",
      "locality":"Redmond","postalCode":"98052"},
      "confidence":"Medium","entityType":"Address",
      "geocodePoints":[{"type":"Point","coordinates":
      [47.64054,-122.12934],"calculationMethod":"Interpolation",
      "usageTypes":["Display","Route"]}],"matchCodes":
      ["Good"]}]}],"statusCode":200,"statusDescription":
      "OK","traceId":"a54a3e7f071b44e498af17b2b1dc596d
      |CH10020545|02.00.152.3000|CH1SCH050110320,
      CH1SCH060052346"
}
```

To run the preceding example, we use a Chrome browser extension called **Postman** (`https://chrome.google.com/webstore/detail/postman-rest-client/fdmmgilgnpjigdojojpjoooidkmcomcm?hl=en`). It provides a good GUI interface to allow executing HTTP Services from within the browser without writing any code. We will use Postman for examples in this book. However, other tools such as **Fiddler** (`http://www.telerik.com/fiddler`) can also be used.

We notice a few things here:

- We did not write a single line of code; in fact, we did not even open an IDE to make to call to the Web API. Yes, it is that easy!
- The Bing API presented the caller with a mechanism to uniquely access a resource through a URI and parameters. The client requested the resource and the API processed the request to produce a well-defined response.
- The example is simple but it is still accessed in a secure manner, the Bing API mandates that an API key be passed with the request and throws an unauthorized failure code if the key cannot validate the authenticity of the caller.

We talk in greater detail about how this request was processed earlier. However, there are two key technologies that enabled the execution of the preceding request, namely, HTTP and REST. We discuss these in greater details in this section.

To explore more free and premium API(s) you can take a look at `http://www.programmableweb.com/`. Programmable web is one of the largest directories of HTTP-based APIs and provides a comfortable and convenient way to discover and search APIs for Web and mobile application consumption.

Getting to know HTTP

Since we concluded in the previous section that Web APIs are based on HTTP, it is important to understand some of the fundamental constructs of HTTP before we delve into other details.

THE RFC 26163 specification published in June 1999 defines the **Hypertext Transfer Protocol** (**HTTP**) Version 1.1. The specification categorizes HTTP as a generic, stateless, application-level protocol for distributed, collaborative, and hypermedia information systems. The role of HTTP, for years, has been to access and handle especially when serving the Web documents over HTML. However, the specification allows the protocol to be used for building powerful APIs that can provide business and data services at hyperscale.

> A recent update to the HTTP 1.1 specification has divided the RFC 2616 specification into multiple RFCs. The list is available at `http://evertpot.com/http-11-updated/`.

An HTTP request/response

HTTP relies on a client-server exchange and defines a structure and definition for each request and response through a set of protocol parameters, message formats, and protocol method definitions.

A typical HTTP request/response interaction looks as follows:

The client made a request to fetch the contents of a resource located at **www.asp.net**, specifying to use HTTP Version **1.1** as the protocol. The server accepts the request and determines more information about the request from its headers, such as the type of request, media formatting, and resource identifier. The server then uses the input to process the results appropriately and returns a response. The response is accompanied by the content and a status code to denote completion of the request. The interaction between the client and server might involve intermediaries such as a proxy or gateway for message translation. However, the message request and response structures remain the same.

HTTP is a stateless protocol. Hence, if we attempt to make a request for the resource at the same address *n* times, the server will receive *n* unique requests and process them separately each time.

HTTP methods

In the preceding request, the first thing a server needs to determine is the type of request so that it can validate if the resource supports this request and can then serve it. The HTTP protocol provides a set of tokens called **methods** that indicate the operations performed on the resource.

Further, the protocol also attempts to designate these methods as **safe** and **idempotent**; the idea here is to make the request execution more predictable and standardized:

- A method is safe if the method execution does not result in an action that modifies the underlying resource; examples of such methods are `GET` and `HEAD`. On the other hand, actions such as `PUT`, `POST`, and `DELETE` are considered unsafe since they can modify the underlying resource.
- A method is idempotent if the side effects of any number of identical requests is the same as for a single request. For example `GET`, `PUT`, and `DELETE` share this property.

The following table summarizes the standard method definitions supported by HTTP Version 1.1 protocol specification:

Method	**Description**	**Safe**	**Idempotent**
`OPTIONS`	This represents the communication options for the target resource.	Yes	Yes
`GET`	This requests data from a specified resource.	Yes	Yes
`HEAD`	This is the same as `GET`, but transfers only the status and header back to the client instead of the complete response.	Yes	Yes
`POST`	This requests to send data to the server, typically evaluates a create request.	No	No
`PUT`	This requests to replace all current representation of the target resource, typically, generally evaluates an `Update` request.	No	Yes
`PATCH`	This applies a partial update to an object in an incremental way.	Yes	No

Method	Description	Safe	Idempotent
`DELETE`	This requests to remove all current representation of the target resource.	No	Yes
`TRACE`	This performs a message loop-back test (echo) along the path to the targeted resource.	Yes	Yes
`CONNECT`	This establishes a tunnel to the server identified by a given URI. This, for example, may allow the client to use the Web server as a proxy.	Yes	Yes

HTTP status codes

HTTP status codes are unique codes that a server returns based on how the request is processed. Status codes play a fundamental role in determining response success and failure especially when dealing with Web APIs. For example, `200 OK` means a generic success whereas `500` indicates an internal server error.

Status codes play a pivotal role while developing and debugging the Web API. It is important to understand the meaning of each status code and then define our responses appropriately. A list of all HTTP status codes is available at `http://en.wikipedia.org/wiki/List_of_HTTP_status_codes`.

Other HTTP goodies

From a Web API perspective, there are some other aspects of HTTP that we should consider.

Header field definitions

Header fields in HTTP allow the client and server to transfer metadata information to understand the request and response better; some key header definitions include:

Field	Description
`Accept`	This specifies certain attributes that are acceptable for a response. These headers can be used to provide specifications to the server on what type of response is expected, for example, `Accept: application/json` would expect a JSON response. Note that as per the HTTP guidelines, this is just a hint and responses may have a different content type, such as a Blob fetch where a satisfactory response will just be the Blob stream as the payload.

Field	Description
`Allow`	The header indicates a list of all valid methods supported by a requested resource (`GET`, `PUT`, `POST`). It is just an indication and the client still may be able to seek a method, not from the `Allow` list. In such cases, the server needs to deny access appropriately.
`Authorization`	This is the authorization header for the request.
`Content-Encoding`	The header acts as a modifier to a content type. It indicates the additional encodings that are applied to the body, for example, Gzip, deflate.
`Cache-Control`	This indicates a cache directive that is followed by all caching mechanisms throughout the request/response chain. The header plays an important role when dealing with server-side cache and CDN.
`Content-Type`	This indicates the media type of the entity-body sent to the server.
`X-HTTP-Method`	The header allows clients or firewalls that don't support HTTP methods such as `PUT` or `DELETE` to allow these methods. The requests tunnel via a `POST` call.

Content negotiation

Content negotiation is a technique to identify the "best available" response for a request when multiple responses may be found on the server. HTTP 1.1 supports two types of negotiations:

- **Pre-emptive or server-driven negotiation**: In this case, the server negotiates with the client (based on the `Accept` headers) to determine the type of response.
- **Reactive or client-driven negotiation**: The server presents the client with the representations available and lets the client choose based on their purpose and goals.

More information about content negotiation can be found at `http://www.w3.org/Protocols/rfc2616/rfc2616-sec12.html`.

HTTP 2.0

HTTP 2.0 is the next planned version of the HTTP protocol specification and is an attempt to optimize the usage of network resources and reduce latency through header compressions and pooling multiple connections over the same channels. The initiative is spearheaded by Google and Mozilla research teams and as of today, is in a working draft state. The good news is that HTTP 2.0 is going to retain all the goodness of HTTP 1.1 while making it more performant over the wire through efficient processing of messages. Since HTTP 2.0 is still in the making, we will refrain from using it for the scope of this book. However, if you are enthusiastic to know more about HTTP 2.0, you can take a look at the current draft of the specification at `http://http2.github.io/http2-spec/`.

For the scope of this book, HTTP always refers to HTTP 1.1 specification of the protocol.

HTTP and .NET

Starting from .NET 4.5, a new namespace and assembly was added as part of the framework, `System.Net.Http`. The resemblance of the types in this namespace may look behaviorally similar to those defined in ASP.NET `System.Web.Http` namespace; however, the addition of this namespace marks a big difference in the development of HTTP services.

Firstly, it enables unified communication over HTTP by providing a set of abstract types. These types allow any .NET application to access HTTP services in a consistent way, for example, now both the client and server can use the same HTTP programming model for better development experience. Secondly, it has been written to target modern HTTP apps such as Web API and mobile development, this signifies the investment of Microsoft in making HTTP services a first-class citizen.

Some of the key types defined in this namespace are:

Type	Description
`HttpClient`	This enables primitive operations for sending HTTP requests and receiving HTTP responses from a resource identified by a URI.
`HttpRequestMessage`	This represents the HTTP request message from a client.
`HttpResponseMessage`	This represents the HTTP response message received from an HTTP request.
`HttpContent`	This is a base class that represents an HTTP entity body and any content headers.

<table>
<tr><th>Type</th><th>Description</th></tr>
<tr><td><code>HttpMessageHandler</code></td><td>This is the base type for all message handlers and this will be used to define all message handlers. Message handlers may be used to create server-side or client-side handlers.

The server-side handler works with the hosted model chain and handles incoming client requests (<code>HttpServer</code> and <code>HttpSelfHostServer</code>). It determines the correct route for the request (<code>HttpRoutingDispatcher</code>) and dispatches the request to the controller (<code>HttpControllerDispatcher</code>).

The <code>HttpClient</code> type uses client-side message handlers to process requests. The default handler <code>HttpClientHandler</code> is responsible to send the request and get the response from the server.

We may, of course, hook our custom controllers in the pipelines, for example, to validate, modify, or log the requests.</td></tr>
</table>

For a complete list of all types available in the `System.Net.Http` namespace, please visit `http://msdn.microsoft.com/en-us/library/system.net.http(v=vs.110).aspx`.

We will see in the later sections that the ASP.NET Web API also leverages some of the `System.Net.Http` types for communication over HTTP.

The rise of REST

When talking about Web APIs, it is imperative to mention the REST framework. Over the years, REST has proven to be a much simplified and efficient web service architecture style as compared to other architectures like RPC-based SOAP. The key reason for this popularity is because of its modern web design patterns and utilization of HTTP transport layer features to the fullest. REST has enabled many modern-world scenarios such as Mobile apps and **Internet of Things (IoT)**, which would be challenging with protocols like SOAP because of its rigid schema-based WSDL structure and bulky XML standards.

A good comparison of REST and SOAP protocols can be found at `http://blog.smartbear.com/apis/understanding-soap-and-rest-basics/`.

The REST style of services

REST stands for **Representational State Transfer** and perhaps the most important thing to realize about REST is that it is an architecture style and not a standard (like SOAP). What do we mean by this?

An architectural style is an accumulation of a set of design elements and constraints that can be tailored to define communication and interaction for a system. The elements in an architecture style are abstracted to ignore the implementation and protocol syntax and focus more on the role of the component. Additionally, constraints are applied to define the communication and extensibility patterns for these elements.

The focus of the REST architectural style is to improve the performance, portability, simplicity, reliability, and scalability of the system. The REST architecture style assumes the system as a whole in its initial state. It then evolves the system by incrementally applying constraints; these constraints allow components to scale efficiently while still maintaining a uniform set of interfaces. It also reduces deployment and maintenance considerations by layering out these components. Note that REST itself is a composition of many other architecture styles. For example, REST utilizes a set of other network architecture styles such data styles, hierarchical styles, and mobile code styles system to define its core architectural constraints. For more information on network architecture styles, please visit `http://www.ics.uci.edu/~fielding/pubs/dissertation/net_arch_styles.htm`.

For a Web API to be RESTful, most or all of the following architectural constraints must be satisfied:

Constraint	**Description**
Client-server	This constraint enforces a separation of concern between the client and server components. The core of this constraint is to promote a distributed architecture where the client can issue requests to a server, and the server responds back with status and the actual response. It enables multiple clients to interact with the server and allows the server to evolve independently.
Stateless	The stateless constraint evolves from the client server but mandates that no session state be allowed on the server component. The client must send all information required to understand the request and should not assume any available state on the server. This pattern is the backbone for enabling scalable Web APIs in a cloud-based environment.

Constraint	Description
Cache	Cache constraint is applied on top of client-server and stateless constraints and allows the requests to be implicitly or explicitly categorized as cacheable and noncacheable. The idea is to introduce a cache intermediator component that can improve latency by caching responses and minimizing interactions over the network. The cache can be employed as a consumer cache or a service side cache.
Uniform interface	The uniform interface constraint is the most critical constraint of a REST architecture style and distinguishes REST from other network architecture styles. The constraint emphasizes a uniform interface or contract between components. REST provides the following set of interface constraints: identification of resources, manipulation of resources through representation, self-descriptive messages, and hypermedia as the engine of application state. A typical uniform interface may be a combination of HTTP methods, media types (JSON, XML), and the resource URI. These provide a consistent interface for consumers to perform the desired operation on the resource.
Layered system	A layered system enables the architecture to be composed of hierarchical layers. These layers expose components to achieve specific behavior or functionality and these components only interact with components within their layer. Having a layered approach promotes extensibility and loose coupling between components.
Code on demand	The code on demand constraint is an optional constraint, and the main idea is to allow clients to be independently updated based on the browser add-on or client scripts.

For a more detailed understanding of REST-based architecture, the one source of truth is Roy Thomas Fielding's dissertation, *Architectural Styles and the Design of Network-based Software Architectures* (`http://www.ics.uci.edu/~fielding/pubs/dissertation/top.htm`).

Web API and Microsoft Azure

Microsoft Azure is a scalable cloud platform that enables organizations to rapidly build, deploy, and manage their applications in a **Platform as a Service (PaaS)** or **Infrastructure as a Service (IaaS)** model. It also provides an array of **Software as a Service (SaaS)** offerings built on Microsoft Azure that further improve the productivity of an organization. Microsoft Azure treats Web APIs as a first-class citizen and all the services and features exposed by Microsoft Azure expose REST-based Web APIs that can be consumed by clients to manage their hosted application and underlying environments.

Some of these APIs are listed here:

Service	**API**
Service Management API	This is the API for managing Azure subscriptions and environment programmatically. For more information, visit `https://msdn.microsoft.com/en-us/library/azure/ee460799.aspx`.
Azure AD	This is the graph API for accessing and managing an Azure AD tenant. For more information, visit `https://msdn.microsoft.com/en-us/library/azure/hh974478.aspx`.
Service Bus	This is the API for managing and accessing Service Bus entities, such as Topics, Queues, and EventHub. For more information, visit `https://msdn.microsoft.com/en-us/library/azure/hh780717.aspx`.
Notification Hubs	This is the API for managing Notification Hubs. For more information, visit `https://msdn.microsoft.com/en-us/library/azure/dn223264.aspx`.
BizTalk Services	This is the API for performing management operations on BizTalk Services. For more information, visit `https://msdn.microsoft.com/en-us/library/azure/dn232347.aspx`.
Azure SQL Database	This is the API for managing SQL databases, server configuration, and firewall associations for the servers. For more information, visit `https://msdn.microsoft.com/en-us/library/azure/gg715283.aspx`.
Mobile Services	This is the API for managing authentication and underlying database CRUD operations. For more information, visit `https://msdn.microsoft.com/en-us/library/azure/jj710108.aspx`.
Storage Services	This is the API for managing storage entities, such as tables, blobs, and file services. For more information, visit `https://msdn.microsoft.com/en-us/library/azure/dd179355.aspx`.
API Management	This is the API for managing the API Management service provided by Microsoft Azure. This allows for management of users, tenants, certificates, authorization servers, products, and reporting capabilities. For more information, visit `https://msdn.microsoft.com/en-us/library/azure/dn776326.aspx`.
Azure Web Sites	This has a REST API but is not currently exposed publicly.

For a list of all Microsoft Azure Web APIs, please refer to Microsoft Azure documentation at `https://msdn.microsoft.com/en-us/library/azure/dn578280.aspx`.

Apart from providing a comprehensive set of REST-based Web APIs, Microsoft Azure provides the tools and environment for customers to build and host their own Web APIs. *Chapter 1, Getting Started with the ASP.NET Web API* to *Chapter 4, Developing a Web API for Mobile Apps* discuss these tools and techniques in detail.

Summary

The Web API market has seen exponential growth since its inception in 2005. Over the last couple of years, the published APIs have increased to more than 12,000 and the number has been increasing each month. Web APIs have given organizations new opportunities to collaborate with partners in a secure and easy way and, at the same time, allowed for rapid development of consumer-based mobile and web-based applications. HTTP and REST provide the backbone for the Web API development, making it widely available and easy to consume. Microsoft Azure has taken special measures to expose services and provide support to easily incorporate the REST-based programming model into customer environments.

In the next chapters, we will dive into the details of the tools and techniques provided by Microsoft Azure and the ASP.NET Web API framework to rapidly build, deploy, and manage scalable Web API services.

1
Getting Started with the ASP.NET Web API

ASP.NET Web API is a framework for building HTTP Services. It is part of the ASP.NET platform, which is a free web framework for building websites and services.

Microsoft Azure makes building web services extremely easy. It provides the backbone for hosting scalable Web APIs and then efficiently managing and monitoring them.

In this chapter, we get to know the ASP.NET Web API framework. We delve into the fundamentals of the components that encompass the ASP.NET Web API, walk through the request-response pipeline of ASP.NET Web API, and also talk about the main features provided by the framework that make development of ASP.NET Web API a breeze. We then begin with the essential step of creating our first ASP.NET Web API and then deploy it in Microsoft Azure.

The ASP.NET Web API framework

ASP.NET Web API provides an easy and extensible mechanism to expose data and functionality to a broad range of clients, including browsers and modern web and mobile apps. The most significant aspect of ASP.NET Web API is that it is targeted to enable support for HTTP and RESTful services. In this section, we will discuss the nuts and bolts of the Web API framework.

> In the context of this book, the words ASP.NET Web API, Web API, and HTTP Services represent the same thing unless explicitly mentioned. This chapter assumes that the reader has knowledge about HTTP, REST, and Web API, in general. For more information on these technologies, please refer to the introduction chapter of this book.

Background

Before we delve into the building blocks and design principles behind ASP.NET Web API, it is important to understand that ASP.NET Web API is an evolution of the existing continuous Microsoft efforts to enable support for HTTP Services. A timeline of events that describe this evolution are outlined next.

Windows Communication Foundation (WCF) (`https://msdn.microsoft.com/en-us/library/ms731082%28v=vs.110%29.aspx`) was launched with .NET 3.0 for SOAP-based services; the primary aim was to abstract the transport layer and enable support for the `WS-*` protocol. No HTTP features were enabled except HTTP `POST` for requests

In NET 3.5, `WebHttpBinding` (`https://msdn.microsoft.com/en-us/library/system.servicemodel.webhttpbinding%28v=vs.110%29.aspx`) was introduced in WCF with the intent to support services that were not based on SOAP. It allowed systems to configure endpoints for WCF services that are exposed through HTTP requests instead of SOAP messages. The implementation was very basic and most HTTP protocol features were still missing or needed to be coded separately.

WCF Starter Kit (`https://aspnet.codeplex.com/releases/view/24644`) preview was launched to provide a suite of helper classes, extension methods, and Visual Studio project templates for building and consuming HTTP REST-based services. A new `WebServiceHost2` type was added to host RESTful services. Also, client HTTP support was added to provide a more natural experience for HTTP programming. The project never got released and eventually migrated into WCF Web API. As of August 2009 the project is in preview status.

During the same time, ASP.NET released some basic support to create REST APIs with its .NET 4.0 release. Its capabilities were limited, and HTTP features such as content negotiation were not available. ASP.NET was still targeted towards building web applications.

WCF Web API (`http://wcf.codeplex.com/wikipage?title=WCF%20HTTP`) was technically the first attempt to create a framework to support HTTP services from the ground up. However, the development efforts still leveraged pieces from WCF REST Starter Kit and .NET 3.5. A new rich, high-level HTTP programming model was adopted that included full support for content negotiation. A variety of traditional formats were supported (XML, JSON, and OData), and server-side query composition, ETags, hypermedia, and much more was enabled. The development was simplified by introducing the use of `HttpRequestMessage` and `HttpResponseMessage` to access requests and responses. The WCF Web API's second release was compatible with ASP.NET and allowed registering routes for Web APIs similar to ASP.NET MVC.

The WCF Web API project merged with the ASP.NET team to create an integrated Web API framework, and ASP.NET Web API was born. It shipped with the MVC4 Beta release in February 2012 and went to RTM in August 2012.

ASP.NET Web API 2 was released in October 2013 with new features such as attribute routing and authorization with OAuth 2.0. Another version, 2.1, was released in January 2014 with improvements to the existing infrastructure and additional features such as global exception handling.

At the time of writing, ASP.NET Web API 2.2 is the current stable version of the ASP. NET Web API framework. It includes more improvements to existing features such as enabling client support for Windows 8.1 devices along with bug fixes.

Building blocks

As described in the previous section, ASP.NET Web API is built on top of existing frameworks and technologies. Web API leverages features from ASP.NET MVC, the core ASP.NET framework, and the .NET framework to reduce the overall learning curve for developers and at the same time provides abstraction to make programming easier. The following figure highlights the key features that make up the ASP.NET Web API framework.

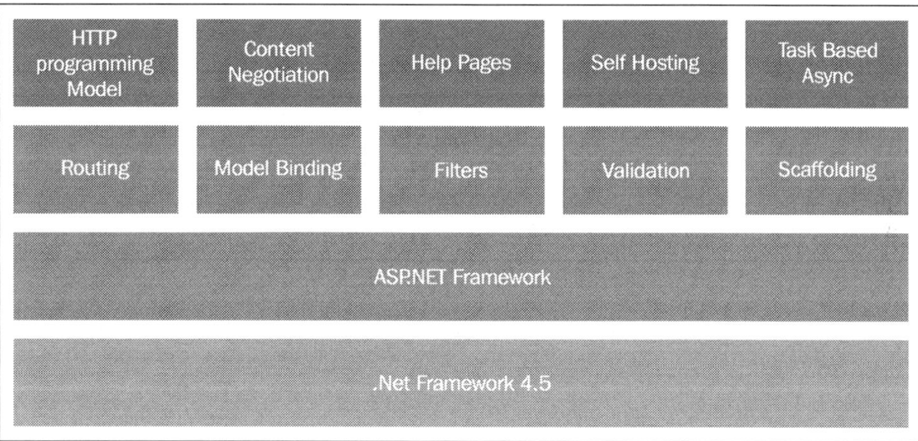

> ASP.NET Web API leverages some standard features from the ASP.NET MVC framework. Though expertise in ASP.NET MVC is not a requirement for developing HTTP Services using ASP.NET Web API, a fundamental understanding of the ASP.NET MVC framework and the MVC design pattern is useful. More information about the ASP.NET MVC framework is available at `http://www.asp.net/mvc`.

Design principles behind the ASP.NET Web API

Now that we understand the intent behind ASP.NET Web API, let's discuss some design principles on which ASP.NET Web API is based:

- **Distributed by design**: ASP.NET Web API considers HTTP as a first-class citizen and has inherent support for REST. It enables a framework for creating distributed services that leverage HTTP features such as stateless, caching, and compression.
- **Russian Doll Model**: This is also called the Matryoshka doll model, which refers to a set of wooden dolls of decreasing sizes placed one inside the other. Architecturally, it denotes a recognizable relationship of nested objects (object within an object). The ASP.NET Web API messaging handlers leverage this principle to define the request-response pipeline. Each handler in the pipeline is responsible for processing the incoming request and then delegating the request to another handler. When a request reaches a handler, it may opt to process it, validate it, and then delegate the request to another handler or break the chain by sending a response. Of course, this is not true for the last handler in the chain since it will not delegate but rather work to get the response back up the chain. The response will follow the same logic but in the reverse direction and each handler will get the response before sending it back to the caller. We will discuss message handlers in detail in the next section. The follow figure describes the Russian Doll model being employed by ASP.NET Web API framework.

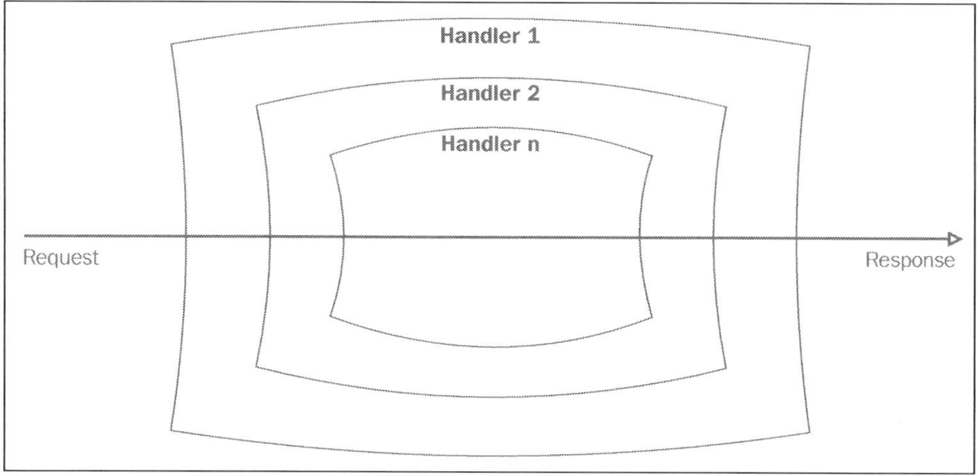

- **Asynchronous to the core**: The ASP.NET Web API leverages the .NET **Task-based Asynchronous Pattern (TAP)** model to the core. TAP is based on the `Task` and `Task<TResult>` types in the `System.Threading.Tasks` namespace, which are used to represent arbitrary asynchronous operations. TAP provides a new pattern to work with both CPU-intensive and non-CPU-intensive asynchronous invocations. It simplifies the overall programming model for asynchronous operations in .NET 4.5 through the `async` and `await` model. Let's look at an example:

```
async Task<int> GetContentLengthAsync(string uri)
{
    int contentLength;
    using (var client = new HttpClient())
    {
        var content = await client.GetStringAsync(uri);
        contentLength = content.Length;
    }

    return contentLength;
}
```

In the preceding example:

- We create an asynchronous method `GetContentLengthAsync` that accepts a web URI and returns the length of the response.
- The return type for this method is `Task<TResult>`, the return type can also be `Task` or `void`.
- An `async` method typically includes at least one `await` call, which will mark a path where the code cannot continue unless an asynchronous operation is completed. It does not block the thread though. Instead, the method is suspended and the control returns to the caller.
- The method execution continues after the response is returned from the asynchronous call.

> A TAP-based pattern simplifies writing asynchronous programming code and improves overall responsiveness of the system.

- ASP.NET incorporates dependency injection at various levels in the core types of the system. The ASP.NET Web API exposes a set of interfaces such as `IDependencyResolver` (`http://www.asp.net/web-api/overview/advanced/dependency-injection`), which enables developers to modify almost everything in the message pipeline by injecting their custom instances. Another good side effect of Dependency Injection in ASP.NET Web API is that we can easily create unit tests for services built on the framework thus improving testability.
- ASP.NET Web API is intended to be an open framework, and it leverages the ASP.NET infrastructure for enabling multiple hosting options. We can host a Web API from a simple console application to a powerful server such as IIS. We will cover the different options in *Chapter 2, Extending the ASP.NET Web API*.

Application scenarios

As mentioned before, ASP.NET Web API enables customers to easily and rapidly develop HTTP-based services that can result in new business opportunities or improved customer satisfaction. Some of these scenarios are described here:

- **Mashup**: This refers to accessing content from more than one service and then creating a new service typically via a user interface. For example, multiple services exposed by the Bing Maps API can be used by a consumer to create a map-plotting user interface that can show the location of nearby location on a map.

- **Smartphone apps**: This is a no-brainer; the mobile app market is one of the most booming markets today. An independent survey suggests that around 56 billion apps were downloaded in 2013 generating revenue of around $20-25 billion, and this number is only going to increase in the coming years. ASP.NET Web API provides multiple client libraries to offer developers with quick and easy ways to create HTTP Services. Moreover, Microsoft Azure Mobile Services provide a robust backend to host mobile apps and Web APIs for multiple platforms, such as iOS, Android, and Windows. It provides baked-in capabilities such as push notifications, social integration, and database management, which seem like a perfect fit for developing mobile applications. We will explore more about Azure Mobile Services and Web API in *Chapter 4, Developing a Web API for Mobile Apps*.
- **Single Page Application (SPA)**: In this, all the necessary code artifacts such as HTML, JavaScript, and CSS are retrieved in a single page load. The appropriate resources are then dynamically rendered by making asynchronous calls to services exposing data and functionality. ASP.NET provides inherent support to populate JS frameworks, such as Knockout.js and Angular JS, and provides full support for HTML5 and Web Sockets (via SignalR). These technologies work together with the backend HTTP Services layer built using ASP.NET Web API and Microsoft Azure websites to provide a comprehensive solution to develop SPA.
- **Intranet and partner integration**: When thinking about Web API, we usually think about publically published APIs; however, there is much value in developing Web API in a corporate or intranet scenario as well. If we go back in history, one of the first Web APIs from Amazon was a byproduct of the work they had been doing in their internal applications. Web API brings reusability, and this brings down the development and testing cost when dealing with multiple teams and large organizations.
- **Internet of Things**: In the past year, **Internet of Things (IoT)** has become the hottest buzzword. It is a phenomena bigger than anything that has happened in the software industry since its inception. IoT coupled with cloud technologies enables scenarios that never existed. For example, a thermostat talking to a cloud service and providing telemetry data to the manufacturer can open avenues of new businesses via predictive maintenance using data analytics or partner integration to provide better customer service. As devices are becoming more powerful, they are no longer restricted to short-range networks or lightweight protocols. HTTP infrastructure and Web APIs can play a pivotal role in such scenarios in the coming years.

Behind the scenes with the ASP.NET Web API

Let's talk about some of the internal workings of ASP.NET Web API and how a request is received and a corresponding response generated.

Anatomy of the API of ASP.NET Web API

Before we understand the request and response lifecycle within ASP.NET Web API, it is important to comprehend some of the principal types and their usage within the pipeline.

The core assemblies for ASP.NET Web API can be installed using the `Microsoft.AspNet.WebApi` NuGet package, which is distributed under the MS license, this will install all the required dependencies to develop an ASP.NET Web API service.

NuGet is the package manager for the Microsoft development platform, including .NET. The NuGet client tools provide the ability to produce and consume packages. NuGet is installed as part of the Visual Studio 2013 release. To know more about NuGet, visit `https://www.nuget.org/`.

To install the runtime packages via the NuGet Package Manager Console in Visual Studio use the following command:

```
PM> Install-Package Microsoft.AspNet.WebApi
```

Alternatively, Visual Studio provides a NuGet user interface dialog that can be used to install the package. For more information on using the NuGet dialog in Visual Studio, visit `https://docs.nuget.org/consume/package-manager-dialog`.

Note that a project created using the ASP.NET Visual Studio 2013 template does not require adding these packages explicitly.

The following figure describes the core assemblies and their dependencies that get downloaded when the `Microsoft.AspNet.WebApi` package is installed. There are other NuGet packages that are published by the ASP.NET Web API team (such as CORS support, Help Pages, OWIN host). This figure provides the bare minimal to get started with ASP.NET Web API development:

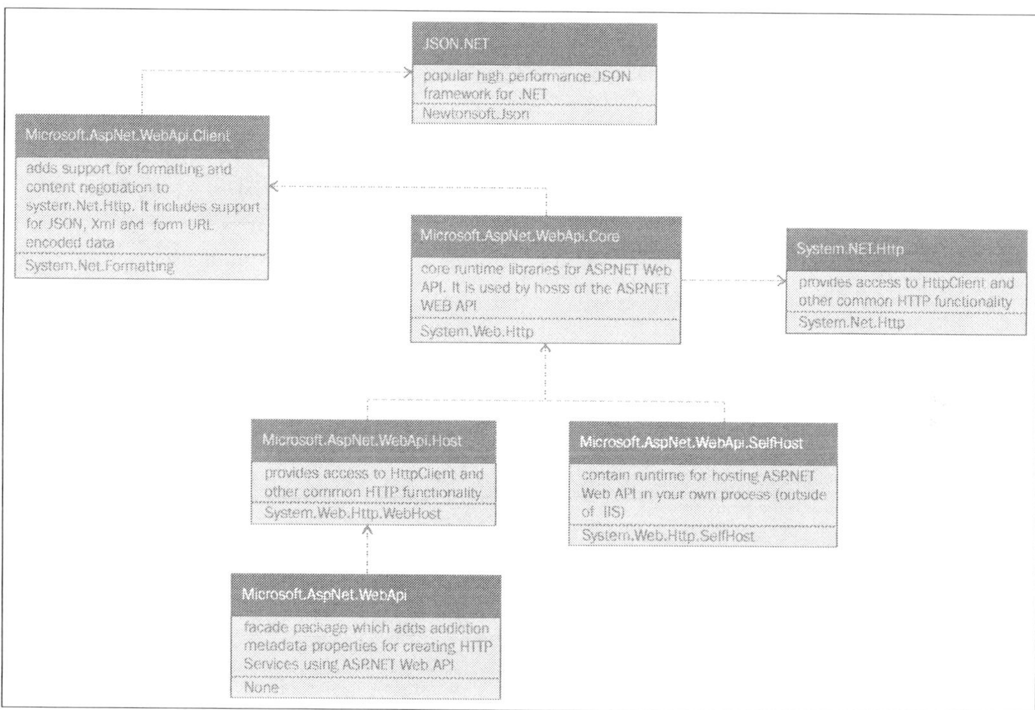

Now, let's look at some of the important runtime types that enable the communication and execution in the ASP.NET Web API pipeline.

DelegatingHandler

As mentioned earlier, the execution of a request implements a Russian Doll Model. A `DelegatingHandler` is a runtime type that enables the creation of a handler that can participate in the chain of request and response pipeline for ASP.NET Web API. Although used heavily by the ASP.NET Web API infrastructure, `DelegatingHandler` is a type defined in `System.Net.Http`.

`DelegatingHandler` is derived from `HttpMessageHandler`, which is the abstract base class for all HTTP message handlers. The most critical method exposed by `HttpMessageHandler` is the abstract `SendAsync` method. It is responsible for maintaining the chain of the request and response pipeline. `DelegatingHandler` can enrich the request message before calling `SendAsync`; once called, it sends the incoming request to the next handler for processing.

```
protected internal abstract Task<HttpResponseMessage>
SendAsync(HttpRequestMessage request, CancellationToken
cancellationToken);
```

`DelegatingHandler` acts as a base type for built-in message handlers such as `HttpServer`. In its base implementation, it enables assigning an inner handler during construction and delegating the `SendAsync` request to the inner handler, thus enabling a chain between the handlers. Any type that inherits from `DelgatingHandler` can then participate in the pipeline by ensuring that `SendAsync` on `DelgatingHandler` is called.

```
public class CustomMessageHandler: DelegatingHandler
{
    protected async override Task<HttpResponseMessage>
      SendAsync(HttpRequestMessage request,
      CancellationToken cancellationToken)
    {
        // Call the inner handler.
        var response = await base.SendAsync(request,
          cancellationToken);
        return response;
    }
}
```

Alternatively, an inherited type may return a response instead of invoking `base.SendAsync`. For example, a handler generating a response. Another useful scenario could be where a handler detects an exception and wants to stop processing the request.

Note that the call to `SendAsync` is asynchronous, thus satisfying the "asynchronous to the core" design principle of REST.

All message handlers in ASP.NET Web API are contained in an ordered collection as part of the `HttpConfiguration.MessageHandlers` collection. What this means is that the handlers are always executed in sequence of their addition. The ASP.NET Web API framework allows for defining message handlers at the configuration level on a per route basis using `HttpRoutingDispatcher`. We discuss more details about this feature in the *Routing and dispatching* section.

HttpRequestMessage

`HttpRequestMessage` is a runtime type defined in the `System.Net.Http` namespace; it acts as an unified abstraction for all HTTP requests irrespective of client or server. Any incoming message is first converted into `HttpRequestMessage` before it traverses through the pipeline; this provides an ability to have a strong type HTTP message throughout the pipeline.

An `HttpRequestMessage` may contain values for the following attributes:

Name	Description
`Method`	This specifies the method of the request (`GET`, `POST`, `PUT`, `DELETE`, `OPTIONS`, `TRACE`, `HEAD`) and returns an `HttpMethod` type.
`Content`	This specifies the body of the request. It is contained in an `HttpContent` object.
`Headers`	This contains all headers in the HTTP request. These can be used to retrieve authorization headers and user agents. The `Content` property also exposes a `Headers` collection, which is useful to define header values for the content itself, such as `ContentType` and `MediaFormatters`.
`Properties`	This represents a dictionary that can contain custom values to be passed as part of the request, such as error details.

HttpResponseMessage

`HttpResponseMessage` represents the other side of the story and provides an abstraction for all responses generated for corresponding HTTP requests. It is also defined in the `System.Net.Http` namespace. Any response within the pipeline will be represented as `HttpResponseMessage` before it gets converted and sent to the caller.

`HttpResponseMessage` may contain values for the following attributes:

Name	Description
`Content`	This specifies the body of the request. It is contained in an `HttpContent` object.
`Headers`	This contains all headers in the HTTP response. It is a key-value pair collection of the `HttpResponseHeaders` type.
`RequestMessage`	This is a copy of the request message (`HttpRequestMessage`) that leads to the response.
`IsSuccessStatusCode`	This is a `bool` value that indicates whether the HTTP response is successful.

Name	Description
`StatusCode`	The HTTP status code for the response (for example, a 202 status code would mean success) returns the `HTTPStatusCode` enum.
`ReasonPhrase`	This is a string description that corresponds to the status code that has been returned (for example, a reason phrase for a 202 status code will be "Accepted").
`Version`	This is the HTTP protocol version; the default is `1.1`, which returns a version type.

`HttpResponse` also exposes the `EnsureSuccessStatusCode` method, which is especially useful in testing scenarios where a successful response is expected. The method throws an exception if `HttpResponseMessage` does not return with a success `HTTPStatusCode` in the range of 200 to 209. Note that in case of a failure response, the `EnsureSuccessStatusCode` internally calls `Dispose` on the stream if the `Content` property for the response is not null. Essentially, we cannot access the `Content` stream post with this method when a failure status code is returned.

ApiController

ASP.NET MVC has the concept of controllers since its inception; conceptually, Web API controllers follow a similar approach to leverage the goodies from the ASP.NET framework. However, Web API controllers are targeted towards providing an abstraction over the HTTP request-response pipeline. Moreover, Web API controllers return only response data in contrast to HTML views in ASP.NET MVC.

All Web API controllers implement the `IHttpController` interface to classify them as Web API controllers. As we will see in the next section, the Web API request dispatch, and route matching pipeline attempts to look for an `IHttpController` instead of a particular controller implementation. The following code snippet shows the definition for the `IHttpController` interface.

```
namespace System.Web.Http.Controllers
{
    public interface IHttpController
    {
        Task<HttpResponseMessage>
          ExecuteAsync(HttpControllerContext
          controllerContext, CancellationToken cancellationToken);
    }
}
```

While we can create our controllers by implementing the `IHttpController` interface, ASP.NET Web API provides a useful base class that abstracts most of the low-level plumbing required for the request-response pipeline.

A typical `APIController.ExecuteAsync` implementation looks like this:

```
public virtual Task<HttpResponseMessage>
  ExecuteAsync(HttpControllerContext controllerContext,
  CancellationToken cancellationToken)
{
    if (this._initialized)
    {
        throw Error.InvalidOperation
          (SRResources.CannotSupportSingletonInstance,
          new object[2]
        {
            (object) typeof (ApiController).Name,
            (object) typeof (IHttpControllerActivator).Name
        });
    }
    else
    {
        this.Initialize(controllerContext);
        if (this.Request != null)
        HttpRequestMessageExtensions.RegisterForDispose
          (this.Request, (IDisposable) this);
        ServicesContainer services =
          controllerContext.ControllerDescriptor.
          Configuration.Services;
        HttpActionDescriptor actionDescriptor =
          ServicesExtensions.GetActionSelector(services)
          .SelectAction(controllerContext);
        this.ActionContext.ActionDescriptor = actionDescriptor;
        if (this.Request != null)
          HttpRequestMessageExtensions.SetActionDescriptor
            (this.Request, actionDescriptor);
        FilterGrouping filterGrouping =
          actionDescriptor.GetFilterGrouping();
        IActionFilter[] actionFilters =
          filterGrouping.ActionFilters;
        IAuthenticationFilter[] authenticationFilters =
          filterGrouping.AuthenticationFilters;
        IAuthorizationFilter[] authorizationFilters =
          filterGrouping.AuthorizationFilters;
        IExceptionFilter[] exceptionFilters =
          filterGrouping.ExceptionFilters;
```

```
            IHttpActionResult innerResult =
              (IHttpActionResult) new ActionFilterResult
              (actionDescriptor.ActionBinding, this.ActionContext,
              services, actionFilters);
            if (authorizationFilters.Length > 0)
              innerResult = (IHttpActionResult) new
                AuthorizationFilterResult(this.ActionContext,
                authorizationFilters, innerResult);
            if (authenticationFilters.Length > 0)
              innerResult = (IHttpActionResult) new
                AuthenticationFilterResult(this.ActionContext,
                this, authenticationFilters, innerResult);
            if (exceptionFilters.Length > 0)
            {
                IExceptionLogger logger =
                  ExceptionServices.GetLogger(services);
                IExceptionHandler handler =
                  ExceptionServices.GetHandler(services);
                innerResult = (IHttpActionResult) new
                  ExceptionFilterResult(this.ActionContext,
                  exceptionFilters, logger, handler, innerResult);
            }
            return innerResult.ExecuteAsync(cancellationToken);
        }
    }
```

The series of actions performed by the API controller in the preceding code is as follows:

1. The API controller invokes the action selection logic for the HTTP request.
2. It then initializes and invokes the registered authentication filters.
3. Subsequently, it initializes and invokes the authorization filters.
4. Next, the action filters are initialized and invoked followed by the exception filters in case of exceptions.
5. In the last step, it invokes the Parameter Binding and content negotiation for the requests and responses.

Finally, the operation is executed.

Other important types

There are other important types in the `System.Net.Http` and `System.Web.Http` namespaces that enrich the ASP.NET Web API framework, these are described as follows:

Type	Description	Assembly
`HttpRoutingDispatcher`	This is the default endpoint message handler, which examines the `IHttpRoute` of the matched route, and chooses which message handler to call. If `Handler` is null, then it delegates the control to `HttpControllerDispatcher`.	`System.Web.Http`
`HttpControllerDispatcher`	This dispatches an incoming `HttpRequestMessage` to an `IHttpController` implementation for processing.	`System.Web.Http`
`HttpControllerContext`	This contains the metadata about a single HTTP operation and provides access to the request, response, and configuration objects for the HTTP operation.	`System.Web.Http`
`HttpParameterBinding`	This provides a definition of how a parameter will be bound.	`System.Web.Http`
`IContentNegotiator`	This is the primary interface for enabling content negotiation by selecting a response writer (formatter) in compliance with header values.	`System.Web.Http`
`IHttpControllerSelector`	This assists in selecting a controller during the request pipeline.	`System.Web.Http`
`HttpActionSelector`	This assists in selecting an action in a controller during request execution.	`System.Web.Http`
`HttpControllerHandler`	This passes ASP.NET requests into the `HttpServer` pipeline and writes the result back.	`System.Web.Http`

Type	Description	Assembly
`MediaTypeFormatter`	This is the base class to handle serializing and deserializing strongly-typed objects. This plays a pivotal role in converting requests and responses to their desired formats.	`System.Web.Http`
`HttpServer`	This defines an implementation of `HttpMessageHandler`, which dispatches an incoming `HttpRequestMessage` and creates an `HttpResponseMessage` as a result.	`System.Web.Http`

We will get into the details of most of these types in later sections and in *Chapter 2, Extending the ASP.NET Web API*.

Message lifecycle

Now that we have some context of the main APIs involved in the Web API request-response pipeline, let's take a look at how a request flows through the Web API pipeline and how a response is directed back to the client.

At a broad level, the message pipeline can be categorized into three main stages:

Let's walk through the message pipeline using a sample Web API. The Web API is a simple Hello World API that allows the client to issue a `GET` request and returns the string `Hello world!` in JSON. For now, don't worry about the implementation details of this Web API. In the next sections, we will get into deeper detail on how to create, test, and deploy a Web API.

Request	`http://localhost:12356/api/hello`
Response	Hello world!

Host listener

A host listener refers to a component listening for incoming requests. For years, Microsoft Web Components had an inherent dependency of using **Internet Information Services (IIS)** as the host. The ASP.NET Web API breaks out of this legacy model and allows itself to be hosted outside IIS. As a matter of fact, we can host a Web API in an executable, which then acts as the server receiving requests for the Web API. There are many options available to host a Web API; we will explore some of them in detail in *Chapter 2, Extending the ASP.NET Web API*. For now, we will focus on using either of the hosting options and enable listening for requests and responding with a response.

Considering the earlier Hello World example, the incoming request will be processed as shown in the following diagram:

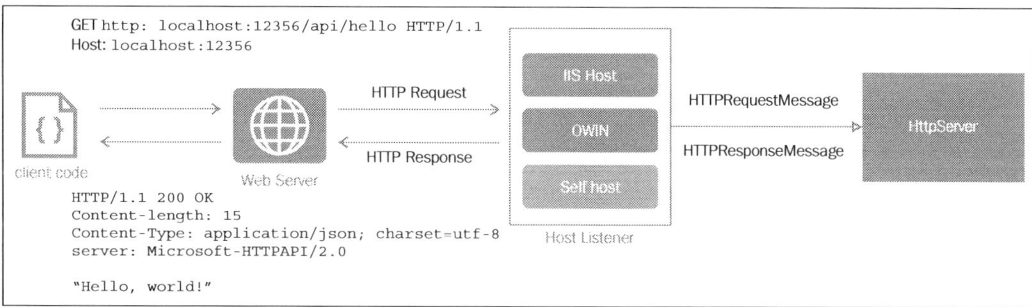

In the preceding diagram:

1. The client code issues a `GET` request using HTTP 1.1 as the protocol. The request is issued to an endpoint, which represents a resource on the server.

   ```
   GET http://localhost:12356/api/hello HTTP/1.1
   Host: localhost:12356
   ```

2. The configured host listener will then receive the request and convert it into `HTTPRequestMessage`. The host inherits from the `HTTPServer` type, which by itself is a message handler and implements `DelegatingHandler`. So, essentially it is just another message handler that delegates the request to the next handler (remember the Russian Doll Model we talked about earlier).
3. The request is then sent through to the routing and dispatching components and then to the controller components for further processing and returning the response.

Routing and dispatching

The routing and dispatching stage primarily involves the execution of a series of message handlers, which process the incoming request and then delegate them to the next message handler for processing. In earlier versions of ASP.NET Web API, we could only configure message handlers globally per application. All the message handlers were added to the `HttpConfiguration.MessageHandlers` collection and were executed for each request. The global configuration was enabled using the `Register` method in the `WebApiConfig.cs` file, which gets added when creating a new ASP.NET Web API project. We talk more about the `WebApiConfig` and `Register` method in the *Creating our first ASP.NET Web API* section. The following snippet show a sample `Register` method definition:

```
public static void Register(HttpConfiguration config)
{

    config.Routes.MapHttpRoute(
       name: "DefaultApi",
       routeTemplate: "api/{controller}/{id}",
       defaults: new { id = RouteParameter.Optional }
    );
    // add a new message handler to all routes
    config.MessageHandlers.Add(new CustomMessageHandler());

}
```

In the preceding code, we configured `CustomMessageHandler()` to be called for all routes in the Web API. While this worked well for most basic scenarios, it became a challenge for applications where specialization for a route was required. For example, specific authorization handlers for a route. Web API 2 introduced a per route handler flow that allows granularity when routing requests to message handlers. The following code is added to `WebApiConfig.cs` to configure a per route custom handler in the ASP.NET Web API 2:

```
public static void Register(HttpConfiguration config)
{
    config.Routes.MapHttpRoute(
        name: "DefaultApi",
        routeTemplate: "api/common/{controller}/{id}",
        defaults: new { id = RouteParameter.Optional }
    );

    config.Routes.MapHttpRoute(
```

```
            name: "CustomDefaultApi",
            routeTemplate: "api/{controller}/{id}",
            defaults: new { id = RouteParameter.Optional },
            constraints: null,
            handler: new CustomMessageHandler()
        );
    }
```

In the preceding code, we configured `CustomMessageHandler`, which inherits from `DelegatingHandler` to a particular route. We also have a global route with API/common that when called will not invoke our custom message handler, it will rather follow a global configuration. The internals of `CustomMessageHandler` have been omitted since they are not necessary at this stage; all we are concerned here is how the internal routing logic works. We will discuss these concepts in greater detail in *Chapter 2, Extending the ASP.NET Web API*.

Let's look at how the per-route message handler routing is performed by ASP.NET Web API 2:

1. When a request is sent, the host listener (`HttpServer`) invokes `HttpRoutingDispatcher`, which acts as the default endpoint message handler. `HttpRoutingDispatcher` is responsible for discovering the route and invoking the corresponding handlers for the route.
2. If no route is matched, `HttpRoutingDispatcher` returns an HTTP standard response code: `Not Found (404)`.
3. If a route is found, the routing handler checks if there is a handler associated with the current route. It does this by checking the `Route.Handler` property on the route.
4. If no handler is specified for the route, it is assumed that the global configuration will be applied, and the request is delegated to `HttpControllerDispatcher` for further processing.

5. If a handler is attached to the route, `HttpControllerDispatcher` attempts to invoke the message handler registered for the particular route. The invoked message handler may then return to the main path and delegate to `HttpControllerDispatcher`, as shown:

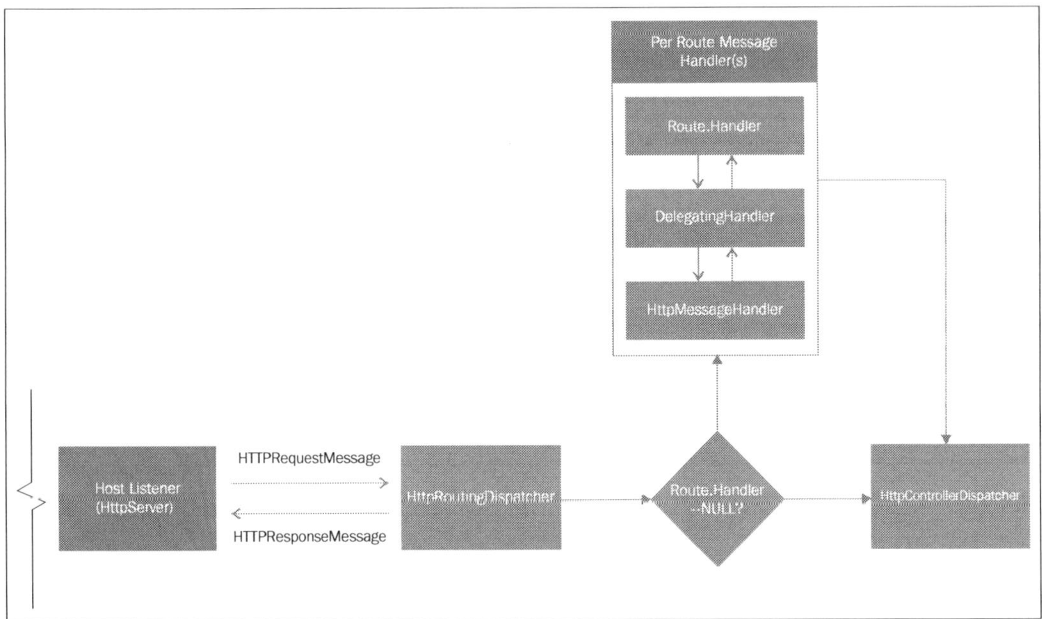

6. `HttpControllerDispatcher` is a message handler, which is then responsible for selecting and creating the controller before delegating the request to the controller, as shown:

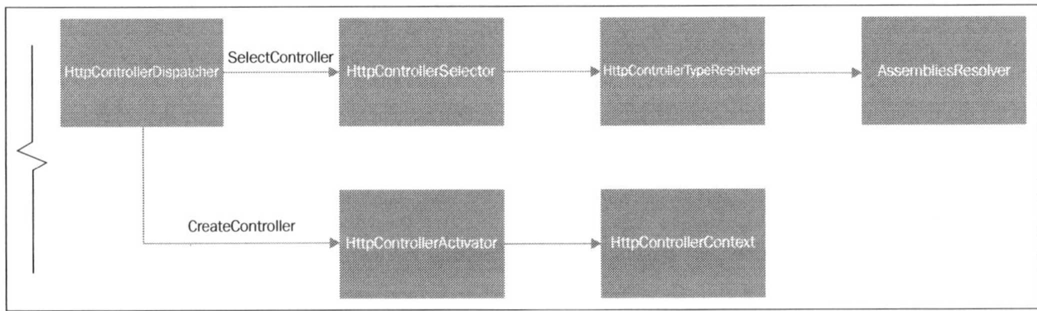

7. If no controller is resolved, a 404 status code is returned by `HttpControllerDispatcher`.

8. Once the controller is created successfully, its `ExecuteAsync` is called to delegate processing of the request:

```
httpResponseMessage = await controller.
ExecuteAsync(controllerContext, cancellationToken);
```

Controller processing

The final and the most exciting stage of the pipeline is processing the request by the controller; this is where all the magic happens to generate the appropriate response for the incoming request. As explained earlier, if the controller inherits from `APIController`, much of the plumbing work is already abstracted from the developer. The following pipeline walks through a controller pipeline that inherits from `APIController`:

1. The controller first determines the action to be invoked:

```
actionDescriptor = ServicesExtensions.
  GetActionSelector(services).
  SelectAction(controllerContext);
```

2. Next, a series of filters is invoked, which provides authentication and authorization. At any point, if there is a failure response (for example, client not authenticated), the filter can invoke an error response and break the response chain, as shown in the following figure:

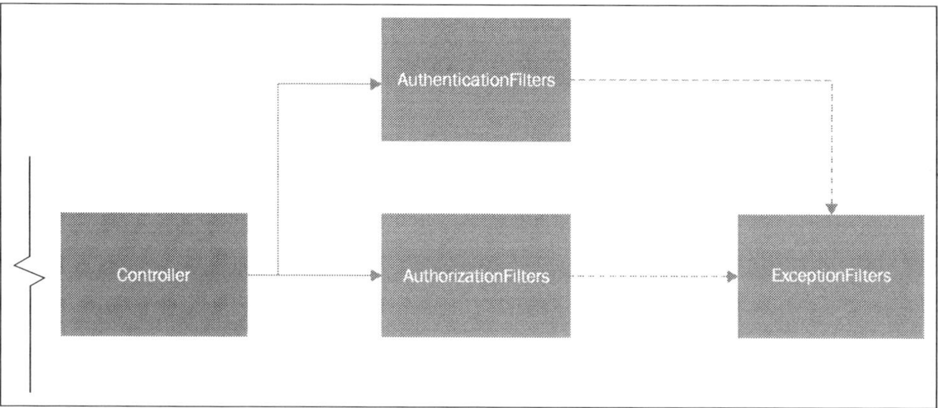

3. The next step is model binding. It is a technique provided by the ASP.NET framework to bind request values to existing models. It is an abstraction layer that automatically populates controller action parameters, taking care of the mundane property mapping and type conversion code typically involved in working with ASP.NET request data. We will explore more about model and parameter binding in *Chapter 2, Extending the ASP.NET Web API*.

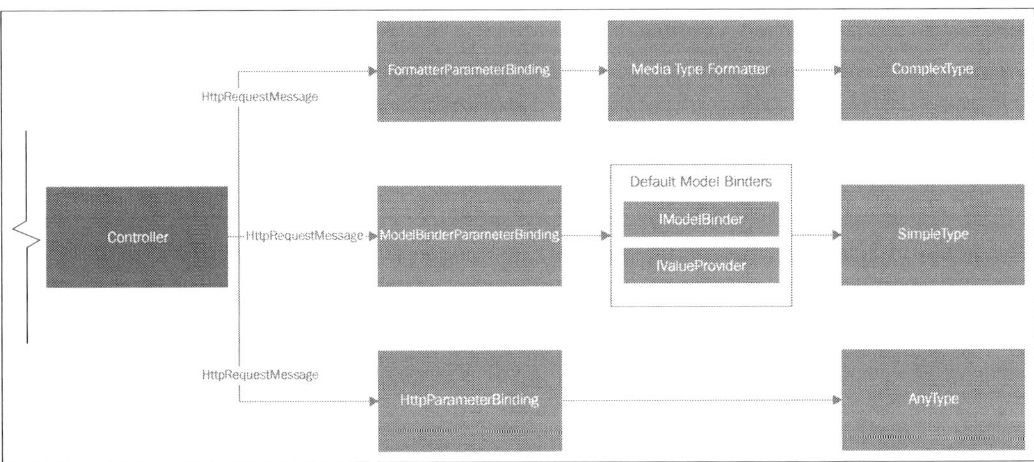

4. Next, the pipeline executes the actual action and any associated action filters. This will process the code that we write in our action method for processing incoming requests. The framework actually provides an ability to execute the action filters as a pre and post step to the actual method execution.

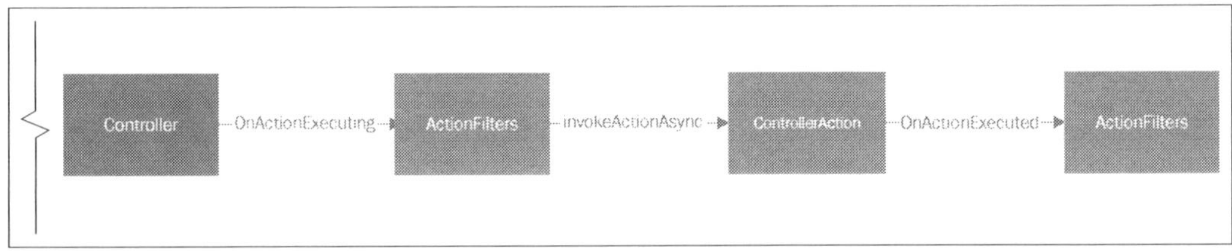

5. Once the controller action and the post filters are executed, the final step is to convert the response generated into an appropriate `HttpResponseMessage` and traverse the chain back to return the response to the client. This is shown in the following figure:

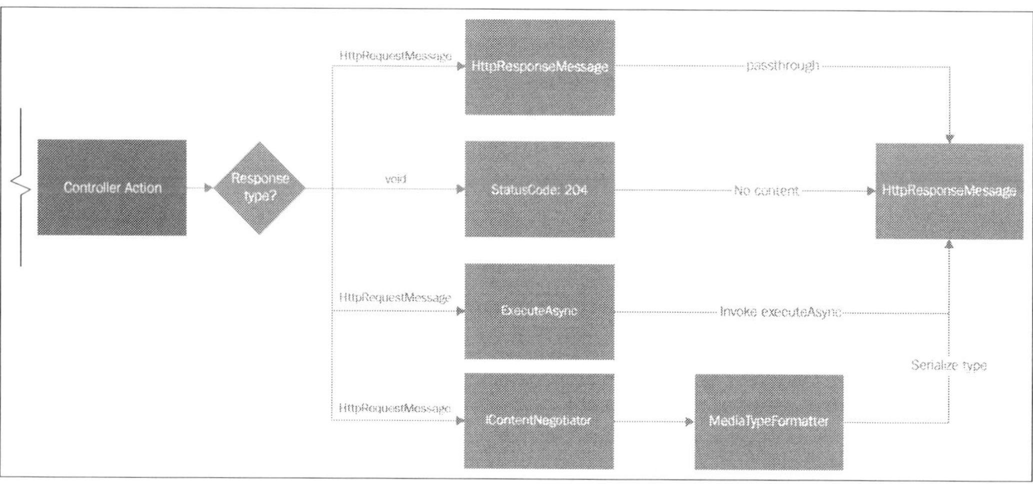

6. Once `HttpResponseMessage` has been created, the response traverses back through the pipeline, and is returned to the client as an HTTP response.

Creating our first ASP.NET Web API

In this section, we will start building our Web API, covering the necessary environment required for creating a Web API. We will also discuss our problem scenario, and then create a Web API from scratch. We will then delve into the details of Microsoft Azure websites and deploy our first Web API in Microsoft Azure.

Prerequisites

The following must be configured to run the example scenarios we discuss in this and following chapters:

- **Developer machine**: We need a development environment that can support Microsoft Visual Studio and ASP.NET Web tools. Although we can create ASP.NET Web API solutions from a local PC, for the purpose of this book, we will host a new virtual machine in Microsoft Azure and use it as our development environment. Setting up and managing an environment on Microsoft Azure is so straightforward and elegant, that it is now used as a preferred way to develop applications.
- **A Microsoft Azure subscription**: We need a Microsoft Azure subscription to host our Web API. A free trial is available at `http://azure.microsoft.com/pricing/free-trial/?WT.mc_id=A261C142F`. For MSDN subscribers, Azure subscription can be activated using their Microsoft Azure credits.

- **Visual Studio 2013**: Once we have the virtual machine up and running, we will need Visual Studio 2013. Any version of Visual Studio Professional 2013 or later should be sufficient for our samples. There is also a free full feature version of Visual Studio referred to as Community Edition, which enables ASP.NET web development. MSDN subscribers can also get access to a set of preconfigured Visual Studio virtual machine images available as part of the Microsoft Azure subscription. The source and samples for this book are built using Visual Studio 2013 Community Edition Update 4.
- **Visual Studio Online**: It is always good practice to use a code management and collaboration system when starting a project. **Visual Studio Online** (**VSO**) is a Microsoft Azure-based service that provides the capabilities of Team Foundation Server in the cloud. We will use VSO for source control throughout all samples, we will also be using Git as our source control system; Visual Studio Online provides integral support for this. VSO also provides integration with Microsoft Azure for **Continuous Integration** (**CI**) and **Continuous Delivery** (**CD**) capabilities.

A free Visual Studio Online account can be created at the following link: `https://www.visualstudio.com/en-us/products/what-is-visual-studio-online-vs.aspx`. To know more about using Git with Visual Studio Online, visit the following link: `https://msdn.microsoft.com/en-us/library/hh850437.aspx`.

An alternative is to use GitHub as a source control strategy as well. For the purpose of this book, we will use VSO and Git.

Now that we have the development tools installed and ready, let's quickly take an example to put these to test. We will build an ASP.NET Web API for a fictitious transport service provider that provides consumers with package tracking abilities. The following figure shows how clients interact with the solution:

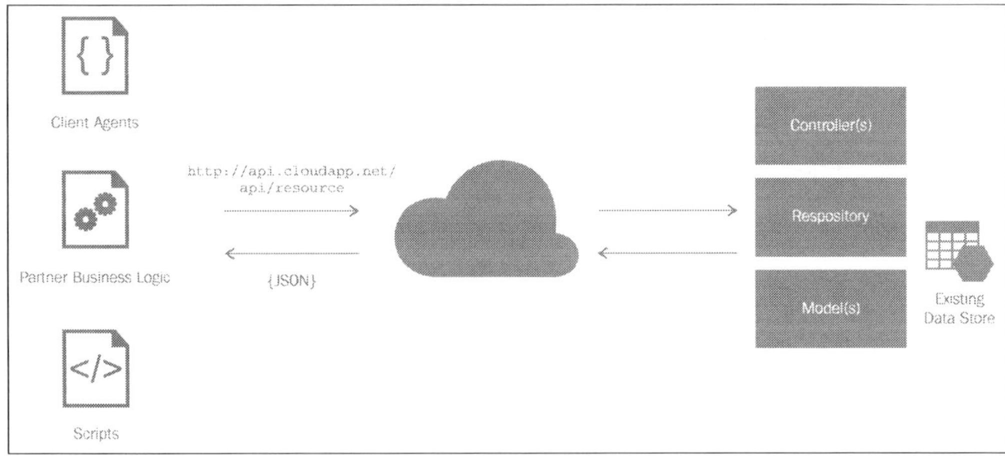

Creating the ASP.NET Web API project

We will start by creating a new ASP.NET Web Application project in Visual Studio.

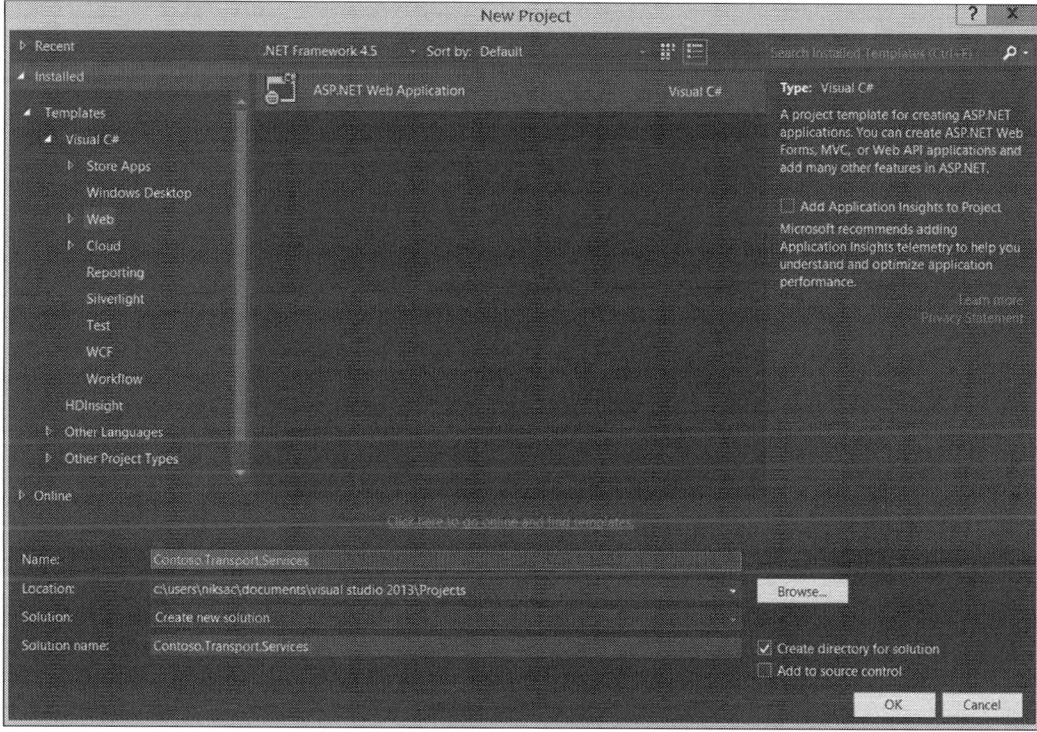

Uncheck the **application insights to project** box for now.

In the new ASP.NET project page, we select the empty template and check **Web API** in the **Add folders and core references for** section. Let **Authentication** be set to **No Authentication** for now. The empty template skips many other sample controllers and folders such as the MVC helper and documentation folders.

Also, we unselect **Host in the Cloud** under Microsoft Azure for now. We will add this in the next section when we talk about the Microsoft Azure website.

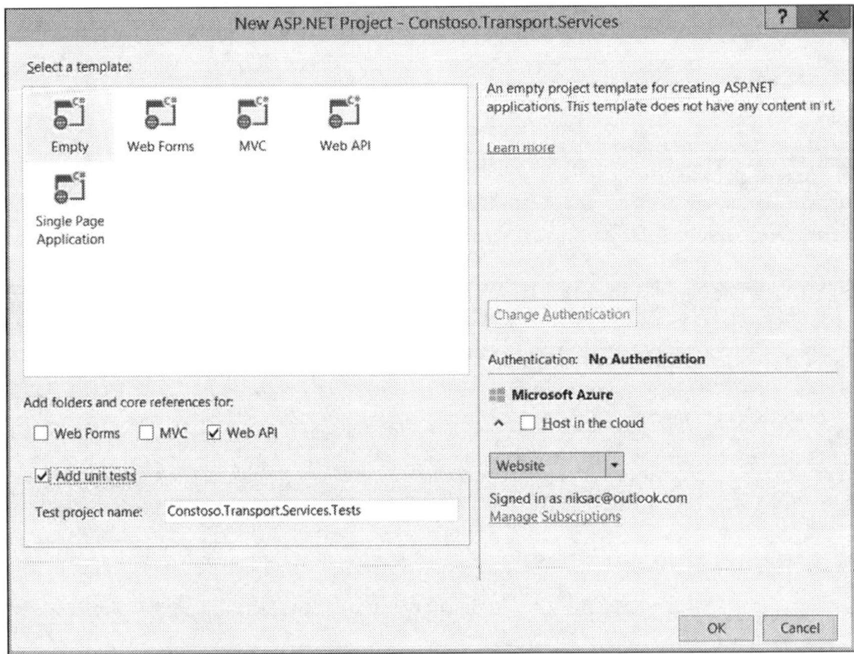

At this stage, the solution should look like this:

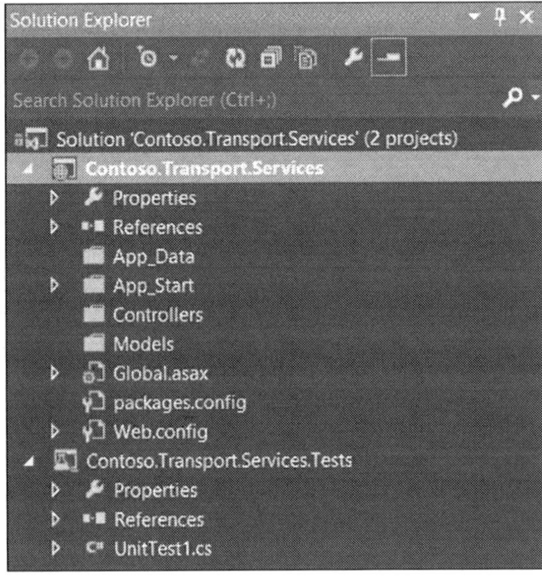

A few things have been added to jump start our Web API project:

A static `WebApiConfig` type has been added to the `App_Start` folder. The `WebApiConfig.cs` file is responsible for registering configuration settings for the Web API during startup. Some of the common uses of `WebApiConfig.cs` are to define default routes, customize the behavior of global and per route matching routes, and define media type formatters.

An important thing to note is the `Register` method that contains the following code:

```
config.Routes.MapHttpRoute(
    name: "DefaultApi",
    routeTemplate: "api/{controller}/{id}",
    defaults: new { id = RouteParameter.Optional }
```

This method defines the default route template for any request; what this means is that any request that has a route `api/{controller}/{id}` will be considered a valid route. In this route we have the following parameters:

- `{controller}`: This refers to the name of the controller class without the suffix, for example, a class with name `PackageController` will be represented as `Package` in the incoming request
- `{id}`: This is used for parameter binding, these together define the controller and action route for the request

With Web API 2, we now have the option to specify attribute-based routes on each API call to provide granular route definitions for our Web API. We will cover this in more detail in *Chapter 2, Extending the ASP.NET Web API*.

The `Global.asax` file has the following defined in `Application_Start`, this registers a delegate for the `WebApiConfig.Register` method in `GlobalConfiguration`. Note that `GlobalConfiguration` belongs to `System.Web.Http.WebHost`, which indicates that we are currently hosting our Web API in IIS, as shown:

```
GlobalConfiguration.Configure(WebApiConfig.Register);
```

Defininig an ASP.NET data model

A model in ASP.NET Web API is similar to a data model defined in the ASP.NET MVC framework. It is a type that represents the entity in the application and manages its state. ASP.NET Web API has inherent capabilities to serialize a model automatically to JSON, XML, or any other format, and then write the serialized data into the body of the HTTP response message. The client can then deserialize the object to obtain the response.

For more information on ASP.NET MVC patterns, visit `https://msdn.microsoft.com/en-us/library/dd381412%28v=vs.108%29.aspx`.

For the scope of this chapter, we will keep the data access very simple. We will have an in-memory store and will define an ASP.NET model to represent it. In later chapters, we will fetch data using tools like Entity Framework and also discuss how expose OData endpoints for building query capabilities from our Web APIs.

We follow these steps to create an ASP.NET model for our solution:

1. Right-click on the `Models` folder. Click on **Add** and then on **New Item**.
2. From the **Add New Item** dialog, add a new C# class. Name it `Package.cs`.
3. Add properties to the data model. The package data model should look like this:

```
namespace Contoso.Transport.Services.Models
{
    public class Package
    {
        public int Id { get; set; }

        public Guid AccountNumber { get; set; }

        public string Destination { get; set; }

        public string Origin { get; set; }

        public double Weight { get; set; }

        public double Units { get; set; }

        public int StatusCode { get; set; }
    }
}
```

Defining an ASP.NET Web API controller

We will now implement a Web API controller that will allow clients to retrieve packages based on a unique package ID. We will use the empty controller template in Visual Studio and then add the following code to our controller type:

1. Right-click on the `Controllers` folder in the `Contoso.Transport.Services` project. Click on **Add** and select **Controller**.

2. Choose an empty Web API 2 controller. Name the controller `PackageController`.

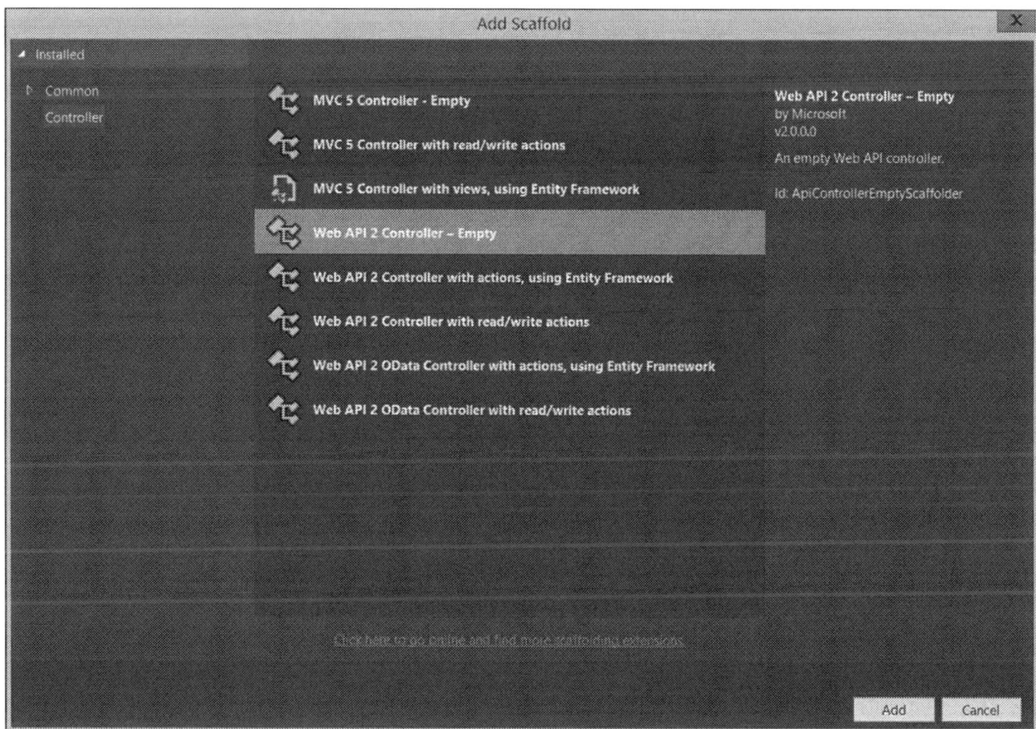

3. Add a reference to the `Contoso.Transport.Service.Models` namespace:

```
using Contoso.Transport.Services.Models;
```

4. Replace the code in `PackageController` with the following code snippet:

```
namespace Contoso.Transport.Services.Controllers
{
    public class PackageController : ApiController
    {
        private static IEnumerable<Package> packages;

        public Package Get(int id)
        {
```

```
            return packages.SingleOrDefault
              (p => p.Id == id);
        }

        protected override void
          Initialize(HttpControllerContext
          controllerContext)
        {
            base.Initialize(controllerContext);

            // Create package for testing purposes. In the real
world use a repository pattern or entity framework to fetch this
data.
            GenerateStubs();
        }

        private static void GenerateStubs()
        {
            packages = new List<Package>
            {
                new Package
                {
                    Id = 1,
                    AccountNumber = Guid.NewGuid(),
                    Origin = "CA",
                    Destination = "TX",
                    StatusCode = 1,
                    Units = 1,
                    Weight = 2.5,
                    Created = DateTime.UtcNow,
                },
                new Package
                {
                    Id = 2,
                    AccountNumber = Guid.NewGuid(),
                    Origin = "AZ",
                    Destination = "AL",
                    StatusCode = 1,
                    Units = 2,
                    Weight = 1,
                    Created = DateTime.UtcNow.AddDays(-2),
                },
                new Package
                {
```

```
                        Id = 3,
                        AccountNumber = Guid.NewGuid(),
                        Origin = "FL",
                        Destination = "GA",
                        StatusCode = 3,
                        Units = 1,
                        Weight = 2.5,
                        Created = DateTime.UtcNow,
                    }
                };
            }
        }
    }
```

The preceding code is relatively straightforward; it creates an in-memory store for packages and a `GET` operation to search for a package based on its ID. A few important things to consider are discussed next.

We override the `Initialize` method for the controller. The method is called when the controller is initialized by the Web API pipeline. It can be used for setting up member variables and populating metadata for a controller.

Note that because this is a sample scenario, we are using an in-memory collection for the data entities. In real-world scenarios, we should use tools such as Entity Framework along with the Repository pattern to make the code more maintainable. The later part of this book discusses the Entity Framework.

The return type here is our `Package` entity, when a response is generated, ASP.NET Web API will serialize the entity using the MediaFormatter configured for the project. To facilitate control over the HTTP Response, ASP.NET Web API also provides additional types such as `IHttpActionResult` and `HttpResponseMessage`. We discuss these in *Chapter 2, Extending the ASP.NET Web API*.

The signature of the `GET` operation matches `HttpRoute` that we defined in the `WebAPIConfig.cs` file (`api/{controller}/{id}`). The signature allows us to determine which HTTP verb needs to be executed for the incoming request. We may define multiple operations for a controller, but each needs to match to a particular route. This approach is also referred to as routing by convention. If no route is found, an exception is thrown. ASP.NET Web API 2 also provides specific routes per controller or even per action through attribute routing. We will discuss these approaches in detail in *Chapter 2, Extending the ASP.NET Web API*.

Next, build the project and that is it! We just created our first Web API. We now have a controller that can search for packages based on IDs and return the package model as a response. In the next section, we put our Web API to test in order to verify our operations.

Testing the Web API

Now that we have a Web API created, we will look at options to validate our Web API functionality. Testing is a crucial stage in the creation of Web API development and publishing. There are a couple of different ways of doing this. We can just test it by requesting the URL in a browser or write code and leverage the `System.Net.HttpClient` type. This section discusses both of these approaches.

Testing in a browser

Testing a Web API is as simple as developing it, since each action in a Web API controller represents a resource, we can just type the URL of the resource and fetch the results.

1. Press *F5* in Visual Studio to launch the Web API in a browser.
2. Visit the following URL:

   ```
   http://localhost:<PORT>/api/package/1
   ```

   Note that the port will be allocated by IIS Express and will be different for each installation.

3. This yields a result similar to the following in the browser:

   ```
   {
       "Id": 1,
       "AccountNumber": "43a2a3eb-e0b8-4840-9e5e-
         192214a79d58",
       "Destination": "TX",
       "Origin": "CA",
       "Weight": 2.5,
       "Units": 1,
       "StatusCode": 1,
       "Created": "2015-03-16T23:57:33.1372091Z",
       "Properties": null
   }
   ```

What happened here?

The client (in this case, the browser) initiated a `GET` request by hitting the URL:

```
GET /api/package/1 HTTP/1.1
Host: localhost:49435
Cache-Control: no-cache
```

When the server received the request, it scanned all controllers to check for a matching route. When the route was found, `PackageController` was selected to respond to the request, and its `Initialize` method was invoked. The `GET` action in `PackageController` was then identified as a route match for the HTTP `GET` request. The method gets called, and `1` is passed as the parameter.

Testing with HttpClient

In the previous section, we discussed how to use a browser to test our Web API. In scenarios where we call our Web API from within a business logic or client application, this may not work. Fortunately, the `System.Net.HttpClient` type can be used to invoke an HTTP-based Web API from a .NET client.

We will use our Visual Studio test project that we created earlier to demonstrate this example:

1. Create a new Unit Test type `PackageControllerTest.cs` in the `Contoso.Transport.Services.Tests` project.

> The Visual Studio ranger's team has built an extension to generate unit tests for class files. It is a useful tool to generate Test methods for multiple methods in the class files. The extensions can be found here: `https://visualstudiogallery.msdn.microsoft.com/45208924-e7b0-45df-8cff-165b505a38d7`.

2. Add the following assembly references to the project:
   - `System.Net.Http` assembly
   - `Contoso.Transport.Services`
3. Add the following NuGet packages to the project:
   - `Newtonsoft.JSON`
4. Replace the code in `PackageControllerTest.cs` with the following code:

```
using System;
using Microsoft.VisualStudio.TestTools.UnitTesting;
using System.Net.Http;
```

```
using Newtonsoft.Json;
using System.Threading.Tasks;
using System.Net.Http;
using Contoso.Transport.Services.Models;

namespace Contoso.Services.Tests
{
    [TestClass]
    public class PackageControllerTests
    {

        [TestMethod]
        public async Task FindPackageByIdNotNullTest()
        {
            var packageid = 1;
            var packageUrl =
              string.Format("http://localhost:
              <PORT>/api/package/{0}", packageid);
            using (HttpClient client = new HttpClient())
            {
                var response = await
                  client.GetStringAsync(packageUrl);
                Assert.IsNotNull(response);
                var package = await
                  Task.Factory.StartNew(() =>
                  JsonConvert.DeserializeObject
                  <Package>(response));
                Assert.IsNotNull(package);
                Assert.AreEqual(packageid, package.Id);
            }
        }
    }
}
```

5. Change `packageUrl` to the URL of the created Web API.
6. At this point, ensure that the Web API is running. Please refer to the *Testing in a browser* section for more details.
7. Build the test project.

8. Right-click on `Test Method` and click on **Run Test** (*Ctrl* + *R* + *T*).

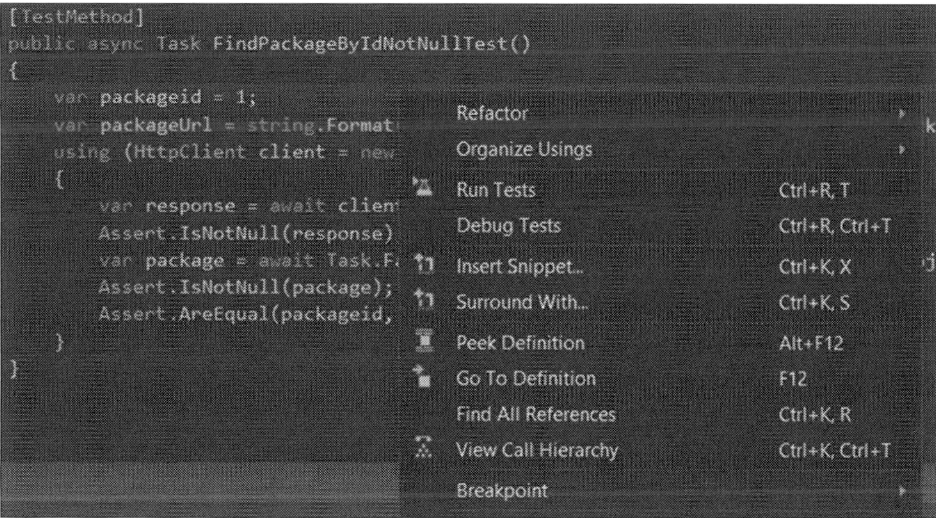

9. The test explorer should display the success results, as follows:

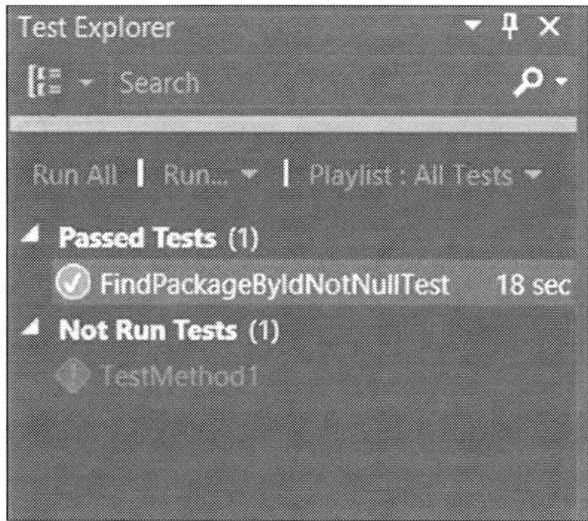

We verified our Web API using a .NET client as well. `HttpClient` exposes a set of utility methods that allow us to perform various HTTP operations. In this case, we used the `GetStringAsync` method that creates an HTTP `GET` request and returns the response as a string.

Committing changes to Git

In the previous section, we built and tested our Web API. Now, we discuss how to use Visual Studio Online and Git for source control management. Note that this section assumes that we have a Git repository created and available. It does not give a walkthrough of setting up a Git repository within VSO.

The Microsoft Virtual Academy has an excellent tutorial for using Visual Studio Online with Git it is highly recommended to understand these concepts before proceeding with this section: `http://www.microsoftvirtualacademy.com/training-courses/using-git-with-visual-studio-2013-jump-start`.

We will now commit the change to Visual Studio Online. Visual Studio 2013 provides a rich integration with Git so we can commit the changes without opening the Git command prompt:

1. Right-click on the `Contoso.Transport.Service` solution file in the `Solution Explorer`, and click on **Add Solution to Source Control**.
2. A dialog box is displayed with options for available source control systems. Select **Git** and click on **OK**.
3. Right-click on the solution again and click on **Commit**.

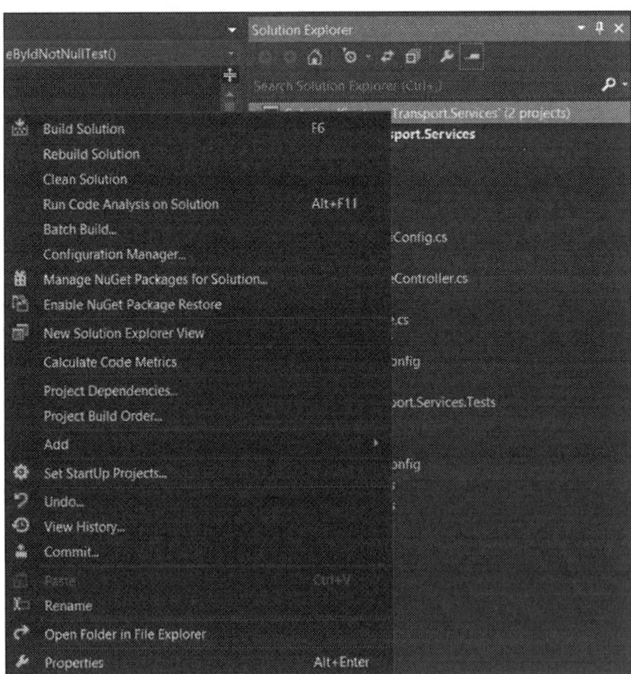

4. Enter comments for the changes, and click on **Commit** to create a local commit.
5. We can now use the **Sync/Push** Git commands from Visual Studio to commit our changes remotely:

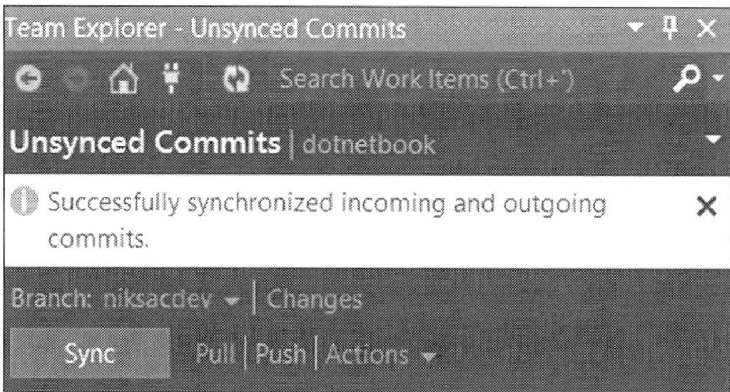

Deploying the ASP.NET Web API using Azure Websites

Microsoft Azure Websites is a **Platform as a Service** (**PaaS**) offering from Microsoft, which allows publishing web apps in Azure. The key focus when building Microsoft websites is to enable a true enterprise-ready PaaS service by allowing rapid deployment, better manageability, global scale at high throughput, and support for multiple platforms. The development of Azure Websites started about 3 years ago under the internal project name *Antares* with the primary intent to create a cheap and scalable web hosting framework for Microsoft Azure. The main target was shared and cross-platform hosting scenarios. The first preview release for Azure Websites came out in June 2012 and went **General Availability** (**GA**) in mid-2013.

> Azure Websites was recently renamed and is now part of Azure App Services. REST based service development is now referred to as API apps. For the scope of this book, we will focus on the existing service implementation. To learn more about App Services, please refer `http://azure.microsoft.com/en-us/services/app-service/`.

There are other PaaS offerings available in Microsoft Azure, such as cloud services that provide Web and worker roles. There is also Microsoft virtual machine through the **Infrastructure as a Service** (**IaaS**), so why choose websites?

Let's look at some of the features provided by Azure Websites, which make them an appealing candidate for Web API and web app deployment:

- **Cloud-First by design**: This is a no-brainer, Azure Websites was started to eliminate the dependency of IIS for cloud developers. Azure Websites leverage SQL Server as a configuration backend, which allows to achieve a greater website density in multitenant environments. It is also intended as a stateless and scalable server architecture.
- **Dynamic provisioning**: The allocation of resources for Azure Websites is determined based on dynamic rules to ensure optimum allocation and performance of the system overall.
- **Network share support**: All instances can leverage shared content storage, this ensures optimum reliability in case the frontend machine goes down.
- **Stateless servers and smart load balancing**: Following the cloud design patterns, all VMs are stateless by design.
- **Build on existing PaaS platform**: Internally, Azure Websites are hosted in PaaS VMs, so it automatically leverages most of the goodies provided by the cloud services platform today. The following figure shows the main components that make up Azure Websites:

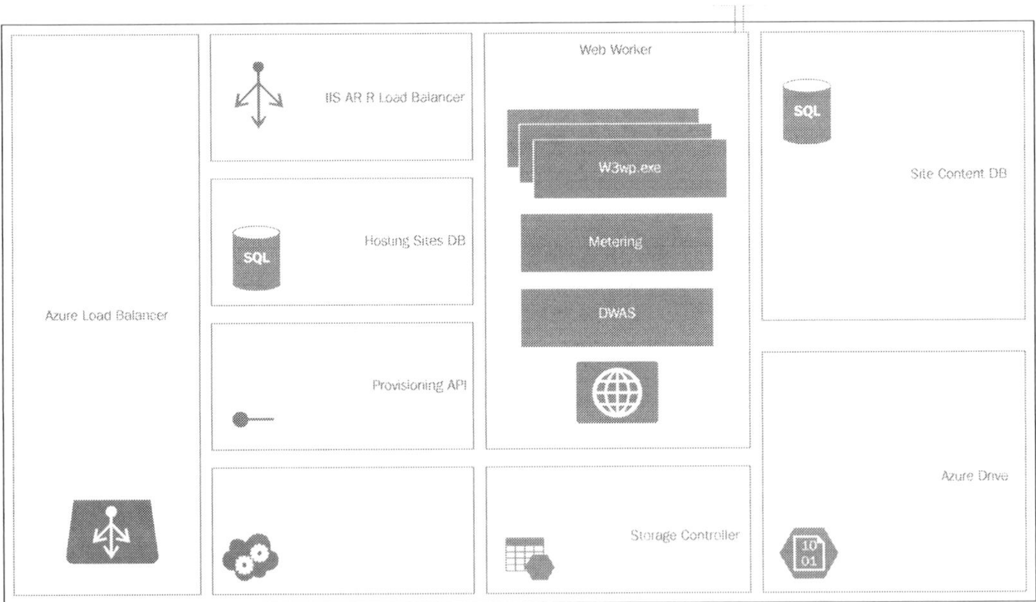

As we can see in the preceding figure, Azure Websites are built on existing technologies, such as Azure storage and web and worker hosting model. It adds additional abstraction to enable rapid deployment and easy configuration management through a set of hosting site and site content databases. Furthermore, Azure load balancers are used in conjunction with IIS **Application Request Routing (ARR)** load balancers to achieve high availability and Hyper Scale. Azure Websites provides the following benefits:

- **Development support**: Websites can be used for developing solutions in an array of languages such as ASP.NET, Java, PHP, Python, and Node.js. Moreover, the development platform does not need to be Windows, OSX, or Linux. CMS solutions such as WordPress, Drupal, and Joomla are fully supported. The integration with code management tools, such as Git, and source control systems, such as VSO and GitHub, is seamless. To add the cherry to the cake, the tools provided by Visual Studio 2013 and above are so easy to use that development, testing, and deployment just take minutes.
- **Built for DevOps**: Azure Websites are targeted to reduce the overall time taken to market and provide an effective TCO. Some of these features include high available environment with automatic patching support, automatic scale, automatic disaster recovery and backups, comprehensive monitoring and alter, and quick and easy deployment.

With such great features, is there any scenario where Azure Websites might not be a good fit?

Well, there are some scenarios where we may be better off using Azure Cloud Services and perhaps even Azure Virtual Machines:

- **Low-level machine access**: Although Azure Websites provide a standard tier that allows its deployment VM, customization that can be done on that VM is still restricted. For example, elevated privileges are not supported as of writing this.
- **Background processes**: There are scenarios where we want to have backend tasks that run complex processing jobs such as math calculations. Worker roles in cloud services seem appropriate for these scenarios. Having said that, from an application perspective, we can still leverage websites as a frontend. For example, a Web API hosted in Azure Websites may push calculation requests to an Azure Service Bus queue, and a backend worker role can then listen to these requests and process them. Another aspect that is supported by Azure Websites is WebJobs, which is associated with an Azure Website, and as of today, can be used for processing lightweight background tasks, such as startup tasks. WebJobs may become more powerful in the future and could then be considered as an alternative for worker roles.

- **Virtual Network support**: Since Azure Websites VMs are controlled by Microsoft PaaS infrastructure, there are minimal options to support Virtual Networks or customer domain integration. As of September 2014, a preview release of supporting websites on Virtual Network has been added as a feature. For the latest information on Virtual Network support, please visit `http://azure.microsoft.com/en-us/documentation/articles/web-sites-integrate-with-vnet/`.
- **Remote desktop**: As of writing of this book there is no support for remote desktop on Azure Websites. It may not be a big limitation though, as websites now support remote debugging from within Visual Studio for all pricing tiers.
- **In-role cache**: Due to the stateless nature of Azure Websites, in-role caching is not supported. However, we can use a distributed cache such as Redis and make it work with websites.

Note that some of the scenarios mentioned here might not be available as of today, but the team may provide support for these in future releases. As a rule of thumb, consider these as recommendations and not protocols. Considerable planning should be conducted based on customer requirements and timelines before making a decision to choose any of the platform options.

Deploying to Azure Websites

Now that we have a fair understanding of Azure Websites' capabilities, let's deploy the Web API we built in the previous section to an Azure Website.

> This sample assumes that the user is signed into an Azure account in Visual Studio. It is required to view the Azure subscription when creating the ASP.NET Web API project. For more information on Azure tools for Visual Studio, please visit `http://msdn.microsoft.com/en-us/library/azure/ee405484.aspx`.

Since we did not associate our Web API project to an Azure Website at the time of its creation, we will now provide details on the Azure subscription and website where we want the deployment to be hosted:

1. Right-click on the Web API project. Click on **Publish** to open the Publish wizard, and select **Microsoft Azure Websites** as the publish target.

2. In the **Microsoft Azure Websites** dialog, click on **New** to create a new Azure Website. Here, we provide details about our Azure subscription and give a name to the website. When deciding on a name, ensure that it is unique; the **Create Site** dialog box validates the fully qualified URL to ensure that there are no existing sites with this name. In case the site name already exists, an error is thrown by the **Create Site** dialog box.
3. By default, the domain name is set to `azurewebsites.net`. It is the default domain for all tiers; we can also provide a custom domain for our deployments (for example, `www.mywebsite.com`).

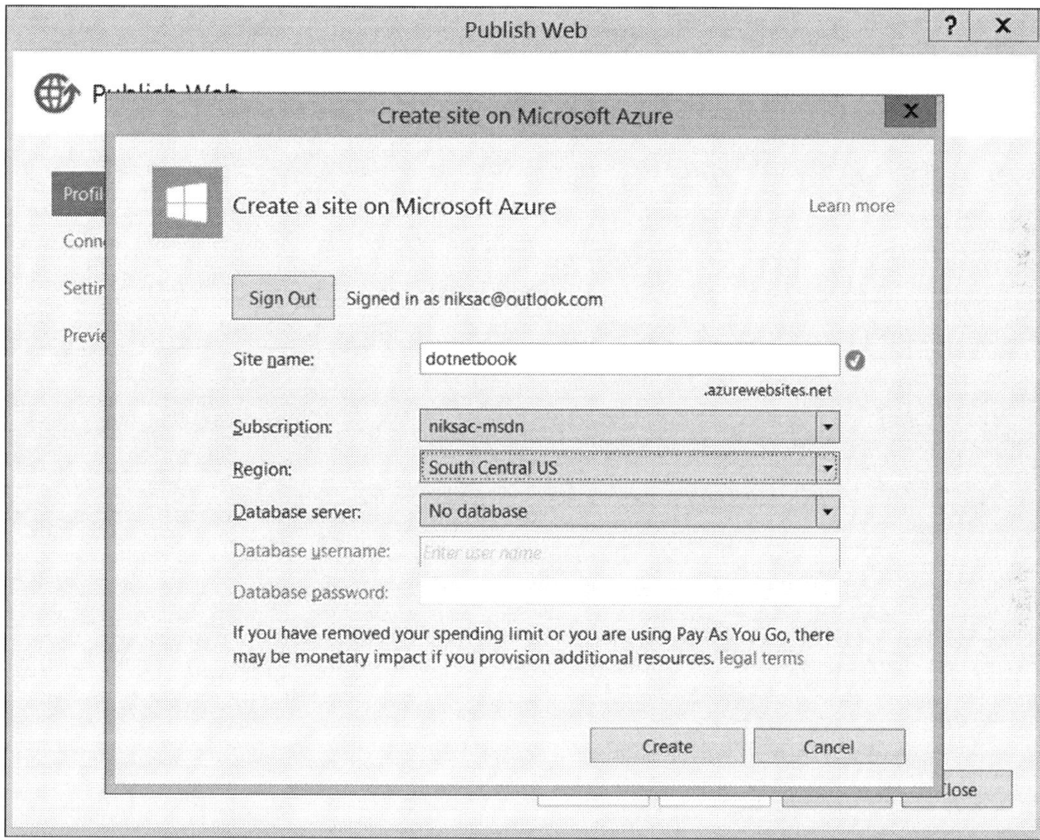

4. Once the Website is created, we are ready to publish our Web API. Azure Websites provides the following publish methods for web applications:
    - **Web deploy**: This is also known as **msdeploy**. It streamlines the deployment of web application to Azure Websites. It enables the packaging of Web application content, configuration, databases, and any other artifacts, which can be used for storage or redeployment. If the package needs to be redeployed to a different environment, configuration values within the package can be parameterized during deployment without requiring modifications to the packages. Use this option to delegate deployment to Azure Websites.
    - **WebDeploy package**: We can use this option when we have an existing `WebDeploy` package.
    - **FTP**: This allows to deploy source from an FTP server.
    - **File system**: This deploys source from a local filesystem location.
5. Once the deployment is complete (should not take more than a few seconds), we will have our Web API running in the cloud.
6. To test the deployment, replace the local domain name we used in the *Testing in a browser* section with the cloud domain name of the Azure Website as shown:

Request	`http://dotnetbook.azurewebsites.net/api/package/1`

Response	`{`
	`"Id": 1,`
	`"AccountNumber": "ac09ae02-00cf-426d-b969-909fae655ab9",`
	`"Destination": "TX",`
	`"Origin": "CA",`
	`"Weight": 2,`
	`"Units": 1,`
	`"StatusCode": 1,`
	`"History": null,`
	`"Properties": null`
	`}`

If we now browse to the Azure management portal and go to the Azure Website we just created, we can right away see incoming requests and how the traffic is being monitored by Azure Websites similar to how it is shown in the following diagram; now that is true PaaS!

> The new Azure portal (currently in preview) provides more detailed statistics about the resources leveraged by Azure Websites. These include storage, network, and compute. The preview portal is accessible at `https://portal.azure.com/`.

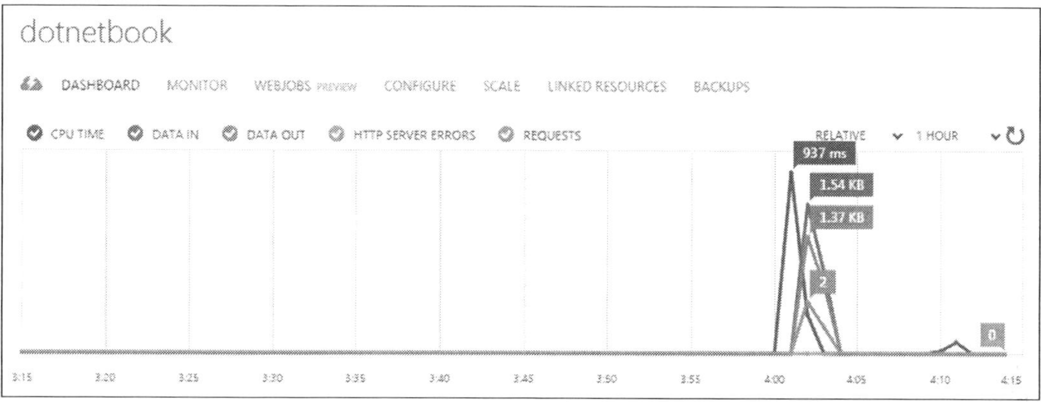

Continuous Deployment using Azure Websites

In the previous section, we used Visual Studio tools to deploy our Web API in Microsoft Azure Websites. The Visual Studio deployment option works well for one-off deployments or small development projects. However, in real-world scenarios, customers prefer integrating builds with automated deployments. Azure Websites provides continuous deployment from source code control and repository tools such as BitBucket, CodePlex, Dropbox, Git, GitHub, Mercurial, and Team Foundation Server. We can, in fact, do a Git deployment from a local machine!

For the purpose of this sample, we use VSO and Git as our repository. Let's take a look at how we can configure Visual Studio Online for our **Continuous Deployments** (CD):

1. Go to the Azure portal and browse to the Azure Website we just created. From the dashboard, select **setup deployment from source control**. When using the new preview portal, this option will be in the **Deployment** section as **Set up continuous deployment**.

2. Select VSO to designate the source code and then select the repository to deploy:

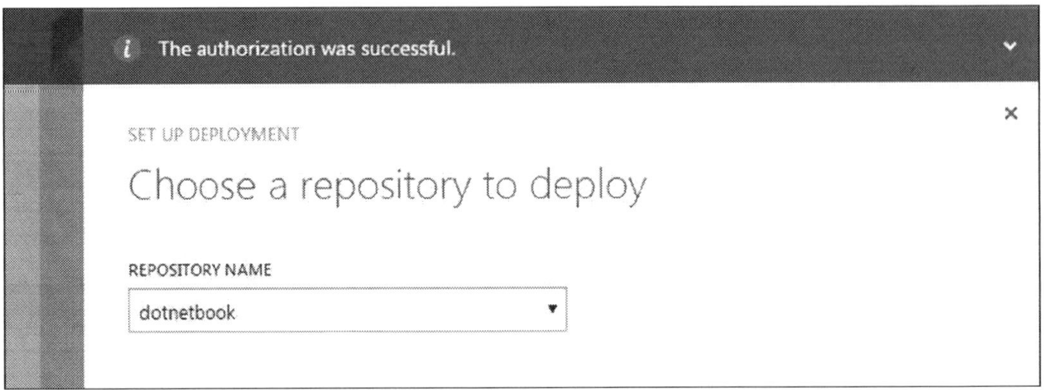

Azure will now create a link to Visual Studio Online. Once the link is established, when a change is committed, it will get deployed to Azure Website automatically. The link creates a build definition for the solution and configures it to run in CD mode. If we go to the build definition in Visual Studio, we can see that a new build definition is added. The linkage also sets the deployment attributes for the build. It ensures that a commit on the solution triggers a deployment. Note that if any unit test projects, which are part of the solution will also automatically get triggered.

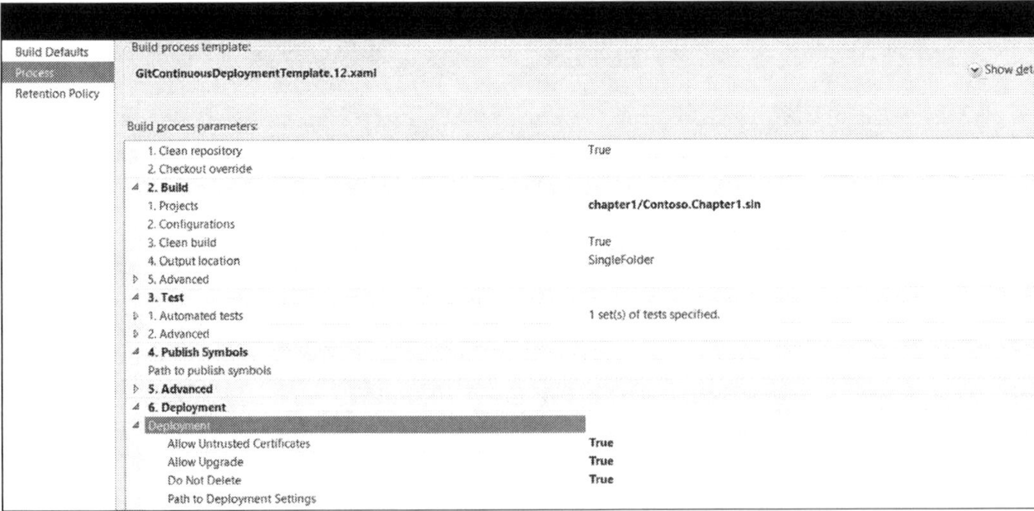

3. Let's make a change to our existing sample to verify this. We will add a new attribute to our Package ASP.NET data model that we created earlier. This attribute will get populated with the current UTC timestamp when the package is created:

```
namespace Contoso.Transport.Services.Models
{
    public class Package
    {
        public int Id { get; set; }

        public Guid AccountNumber { get; set; }

        public string Destination { get; set; }

        public string Origin { get; set; }

        public double Weight { get; set; }

        public double Units { get; set; }

        public int StatusCode { get; set; }

        public DateTime Created { get; set; }
    }
}
```

We will also update the in-memory collection in `PackageController` to ensure that a created timestamp is associated with each record. The code for updating the controller is left as an exercise.

4. When we make a commit and push to the Visual Studio Online repository, the build definition will invoke a new build, which will also update the deployment in our existing Azure Website. This can be verified by looking at the build report:

dotnetbook_CD_20140914.4 - Build succeeded

View Summary | View Log - Open Drop Folder | Diagnostics ▾ | <No Quality Assigned> ▾ | Actions ▾

Nikhil Sachdeva triggered dotnetbook_CD (dotnetbook) for branch refs/heads/master (9eb33bd)
Ran for 2.2 minutes (Hosted Build Controller), completed 6 seconds ago

Latest Activity

Build last modified by Elastic Build (niksacdev) 6 seconds ago.

Request Summary

Request 5, requested by Nikhil Sachdeva 3 minutes ago, Completed

Deployment Summary

Your Website was deployed to : http://dotnetbook.azurewebsites.net/

Summary

Debug | Any CPU

0 error(s), 0 warning(s)

▷ C:\a\src\chapter1\Contoso.Chapter1.sln compiled

▷ 1 test run completed - 100% pass rate

No Code Coverage Results

5. Now, if we again call the same end point, we should get the `Created` attribute as part of the response:

Request	`http://dotnetbook.azurewebsites.net/api/package/1`
Response	{ "Id": 1, "AccountNumber": "48e89bcd-cfaa-4a47-a402-9038ca2dd69b", "Destination": "TX", "Origin": "CA", "Weight": 2.5, "Units": 1, "StatusCode": 1, "Created": "2014-09-14T22:17:32.8954157Z", "History": null, "Properties": null }

Our Web API is now successfully deployed in Microsoft Azure Website and configured for CD.

Summary

This chapter provided an overview of the what, why, and how of an ASP.NET Web API. ASP.NET Web API is a next generation service that enables support for a first-class modern HTTP programming model. It provides abundant support for formats and content negotiation, and request validation.

We talked about the foundational elements of a Web API. We then discussed its usage scenarios and components, and also discussed the classes that make up the API. We went through the request-response pipeline and walked through the message lifecycle of a request. We then created our first simple Web API for a simplified customer scenario and walked through its development, testing, and deployment using Azure Websites. In the next chapter, we will look into advanced capabilities of ASP.NET Web API, and see how these capabilities can be used to customize different aspects of the ASP.NET Web API request-response pipeline.

2
Extending the ASP.NET Web API

The previous chapter was an introduction to the building blocks of a Web API. We discussed how easy it is to create and deploy an ASP.NET Web API using the tools available in Microsoft Visual Studio and Microsoft Azure. In this chapter, we look at some of the features provided by the ASP.NET Web API framework that allow us to customize the Web API pipeline and solve real-world problems.

Attribute routing

In *Chapter 1, Getting Started with the ASP.NET Web API*, we discussed `HttpRoutingDispatcher` and how we can define a route template in the `WebApiConfig.cs` file. This method is referred to as "convention-based routing". It allows developers to define multiple route templates at a global configuration level for all controllers. Every incoming request is then matched to one of these routes to determine the controller and action that will process the request. If no paths match, an `HTTP 404 Not Found` error is issued. Convention-based routing works great for simplistic route matching. However, it becomes cumbersome to maintain a routing table, for example, in situations where we may want to provide nested URI matching. Also, REST architecture constraints recommend having unique explicit paths for recognition of any single resource. Starting with ASP.NET Web API 2, the attribute routing scheme was introduced to tackle such situations.

Attribute routing enables a more granular-level control over route matching. It allows developers to specify routes declaratively within the context of the action. Let's understand this using an example.

We will extend our scenario from *Chapter 1, Getting Started with the ASP.NET Web API*, to leverage attribute routing. To recollect, in *Chapter 1, Getting Started with the ASP.NET Web API*, we developed a Web API for Contoso Transport Corporation that allows them to track packages. We created a package data model that provided metadata for each package; we will now extend this data model and also add a few additional types.

Add a new type `Event` that will represent a point in time record for the status of the package.

Follow these steps to create the `Event` type:

1. Right-click on the `Models` folder and navigate to **Add | New Item**.
2. From the **Add New Item** dialog, add a new C# class. Name it `Event.cs`.
3. Add properties to the data model. The `Event` type should look like this:

```
namespace Contoso.Transport.Services.Models
{
    public class Event
    {
        public string Description { get; set; }
        public DateTime Created { get; set; }
        public Guid Id { get; set; }
        public string Location { get; set; }
    }
}
```

The package data model did not provide status updates earlier. We will add a new property `Status`. The `Status` property in the `Package` type provides an event log of the status of the package; think of the tracking information that is shown on popular online shopping portals. The updated package model now looks like this:

```
namespace Contoso.Transport.Services.Models
{
    public class Package
    {
        public int Id { get; set; }

        public Guid AccountNumber { get; set; }
        public string Destination { get; set; }
        public string Origin { get; set; }
        public double Weight { get; set; }
        public double Units { get; set; }
        public int StatusCode { get; set; }
```

```
        public DateTime Created { get; set; }
        public IEnumerable<Event> Status { get; set; }
    }
}
```

We also modify `PackageController` to provide a method that returns the status of a package based on its identifier. For example, a developer will be able to invoke the API to monitor the status of the package using a URI like this:

`/api/package/1/status`

The first task is to enable attribute routing in our project. Attribute routing is enabled by default for all Web API projects when using the ASP.NET template in Visual Studio (2013 or greater). The `WebAPiConfig.cs` file has the following code that allows attribute routing for our Web API:

```
public static void Register(HttpConfiguration config)
{
    // Web API configuration and services

    // Web API routes
    config.MapHttpAttributeRoutes();

    config.Routes.MapHttpRoute(
        name: "DefaultApi",
        routeTemplate: "api/{controller}/{id}",
        defaults: new { id = RouteParameter.Optional }
    );
}
```

The preceding line of code `config.MapHttpAttributeRoutes();` calls the `AttributeRoutingMapper.MapAttributeRoutes` static method that scans through all controllers and evaluates their actions to generate a URL map for all routes decorated with attribute routing attributes.

Alternatively, we can customize the route discovery by passing a type that implements the `IInlineConstraintResolver` or `IDirectRouteProvider` interface to the `MapHttpAttributeRoutes` method. We will look at this in a moment.

Adding attribute routing to our Web API controller is easy; the framework provides attributes at the action and controller level. This allows a declarative way to define resource URLs at a granular level:

- `Route`: This attribute can be used to decorate an action within a controller. The `Route` attribute is a string parameter that acts as a URI template; the Web API framework then leverages this template URL to create a route entry map for the annotated action in the controller.
- `RoutePrefix`: The `RoutePrefix` attribute allows for route definitions at the controller level. It can be used to provide a base URL for the controller.

Now, let's update `PackageController` to leverage both these attributes.

We add a new action to our existing controller; the functionality of this action is to provide a history of events that have occurred to track a package's current status. We will define a unique route for this action and leverage the updated package data model we just modified. The implementation will look as follows:

```
public IHttpActionResult GetStatus(int id)
{
    // find the package
    var package = packages.SingleOrDefault(p => p.Id == id);
    if (package == null)
    {
        throw new HttpResponseException
          (Request.CreateResponse(HttpStatusCode.NotFound));
    }

    return new PackageResult(package.Status, Request);
}
```

The `GetStatus` method takes an integer ID as a parameter and then performs a search for the existing data store (in our case, the in-memory collection). If there is a match, the current status of the package is returned to the client, or else a `NotFound` HTTP status code is returned. Note that we have `IHttpActionResult` as our return type. The `IHttpActionResult` type was introduced in Web API 2 that provides an abstraction over the `HttpResponseMessage` type. It is especially useful when unit testing a Web API as it acts as a factory for response messages, and we can manipulate our response message before returning the result to the client.

In case you are creating an Asynchrnous operation, you can also return the IHttpActionResult using the Task pattern (`Task<IHttpActionResult>`) in the **Task Processing Library** (TPL).

In the preceding code, we used a custom `IHttpActionResult` implementation that represents a response for `PackageController`:

```
public class PackageResult : IHttpActionResult
{
    IEnumerable<Event> package;
    HttpRequestMessage _request;

    public PackageResult(IEnumerable<Event> value,
      HttpRequestMessage request)
    {
        package = value;
        _request = request;
    }

    public async Task<HttpResponseMessage>
      ExecuteAsync(System.Threading.CancellationToken
      cancellationToken)
    {
        var response = new HttpResponseMessage()
        {
            Content = new ObjectContent
              <IEnumerable<Event>>(package, new
              JsonMediaTypeFormatter()),
            RequestMessage = _request,
            StatusCode = HttpStatusCode.OK,
        };

        return response;
    }
}
```

Next, we define the route for our new action. Decorate the action method with the following attribute:

```
[Route("api/package/{id}/status")]
```

When the Web API executes, it generates an URL map based on the `Route` attribute we decorated for our action. Now run the sample and enter the following in a web browser:

```
http://localhost:49675/api/package/1/status
```

We will see a result similar to this:

```
[
    {
        "Description":"At Seller location",
        "TimeStamp":"2014-11-25T05:26:45.5487368Z",
        "Id":"36b7b36b-1838-4b7a-8537-43da9314711b",
        "Location":"CA",
        "Properties":null
    }
]
```

The Web API framework did the mapping of the routes for the incoming request and then used this map to associate it with the designated action.

Note that we had to provide the absolute URL path in our `Route` attribute template to ensure that the Web API maps to our action. A more efficient way to decorate such attributes is to abstract any standard URI prefix and apply it to the entire controller. We use the `RoutePrefix` attribute to designate a controller-level URL route. The following snippet implements the `RoutePrefix` attribute to `PackageController`:

```
[RoutePrefix("api/package")]
    public class PackageController : ApiController
    {
.....
        private static ICollection<Package> _packages;

        /// <summary>
        /// Gets the status.
        /// </summary>
        /// <param name="id">The identifier.</param>
        /// <returns></returns>
        [Route("{id}/status")]
        public IHttpActionResult GetStatus(int id)
        {
            // find the package
            var package = packages.SingleOrDefault
              (p => p.Id == id);
            if (package == null)
            {
                throw new HttpResponseException
                  (Request.CreateResponse
                  (HttpStatusCode.NotFound));
```

```
            }

            return new PackageResult(package.Status, Request);
        }
......
```

The key thing to notice in the preceding code is that we have dissected our route URL into two sections:

Entity	Attribute	Description
Controller	`[RoutePrefix("api/package")]`	This applies to all actions in this controller
Action	`[Route("{id}/status")]`	This applies to a specific action in the controller

Now run the Web API and make a request:

```
http://localhost:49675/api/package/1/status
```

The `GetStatus` method will get executed, and we will see a similar result:


```
[
   {
      "Description":"At Seller location",
      "TimeStamp":"2014-11-25T05:26:45.5487368Z",
      "Id":"36b7b36b-1838-4b7a-8537-43da9314711b",
      "Location":"CA",
      "Properties":null
   }
]
```


The Web API framework matched the controller URL and the action URL to generate a unique URL that matched the request and then executed the action to display our JSON response.

Custom route discovery using IDirectRouteProvider

In the previous section, we talked about `MapHttpAttributeRoutes` and how it creates a route map by traversing the `Route` attribute decorated action methods within a controller. The type that does the magic of generating and registering these routes is `DefaultDirectRouteProvider` and is an ASP.NET Web API provided by the default implementation of the `IDirectRouteProvider` interface.

The `IDirectRouteProvider` interface allows developers to customize the algorithm responsible for registering routes for all the actions and controllers of the Web API. It is useful in scenarios where we may have specialized routing requirements such as attribute inheritance or when we want to perform centralized operations for the route mapping of all controllers.

Instead of writing an `IDirectRouteProvider` implementation from scratch, we can inherit from `DefaultDirectRouteProvider` that provides a base implementation along with overrides for most methods.

Let's incorporate this into our packaging Web API scenario. We will incorporate `BaseController` that provides a common set of APIs for each controller in our project. These APIs will provide metadata about the controller such as the company name, module name, and version. All controllers must implement the abstract `BaseController` to enable these APIs. Note that we can pass such information as part of the response headers as well. However, we will use an API call to demonstrate the usage of the `IDirectRouteProvider` in our sample.

The `BaseController` looks as follows:

```
using System.Web.Http;
public abstract class BaseController : ApiController
{
    /// <summary>
    /// Gets the information.
    /// </summary>
    /// <returns></returns>
    [Route("info/company")]
    public virtual string GetCompany()
    {
        return "Contoso Packaging LLC";
    }

    /// <summary>
    /// Gets the version.
    /// </summary>
    /// <returns></returns>
    [Route("info/version")]
    public virtual string GetVersion()
    {
        return "1.0.0.0";
```

```
    }

    /// <summary>
    /// Gets the module.
    /// </summary>
    /// <returns></returns>
    [Route("info/module")]
    public abstract string GetModule();
}
```

We will also modify `PackageController` now to implement `BaseController` instead of the `APIController` type:

```
[RoutePrefix("api/package")]
public class PackageController : BaseController
{
    /// <summary>
    /// The packages.
    /// </summary>
    private static ICollection<Package> packages;

    .....

[Route("{id}/status")]
        public IHttpActionResult GetStatus(int id)
        {
            // find the package
            var package = packages.SingleOrDefault(p => p.Id == id);
            if (package == null)
            {
                throw new HttpResponseException(Request.
CreateResponse(HttpStatusCode.NotFound));
            }

            return new PackageResult(package.Status, Request);
        }
....
```

Let's run our sample to verify our changes. We will call one of the `BaseController` APIs to get the company name:

/api/package/info/company

The preceding request returns the following result:

```
HTTP/1.1 404 Not Found
Cache-Control: private
Content-Type: text/html; charset=utf-8
Server: Microsoft-IIS/8.0
X-SourceFiles: =?UTF-8?B?RDpcUHJvamVjdHNcZG90bmV0Ym9va1xDb250b3NvLkNoYXB0
ZXIzXENvbnRvc28uU2VydmljZXNcYXBpXHBhY2thZ2VcaW5mb1xjb21wYW55?=
X-Powered-By: ASP.NET
Date: Tue, 25 Nov 2014 07:21:47 GMT
Content-Length: 4969
```

Why did we get a HTTP Not Found (404) instead of the desired result?

`DefaultDirectRouteProvider` The issue here is that DefaultDirectRouteProvider does not honor attribute inheritance. Although we had it inherited from `BaseController`, there were no matching URLs created for the path: `/api/package/info/company`.

Let's fix this issue by introducing our custom direct route provider. Since `DefaultDirectRouteProvider` provides most of the logic we need, we inherit from the default implementation.

Add the following references to the `WebApiConfig.cs` file in the Web API project:

```
using System.Web.Http.Routing;
using System.Web.Http.Controllers;
```

Add the following type to the `WebApiConfig.cs` file:

```
internal class CustomDirectRouteProvider :
  DefaultDirectRouteProvider
{
    protected override IReadOnlyList<IDirectRouteFactory>
      GetActionRouteFactories(HttpActionDescriptor
      actionDescriptor)
    {
        return actionDescriptor.GetCustomAttributes
          <IDirectRouteFactory>(true);
    }
}
```

The preceding implementation enables attribute inheritance by setting the inherit flag to `true` when defining route mapping for all actions in all controllers:

```
actionDescriptor.GetCustomAttributes<IDirectRouteFactory>(true);
```

Next, we want to ensure that `CustomDirectRouteProvider` is used instead of the default provider. We modify `Register()` in `WebApiConfig.cs` to include our custom provider during registration:

```
config.MapHttpAttributeRoutes(new CustomDirectRouteProvider());
```

Let's run our sample again and call the `BaseController` API to get the company name:

```
/api/package/info/company
```

The request now correctly returns the company name as the result:

```
HTTP/1.1 200 OK
Cache-Control: no-cache
Content-Type: application/json; charset=utf-8
Server: Microsoft-IIS/8.0
Content-Length: 23

"Contoso Packaging LLC"
```

The preceding scenario was simplistic, but we can see how custom routing scenarios can be easily enabled using the ASP.NET Web API framework.

Content negotiation

Content negotiation is an HTTP technique to identify the "best available" response for a client request when multiple responses may be available on the server.

The RFC 2616 (`http://www.w3.org/Protocols/rfc2616/rfc2616-sec12.html`) specification for HTTP allows server-driven, agent-driven, and transparent negotiations. For the scope of this chapter, we focus on server-driven negotiations.

The negotiation between the client and the server is accomplished through a set of HTTP headers. These header fields are used by the client to express the desired content type or media type, this information is then used by the server to format the response in a way the client can understand:

Field	Description
`Accept` headers	These specify certain attributes that are acceptable for a response. These headers specify to the server the type of response expected. For example, `Accept: application/json` will expect a JSON response. Other `Accept` headers include `Accept-Charset`, `Accept-Encoding`, and `Accept-Language`. Note that as per the HTTP guidelines, this is just a hint and responses may have a different content type such as a blob fetch where a satisfactory response will just be the blob stream as the payload.
`Content-Type`	This indicates the media type of the entity-body such as `application/json`.
`Content-Encoding`	This is used as a modifier to a content type; it shows the additional encodings that have been applied to the body, for example, `gzip`, `deflate`.

The response chain of the ASP.NET Web API pipeline invokes the content negotiation process: This is depicted in the diagram below:

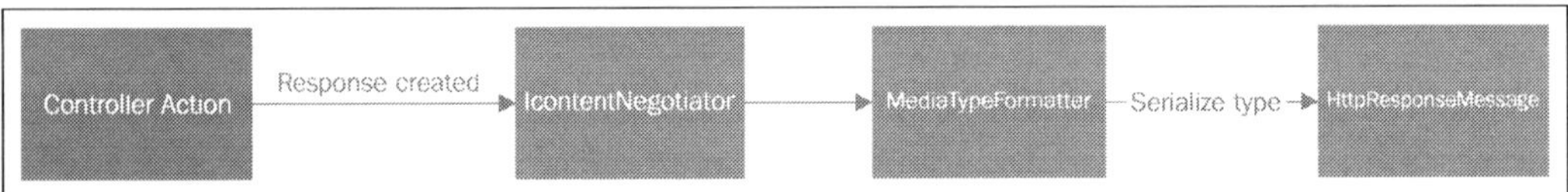

The controller action sends the response stream. An implementation of the `IContentNegotiator` interface is then invoked to determine and apply the appropriate media type formatting. Finally, the content is serialized and delivered as a response to the client:

```
public interface IContentNegotiator
{
    ContentNegotiationResult Negotiate(Type type,
      HttpRequestMessage request,
      IEnumerable<MediaTypeFormatter> formatters);
}
```

The `IContentNegotiator` interface has only one method, `Negotiate`; it performs content negotiation by selecting `MediaTypeFormatter` from the available collection and then processes the content using the media formatter. The ASP.NET Web API ships with a default implementation (`DefaultContentNegotiator`) of the `IContentNegotiator` interface that executes the process of selecting the media formatter, selecting the content encoding, and serializing the content in the requested format.

While content negotiators provide a means to discover the formatting and encoding, media formatters provide more granular control over how responses will be serialized and deserialized. The `MediaTypeFormatter` abstract type in the `System.Net.Http.Formatting` namespace enables support for media formatters in the ASP.NET Web API. It is the base class for serializing and deserializing any strong typed object. Some of the key APIs available in the type include:

Name	**Description**
`ReadFromStreamAsync`	This deserializes an object using the incoming stream asynchronously.
`WriteToStreamAsync`	This serializes an object using the incoming stream asynchronously.
`SelectCharacterEncoding`	This parses the content headers to determine the best character encoding when serializing or deserializing the content body.
`CanWriteType`	This specifies the types that the media formatter can serialize.
`CanReadType`	This specifies the types that the media formatter can deserialize.

The `System.Net.Http.Formatting` namespace also provides out-of-the-box support for most modern media types:

Name	**Description**
`JsonMediaTypeFormatter`	This is the formatter to handle JSON requests: `application/json`. By default, this leverages the NewtonSoft JSON.NET serializer and deserializer. This also has the option to use `DataContractJsonSerializer`.
`BsonMediaTypeFormatter`	This is the formatter to handle BSON requests: `application/bson`. By default, this leverages the NewtonSoft JSON.NET serializer and deserializer.

Name	Description
`XmlMediaTypeFormatter`	This is the formatter that handles XML requests: `application/xml`. It leverages `System.Xml.Serialization.XmlSerializer`.
`FormUrlEncodedMediaTypeFormatter`	This is the formatter that handles HTTP for URL-encoded requests: `application/x-www-form-urlencoded`. This leverages a custom `FormUrl` encoding parser to process the incoming request as key-value pairs.
`BufferredMediaTypeFormatter`	This is a helper class to allow for synchronous operations on a media formatter.

To demonstrate how content negotiation works, we use the example we developed in the previous section *Attribute routing*. We will run the sample using a Chrome extension `PostMan`:

When sending the request, we add an `Accept` header field only to accept `application/json`:

```
GET /api/package/info/company HTTP/1.1
Host: localhost:49675
Accept: application/json
```

The content negotiation process will honor this attribute and use the `JsonMediaTypeFormatter` to serialize and send back a response in JSON format:

```
HTTP/1.1 200 OK
Cache-Control: no-cache
Pragma: no-cache
Content-Type: application/json; charset=utf-8
Expires: -1
Server: Microsoft-IIS/8.0
Content-Length: 23
"Contoso Packaging LLC"
```

We can see that the `Content-Type` returned by the server is in JSON format. Note that the default content encoding (UTF-8) was automatically applied to the response; we can specify content encoding headers in the HTTP request to make the response more selective.

In this section, we discussed out-of-the-box options for content negotiation and media formatters. Let's look at some of the customization options for these features in the ASP.NET Web API infrastructure.

Customizing content negotiation

The `DefaultContentNegotiator` works for most scenarios; however, the framework is extensible to allow for hooking a custom content negotiator if required. We can create a custom content negotiator by inheriting the `DefaultContentNegotiator` type or implementing the `IContentNegotiator` interface and then associating it in the Web API pipeline:

```
GlobalConfiguration.Configuration.Services.Replace(typeof(IContentNego
tiator), new YourCustomContentNegotiator());
```

Customizing media formatters

We can customize or extend the out-of-the-box media formatter by attaching or removing behavior to these adapters. For example, to ensure that our Web API always uses JSON as the default media type, we can add the following code:

```
config.Formatters.JsonFormatter.SupportedMediaTypes.Add(new
MediaTypeHeaderValue("text/html") );
```

The content negotiator will now use the `JsonMediaTypeFormatter` for all HTTP requests that do not have a content encoding specified.

For scenarios that involve proprietary media types or require more control on the serialization and deserialization of HTTP content, we can create our custom media formatter and attach it to the Web API pipeline. Creating a custom media formatter involves the following:

- Inherit from `MediaTypeFormatter` or `BufferredMediaTypeFormatter`. The latter is a synchronous abstraction and can block threads. The `MediaTypeFormatter` provides asynchronous reads and writes.
- Define the supported media types, for example, `text/mymedia`. During content negotiation, we will match this value against the header field values. These can be multiple media types that a media formatter may support encoding variations.

- Define the character encoding for the media formatter (for example, UTF-8 encoding). We can then choose the encoding based on the incoming request by implementing the `SelectCharacterEncoding` method.
- Implement the serializer (`WriteToStream`) and de-serializer (`ReadToStreamAsync`). Note that not all media formatters support de-serialization, so we can use the default base implementation for `ReadToStreamAsync` as well.

> An example of a custom media formatter is available on the ASP.NET portal at:
> `http://www.asp.net/web-api/overview/formats-and-model-binding/media-formatters`

Once we have the media formatter created, we can attach it to the Web API pipeline by adding it to the media formatter collection:

```
config.Formatters.Add(new CustomFormatter());
```

The preceding code adds a custom media formatter to the media formatters collection. During content negotiation, the `IContentNegotiator` implementation determines the media formatter; this is done by a match of the incoming HTTP request media type header field. If the request has `Content-Type: text/mymedia`, it will match our `CustomFormatter` and will be serialized using our custom media formatter.

In this section, we discussed enabling and customizing content negotiation between the client and server; now let's look at some of the security features that the ASP.NET Web API provides.

Securing the ASP.NET Web API

Multiple extension points in the ASP.NET Web API enable developers to implement a feature in different ways. Some features can be provided by the hosting platform while some are available as part of the ASP.NET Web API framework. In this section, we discuss options available for Web API authentication and authorization and delve into the details of some of the features provided by the ASP.NET Web API framework.

The following table lists the various options that can be used to secure an ASP.NET Web API:

Option	Description
Authentication filters	These provide a clean and granular way of implementing authentication for Web API controllers and actions. For example, they allow us to enable multiple authentication schemes for each controller or even for a particular action. We discuss authentication filters later in this section.
Authorization filters	These are used to determine access to a resource based on incoming user credentials. We discuss authorization filters later in this section.
Message handlers	As we discussed in *Chapter 1, Getting Started with the ASP.NET Web API*, message handlers can be hooked into the Web API pipeline and will be executed in an ordered fashion when processing the incoming requests. We can use this option when the security requirements for a particular route are global or common irrespective of the controllers and actions, and when granular access control is not required.
HTTP modules	These have been long used for extending ASP.NET requests running on IIS, and are a .NET assembly that is called on every request made to the Web API. This is not a flexible approach for Web API since the security is applied to all requests without much granular control. Moreover, this option is not available in non-IIS frameworks.
Host providers	Since the ASP.NET Web API allows for different hosting models (for example, OWIN), we can also leverage features already available in the hosting providers. Further, they can also be combined with filters to provide an additional level of customization.

Let's discuss some of these options in detail.

Authentication and Authorization filters

Authentication and Authorization filters allow for a cleaner separation of concerns between authentication and authorization, and, at the same time, provide granular control for controllers and actions. These filters can be applied to the action scope, controller scope, and global scope.

> Authentication filters were a much-awaited feature introduced in ASP.NET Web API 2. In the previous version, authorization filters were used for both authentication and authorization. While this enabled granular control over security, it was confusing and sometimes resulted in unpredictable results because of their flow of execution in the Web API pipeline.

Being a core part of the ASP.NET Web API framework, these filters are invoked by the pipeline during request processing. The following diagram shows how authentication and authorization filters can be hooked into the ASP.NET Web API pipeline:

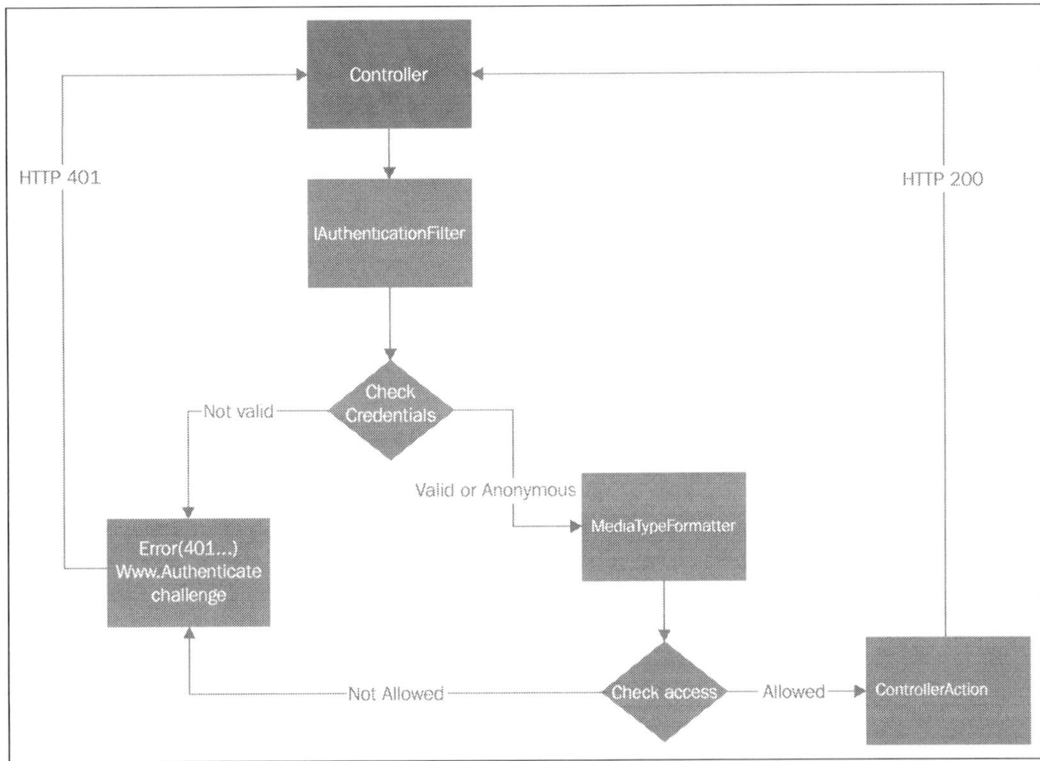

Let's discuss this in greater detail:

1. All incoming requests for a secure resource go through the authentication filter.
2. The authentication filter checks for credentials to validate the incoming user:
    - If the user is valid, it creates a `Principal` (`https://msdn.microsoft.com/en-us/library/system.security.principal.iprincipal%28v=vs.110%29.aspx`) object and attaches it to the context. The `Principal` object is used by the authorization filter later to authorize the user.
    - If the credentials are not valid, an error is attached to the context and an `UnAuthorized` exception (HTTP 401) may be sent to the client.
    - In case of an anonymous user, the user does not send any credentials at all. In this case, the filter can interrupt request processing or decide to pass an empty `Principal` object and let the filters determine what action to perform.
3. If the credentials are verified successfully, the request flows through the authorization filter, which verifies user access for the particular controller or action.
4. If access is granted the request is forwarded to other action filters or to the controller action for building the response. In case, the request is not verified an unauthorized exception (HTTP 401) may be sent to the user.

Now that we have an understanding of authentication and authorization filters, let's extend our sample to demonstrate their usage.

We can create our implementation of the `IAuthentication` and `IAuthorization` filters. However, we will leverage some popular existing technologies to do this work for us:

Technology	**Description**
Azure Active Directory	This is a Microsoft Identity Service in the cloud. It is a scalable multi-tenant service that provides enterprise-grade capabilities to secure our resources. We will leverage Azure Active Directory as our Authority Service. It will primarily authenticate and authorize the user based on the token sent as part of the incoming request headers. To know more about Azure Active Directory, visit `http://azure.microsoft.com/en-us/documentation/articles/active-directory-whatis/`.

Technology	Description
OWIN	This stands for Open Web Interface for .NET. It acts as a middleware between web servers and web applications, decoupling the dependencies of applications on the underlying host. To know more about OWIN, visit `https://github.com/owin/owin`.
Project Katana	Katana can be thought of as IIS running on open source. It is an implementation of a web server providing IIS capabilities but leveraging OWIN as an underlying platform. The next version of ASP.NET (Version 5) is strongly influenced by Katana and OWIN as the core infrastructure. To know more about Katana, visit `http://www.asp.net/aspnet/overview/owin-and-katana/an-overview-of-project-katana`.

Creating an Azure AD directory

We will need an Azure AD directory tenant that will act as our user store and also our token issuer authority. A default Active Directory is automatically associated with an Azure subscription when it is created. We will leverage the existing directory for our sample.

We can also associate a different directory to our subscription by modifying settings for our subscription in the Azure Management Portal. More information can be found at `http://blogs.technet.com/b/ad/archive/2013/11/08/creating-and-managing-multiple-windows-azure-active-directories.aspx`.

Enabling authentication for the Web API project

Visual Studio 2013 provides an intuitive ASP.NET Web API template that allows you to configure authentication when creating a new Web API project. The authentication option automatically adds all the necessary infrastructure and code to configure the Web API for the selected organization or user account. As of today, this support is only available when creating new ASP.NET Web API projects.

For our sample, we will be extending our existing Web API project hence we will not use the authentication scaffolding option. Instead, we will configure the authentication for the project manually.

> Visual Studio 2013's tooling support is recommended for all new project creations. To know more about how to use the out-of-the-box option provided by Visual Studio 2013, please visit `http://www.asp.net/web-api/overview/security/individual-accounts-in-web-api`.

First, we ensure that all NuGet package references are added to our project. We will need the following packages to be installed in our Web API project:

Package	Description
`Microsoft.Owin`	This provides helper components for OWIN Components.
`Microsoft.Owin.Security`	This is the shared infrastructure for all OWIN supported security providers.
`Microsoft.Owin.Security.OAuth`	This enables OAuth authentication for the Web API. The `Owin.ActiveDirectory` module utilizes the types in this package.
`Microsoft.AspNet.WebApi.Owin`	This allows for hosting an ASP.NET Web API in an OWIN server.
`Microsoft.Owin.Host.SystemWeb`	This allows OWIN-hosted application to run on ISS and leverage the ASP.NET request pipeline.
`System.IdentityModel.Tokens.Jwt`	This provides the infrastructure to generate, parse, and validate **JSON Web Tokens (JWT)**.
`Microsoft.Owin.Security.Jwt`	This is the OWIN middleware to validate and parse JWT.
`Microsoft.Owin.Security.ActiveDirectory`	This provides interfaces and logic to leverage Azure Active Directory as an authority and authentication service when using OWIN middleware.

Next we will add some classes to enable Azure AD authentication for our Web API.

Right-click on the project and navigate to **Add** | **Class** to create a new class. Name the class as `Startup.cs`.

An OWIN application requires a `StartUp` class that allows for defining the components of the application pipeline.

Add the following code to the `Startup` type we just created:

```
using System;
using System.Collections.Generic;
using System.Linq;
```

```
using Microsoft.Owin;
using Owin;

[assembly: OwinStartup(typeof(Contoso.Transport.Services.Startup))]

namespace Contoso.Transport.Services
{
    public partial class Startup
    {
        public void Configuration(IAppBuilder app)
        {
            ConfigureAuth(app);
        }
    }
}
```

The `Configuration` method is executed when the Web API is invoked:

- The `Configuration` method in turn invokes the `ConfigureAuth` method that is responsible for setting up the authentication providers before the Web API can receive a request. We will now define the `ConfigureAuth` method.
- The `ConfigureAuth` method is defined in a partial class for startup. We will create a new class in the `App_Start` folder and name it `StartUp.Auth.cs`. When using the VS 2013 Project Wizard for authentication, the `ConfigureAuth` method enables support for an OAuth 2.0 bearer token. While this can be used to support Azure AD, we will add code to support the Azure AD OWIN abstraction. The Azure AD OWIN components are available as part of the `Microsoft.Owin.Security.ActiveDirectory NuGet` package and simplify much of the underlying configuration:

  ```
  using System.Configuration;
  using System.IdentityModel.Tokens;
  using Microsoft.Owin.Security.ActiveDirectory;
  using Owin;
  public partial class Startup
  {
      public void ConfigureAuth(IAppBuilder app)
      {
          var validationParameters = new
            TokenValidationParameters
          {
              ValidAudience =
  ```

```
                ConfigurationManager.AppSettings
                  ["ida:Audience"]
            };

            app.UseWindowsAzureActiveDirectory
              BearerAuthentication(
            new WindowsAzureActiveDirectory
              BearerAuthenticationOptions
            {
                TokenValidationParameters =
                  validationParameters,
                Tenant = ConfigurationManager.
                  AppSettings["ida:Tenant"]
            });
        }
    }
```

- In the above code, the long named method `app.UseWindowsAzureActiveDirectoryBearerAuthentication` adds support for an Azure AD issued bearer token to be consumed by our Web API. The method is simply an abstraction to use Azure AD, and under the hood, it uses the OWIN `app.UseOAuthBearerAuthentication` method to set up the authentication infrastructure for Azure AD generated OAuth tokens.
- Additionally, there are two configuration values that will be used at runtime to determine the audience and tenant for the Azure AD application. We will update this configuration in the next section where we configure our Web API in Azure AD.

Our Web API is now configured to use Azure AD security and OWIN middleware. Let's configure our Web API in Azure AD.

Configuring the Web API in Azure AD

Azure AD provides an application security model for the Web and native applications. The applications can register themselves, define policies such as read/write access and single sign-on capabilities, and grant access to other applications. We will now leverage the Azure Management portal to register our Web API with our Azure AD directory:

1. Go to **Active Directory** | **Applications** and click on **Add An Application**.

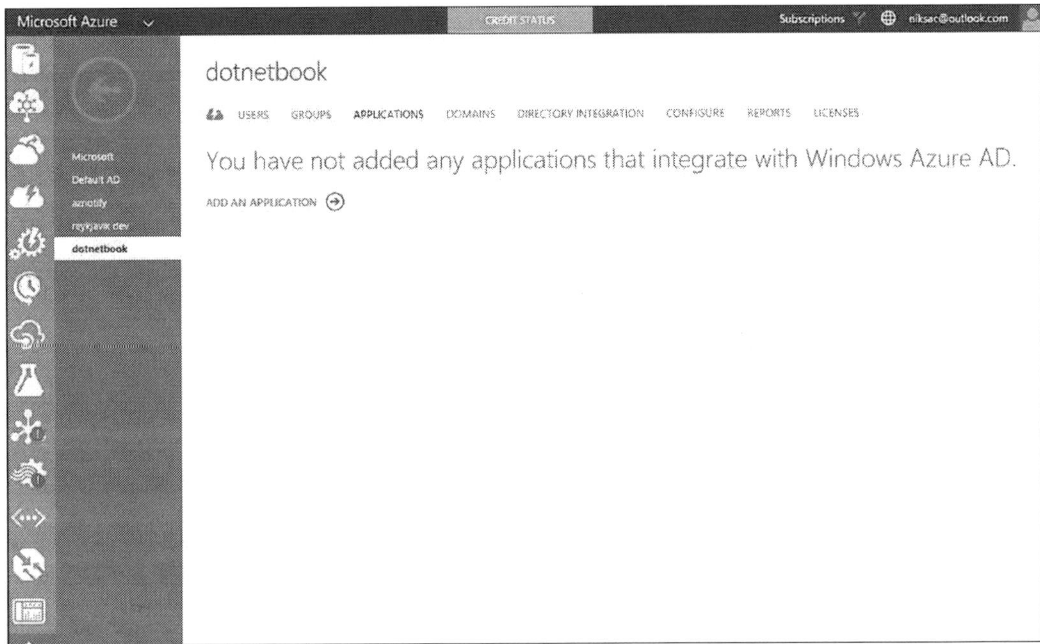

2. Choose **Add an application my organization is developing**:

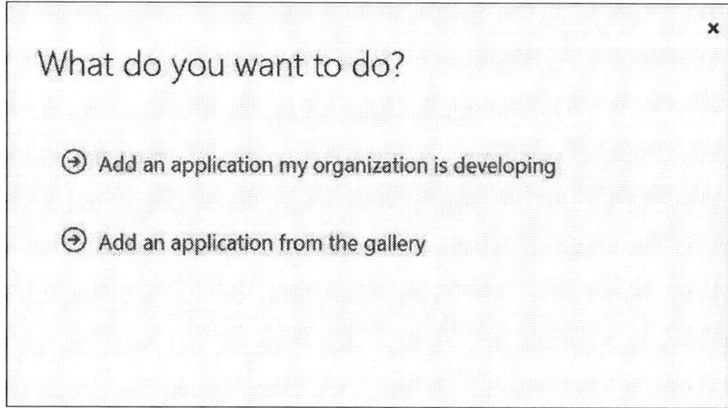

3. In the next section, enter a name for the application and choose **Web Application and/or Web API** as the type:

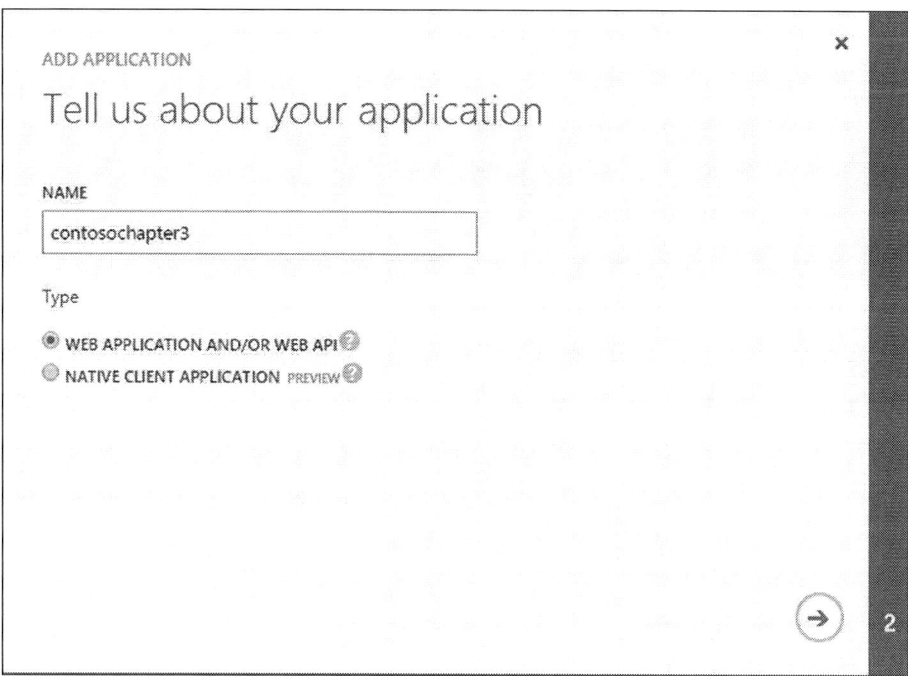

4. In the next screen, we will configure properties for our application. Azure AD uses the following information to create a service principal for our Web API:
    - The **Sign-On URL** for our Web API, which is typically the default or root URL of the Web API.
    - The **App ID URI** is used by Azure AD to create something similar to a realm. The APP ID URI needs to be unique within the directory tenant. A way of defining unique APP ID URIs is to use the tenant name as the base URI and append a suffix per environment (`Dev`, `Test`, `QA`). Note that since App ID is a URI and not a URL, it does not need to resolve to an addressable endpoint.

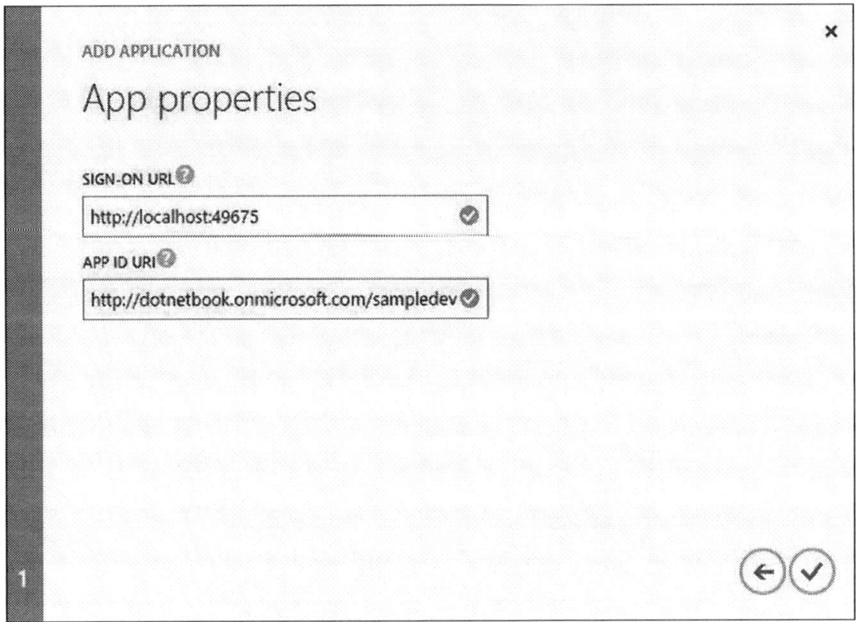

In the preceding example, we used localhost and an IIS Express port number for the Sign on URL. Since these can frequently change, it is recommended to deploy applications to Windows Azure or use dedicated port numbers.

5. If we now go to the **Configure** tab for our application created in Azure AD, we will see a **Client ID** generated for the application. It is the service principal ID and will now be used uniquely to identify our Web API instance within Azure AD.

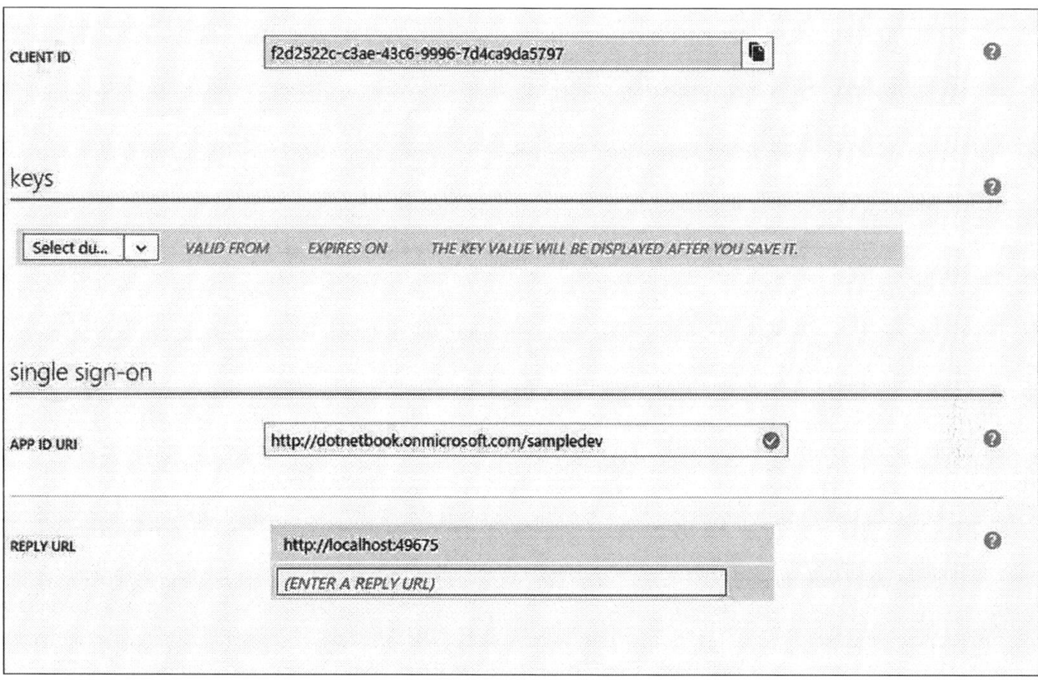

6. The final step in the Azure AD configuration is to define a permission set for our Web API.

Azure AD provides a JSON manifest file that can be used to create permission policies for an application. The following steps describe how to configure permissions for the application:

1. Download the manifest for the Web API application we configured:

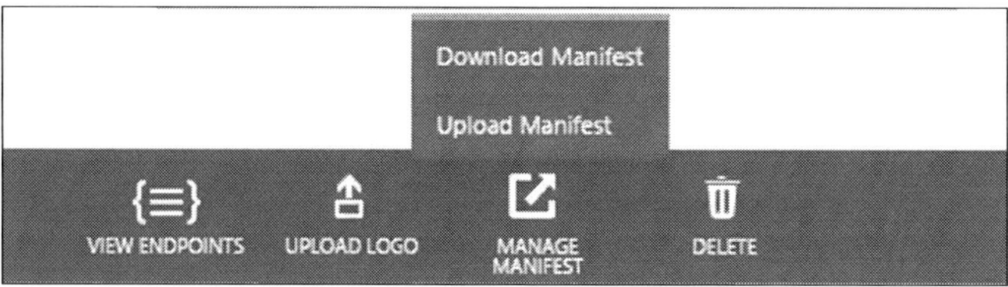

2. Open the downloaded manifest file and replace the `oauth2Permissions` node with the following snippet:

```
"oauth2Permissions": [{
    "adminConsentDescription": "Allow the application
      full access to the Packaging Web API on behalf
      of the signed-in user",
    "adminConsentDisplayName": "Have full access
      to the Packaging Web API",
    "id": "255b6da8-739b-41f5-ae31-01aaab71cd74",
    "isEnabled": true,
    "origin": "Application",
    "type": "User",
    "userConsentDescription": "Allow the application full
      access to the Packaging Web API on your behalf",
    "userConsentDisplayName": "Have full access to the
      service",
    "value": "user_impersonation"}],
```

   This snippet introduces a user impersonation permission scope for our Web API. Any client that presents a valid access token with this scope will be able to access the Web API. Note that the ID attribute must be changed to a new `Guid` value to avoid conflicts.

3. Upload the complete JSON manifest using the Azure management portal.

We have now configured our Web API to work with Azure AD. However, we need to update the tenant and audience in our Web API project so we can link the Web API with the Azure AD tenant. Add the following settings in the root `web.config` of the Web API project:

```
<appSettings>
    <add key="ida:Tenant" value="<Your Azure AD tenant name>"
      />
    <add key="ida:Audience" value="<Your App ID URI>" />
</appSettings>
```

Note that `Tenant` should only include the name of the tenant without any special characters, for example, `dotnetbook.onmicrosoft.com`.

Our web API is now configured to authenticate with Azure AD. However, we still need to set access control on our controllers to ensure that only valid requests are permitted to access resources. In the next section, we add authorization for our Web API controller.

Enabling Authorization for the controller

Adding authorization filters to our Web API is fairly simple; we leverage the `Authorize` attribute to use the default authorization filter. The `Authorize` attribute inherits from an abstract class `AuthorizationFilterAttribute`, which is an implementation of the `IAuthorizationFilter` filter. The `Authorize` attribute can be applied at the controller or action level thus providing granular control over how security needs to be implemented. Some of the principal methods provided by this filter are given in this table:

API	**Description**
`OnAuthorization`	This method is called when an action is being authorized. It uses the user principal in the current context to validate user access. Authorization is denied in the following cases: • The request is not associated with any user • The user is not authenticated • The user is authenticated but is not in the authorized group of users collection • If the user is not in any of the authorized roles collection For more details, please visit `https://msdn.microsoft.com/en-us/library/system.web.http.authorizeattribute.onauthorization(v=vs.118).aspx`
`HandleUnauthorizedRequest`	This method determines how to handle requests when an authorization is denied. The default response is to generate an unauthorized user response (401).
`ExecuteAuthorizationFilterAsync`	This is the only method in the `IAuthorizationFilter` interface and is responsible to execute the authorization filter.

Let's add this attribute to our `PackageController`:

```
[Authorize]
[RoutePrefix("api/package")]
public class PackageController : BaseController
    {...}
```

The preceding attribute will now deny access to any requests for the controller that do not have a valid authorization header. If we now try to access a resource in our Web API, we will get an HTTP 401 unauthorized response:

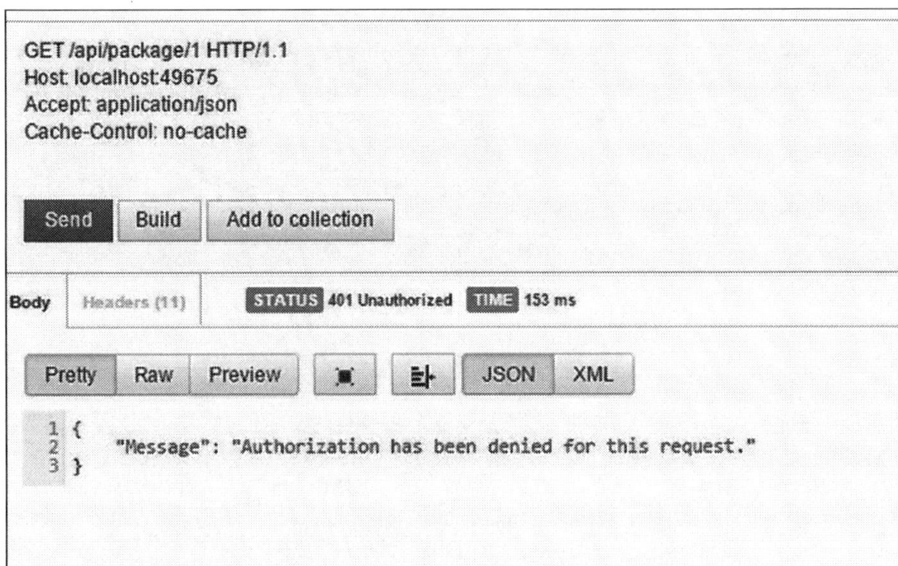

In the next section, we will create a test client and configure its security permissions to ensure that it can access our secure Web API.

Testing our secure Web API

In the previous section, we enabled our Web API to leverage Azure AD as an identity and access control store. Any caller must provide appropriate credentials to access the Web API resources, or else an HTTP 401 status response is returned.

So what is an appropriate credential for our Web API?

Azure AD is based on an implementation of the OAuth 2.0 RFC 6749 specification. In this framework, a client requests an Auth code from an authorization server (in this case, Azure AD) based on user credentials. This is typically done through a user agent as a redirection to the identity provider login page or through the use of service credentials. Once the Auth code is granted, the client uses the Auth code to request for an access token. The authorization server issues an access token based on the permission policies for the current user. The client can then send this token as part of the HTTP headers to access resources for endpoints protected using the authorization server.

> A more detailed explanation of the **Authorization Grant Flow** in Azure AD is available at `https://msdn.microsoft.com/en-us/library/azure/dn645542.aspx`.

We will leverage the preceding concepts to create a native test client that allows us to issue authenticated requests to our Web API.

Creating the test client

The first step is to create a test client. In *Chapter 1, Getting Started with the ASP.NET Web API*, we created a unit test project. We will use the project to create an integration test that will allow us make a request to our secured packaging Web API.

In a real-world scenario, we will use a web application or a mobile app as a client for our Web API.

Configuring the test client in Azure AD

We will leverage the application module of Azure AD to register the test client in Azure AD. Azure AD simplifies the permission model by establishing a trust between the test client and the Web API. In the *Configuring the Web API in Azure AD* section, we created a permission scope in Azure AD for our Web API; we will now use the scope to associate the test client with our Web API:

1. Navigate to the **Azure AD | Application** module and choose **Add an application my organization is developing**:

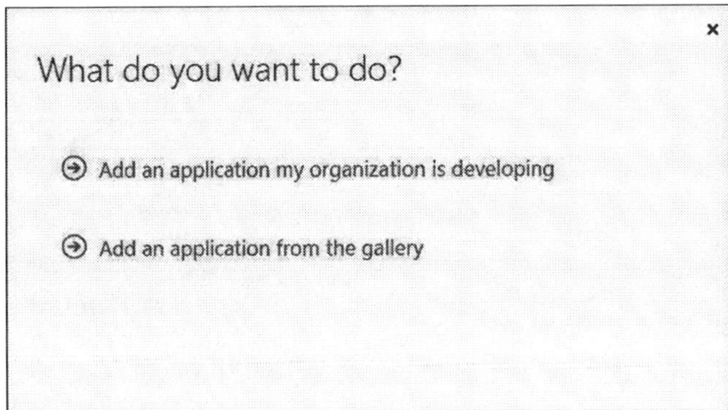

2. In the next section, enter a name for the application and choose **Native Client Application** as the type.

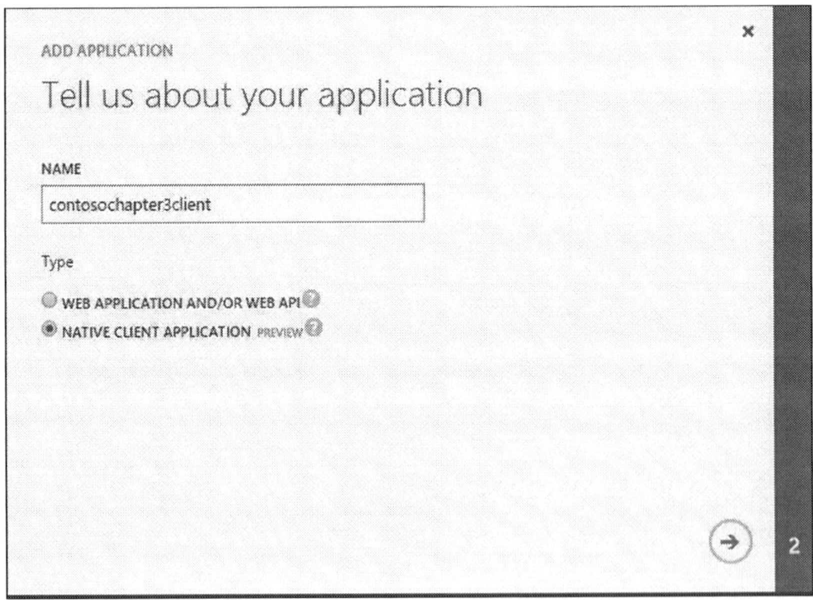

3. On the next screen, specify a URI for our native application. It does not need to be an addressable resource.

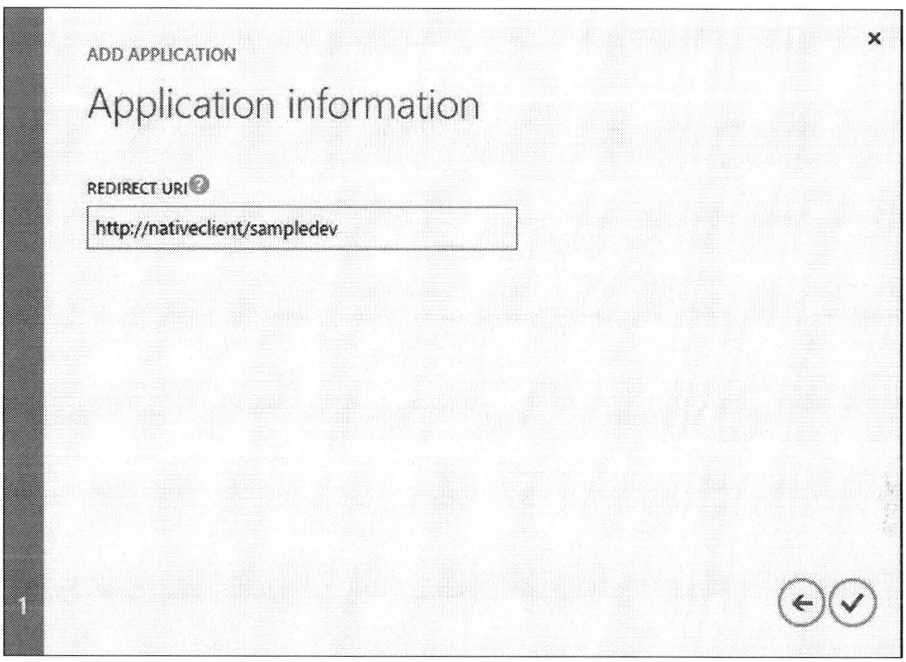

4. If we now go to the **Configure** page, we will see a similar configuration as we saw when configuring our Web API. In this, however, we will also configure a permission scope for our test client.
5. Scroll down to the **permission to other applications** section. From the applications list, select our Web API application. Also from the **Delegated Permissions** list, choose the only permission scope available:

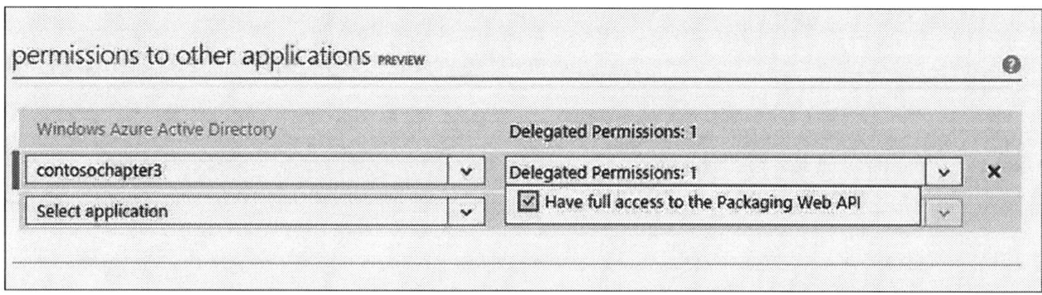

6. Save the configuration.

Now we have our test client configured in Azure AD. Next we will update our test client to make an authenticated request.

Updating the test client

Azure AD provides a set of client interfaces that facilitate getting the access token for a set of valid credentials. The NuGet package that facilitates this API is ADAL or Active Directory Authentication Library. Let's leverage the client API available in this package to make a request to our Web API:

1. Add the ADAL (`Microsoft.IdentityModel.Clients.ActiveDirectory`) NuGet package to the unit test project.
2. The following code snippet connects to Active Directory and fetches a bearer token based on a set of valid user credentials:

```
private async Task<string> GetAuthTokenAsync()
{
    ServicePointManager.ServerCertificateValidationCallback
      += (sender, cert, chain, sslPolicyErrors) => true;

    // Create the Azure AD auth context based on
      //the directory tenant
    var authContext =
    new AuthenticationContext(
        string.Format(
            "https://login.windows.net/{0}",
            ConfigurationManager.
              AppSettings["ida:Tenant"]));

            // Get token by prompting the user
            //for credentials
            // Alternatively use AcquireTokenSilent to pass
            //in user credentials without prompting
            var result = authContext.AcquireToken(
                ConfigurationManager.AppSettings
                  ["ida:WebAPIAppIdURI"],
                ConfigurationManager.AppSettings
                  ["ida:NativeClientId"],
                new Uri(ConfigurationManager.AppSettings
                  ["ida:NativeAppRedirectUri"]),
                PromptBehavior.Auto);

            // get the authorization header
```

```
            return result.CreateAuthorizationHeader();
}

// Now we create a HttpClient and pass in the
  //bearer token generated in the previous step as an
  //Authorization Header
// Get the client token
var authtoken = this.GetAuthTokenAsync().Result;

using (var client = new HttpClient(handler))
{
    // add an authorization header
    client.DefaultRequestHeaders.Authorization =
      new AuthenticationHeaderValue
    ("Authorization", authtoken);

    // get the response
    var response =
      client.GetStringAsync(string.Format
      ("{0}/api/package/{1}",
      ConfigurationManager.AppSettings["BaseUrl"],
      Packageid)).Result;
    Assert.IsNotNull(response);
    var package = Task.Factory.StartNew(() =>
      JsonConvert.DeserializeObject
      <Package>(response)).Result;
    Assert.IsNotNull(package);
    Assert.AreEqual(Packageid, package.Id);
}
```

3. We need to populate the `app.config` file with the correct values for the following:

Value	Description
`BaseUrl`	This is the root URL for the deployed Azure Website
`WebAPIAppIdURI`	This is the app ID URI as defined in the configuration of the Web API in Azure AD
`NativeCleintId`	This is the client ID of the Native application configured in Azured AD
`NativeAppRedirectUri`	This is the redirect URI as described in the configuration for the native client in Azure AD
`Tenant`	This is the Azure AD tenant

4. If everything goes well, we will see a response as shown here:

```
HTTP/1.1 200 OK
Content-Type: application/json; charset=utf-8
Expires: -1
Content-Length: 364
{
    "Id": 1,
    "AccountNumber": "03d99961-7fdf-47b8-
      97fd-8d4d726ac73d",
    "Destination": "TX",
    "Origin": "CA",
    "Weight": 2.5,
    "Units": 1,
    "StatusCode": 1,
    "Created": "2014-12-01T08:36:40.7298855Z",
    "Status": [
        {
            "Description": "At Seller location",
            "TimeStamp": "2014-12-
              01T08:36:40.7298855Z",
            "Id": "015a1024-012f-4e42-
              a64c-7f00dfce7377",
            "Location": "CA",
            "Properties": null
        }
    ],
    "Properties": null
}
```

In this section, we demonstrated how we can authenticate and authorize a Web API using enterprise-grade stores such as Azure AD. Although the preceding example was confined to Azure AD, the OWIN framework provides inherent support for other identity providers such as Google, Yahoo, Facebook, and Custom stores. The OWIN libraries can be easily used in conjunction with this store to enable highly customizable and granular access control policies for the ASP.NET Web API.

In the next section, we discuss hosting options for our Web API.

Hosting

In *Chapter 1, Getting Started with the ASP.NET Web API,* we discussed the concept of a Host Listener. It listens for incoming requests, transforms them into an appropriate `HttpRequestMessage`, and then sends it through the Web API `MessageHandler` pipeline. The plug and play model of a Host Listener in the ASP.Net Web API provides considerable flexibility in determining how we want to host our Web API. There are two broad categories to host a Web API:

Type	Description
Web or IIS hosting	Web hosting refers to using the legacy ASP.NET pipeline in IIS for hosting the Web API. The `Microsoft.AspNet.WebApi.Host` assembly contains the components to host a Web API using IIS. The `HttpApplication` object passes all Web API route requests to `HttpControllerHandler`. This handler is then used to process incoming Web API requests and transform them into `HttpRequestMessage`. The messages are then sent through the Message Handler chain of execution and finally to the controller to execute the appropriate action.
Self-hosting	This has become a widely popular option for hosting the ASP.NET Web API primarily because of its applicability to non-IIS environments. It has also opened new scenarios for hosting the ASP.NET Web API in non-Windows environments such as Linux by leveraging the Mono framework for .Net. The `Microsoft.AspNet.WebApi.SelfHost` assembly contains the runtime components to host a Web API using IIS. The OWIN runtime that we have been using throughout this chapter is an implementation of the ASP.NET Web API Self-Hosting model. It is the default hosting model being used in Web API 2 and is going to become more prominent with ASP.NET 5 and later.

Choosing between hosting providers entirely depends upon customer requirements. IIS hosting provides the existing capabilities of IIS such as management tools, security, health, and diagnostics. Self-hosting our Web API gives the flexibility to make it platform agnostic and enable scenarios such as using non-Windows platforms or even hosting in device controllers for Internet of Things scenarios. A balanced option is to use OWIN components with Katana, which tends to provide the best of both worlds. In the next Version of ASP.NET 5, it tends to progress toward this as the default options, and so green field applications should consider this seriously before proceeding with IIS as standard.

Summary

In this chapter, we discussed some of the primary extensibility features provided by the ASP.NET Web API framework. We discussed attribute routing and how we can easily customize the routing behavior of our Web API resources at a very granular level. We talked about extending the content negotiation and media formatters and how we can support custom formatters for processing proprietary media formats. We then considered enabling security for our Web API; we leveraged the APIs provided by the OWIN framework and Azure AD to create a powerful and scalable security infrastructure for our Web API. Finally, we discussed the multiple hosting options available for Web API.

In the next chapter, we discuss what API Management is and how we can leverage out-of-the-box services in Azure to securely publish and monitor our Web APIs.

3
API Management

In the previous chapters, we discussed developing, extending, and deploying our Web APIs using ASP.NET and Microsoft Azure. Publishing a Web API that meets customer requirements and quality benchmarks is essential. However, managing, marketing, and maintaining the Web API is equally important. In this chapter, we explore Azure API Management, which provides a set of tools for rapid publishing and continuous monitoring of a Web API.

Azure API Management

Let's face it, developing and deploying a Web API (and for that matter, any product) does not make it successful. There are multiple other factors that influence the success of a Web API:

- It should provide high availability and scalability
- It should provide a support model and a seamless update process to ensure business continuity
- It should provide monitoring support for customers to understand usage and cost patterns
- It should provide a consistent and variant costing model through policies for businesses to experiment with and implement
- It needs to be backed with robust documentation and an easy-to-consume reference
- It should be available for multiple platforms to reach a large developer community
- The idea needs to be marketed to sell to a wider audience

There are many other factors such as compliance, constraints, and geo-distribution that need to work to ensure the success of a production quality Web API. One of the key terms in developing and managing software efficiently is DevOps. It provides a workflow for predictable and repeatable development of the service and at the same time ensures quicker development cycles through learning and feedback. There are some excellent books for understanding DevOps, such as *Building Cloud Apps with Microsoft Azure, Microsoft Press*, which discusses the development cycle from a Microsoft Azure perspective.

Azure API Management provides a set of features that alleviate most of the preceding considerations and let API developers focus on their business functionality:

- Generation of documentation and code samples in multiple languages.
- Discovery packaging and subscription management for billing and monitoring consumer access.
- Security and compliance through policy management and support for multiple authorization formats.
- Monitoring of Web API health and usage through analytics and operation logs. Also, generating trend analysis reports to facilitate API upgrades and projections.
- Forums for discussion of issues and bugs for the API.

The beautiful thing about API Management is that it is not targeted only towards public APIs. It also provides the infrastructure that can be leveraged for private or partner APIs as well.

API Management was the outcome of the acquisition of **Apiphany** by Microsoft in fall 2013 (`http://azure.microsoft.com/blog/2013/10/23/microsoft-acquires-apiphany/`).

Let's discuss the tools provided by Azure API Management to facilitate management of our Web APIs:

- **Publisher portal**: Organizations use the publisher portal to publish, monitor, and manage their existing APIs. It provides the following features:

Feature	Description
API	This is the fundamental construct that represents the operations and parameters for the Web API. The operations defined in the API section are available for consumers to access their client applications. Internally, an API is an abstraction to the actual Web API action.
Products	These determine how the API will be made available to consumers. Administrators can package one or more APIs into a product and define group policies, access, and organization terms and conditions for those APIs.
Policies	Administrators can define granular policies that determine how the API is consumed. Policies are applied to the product, API, or API operation, and can either be an access or transformation policy: • Access policies define limits or boundaries on how the API is consumed. For example, for a free tier, an administrator can set a quota on the number of requests or bandwidth consumption. • Transformation policies can be applied to change the format of the request or response—for example, Convert XML to JSON.
Analytics	The publisher portal provides a detailed and in-depth analysis of how the API is being consumed. This includes metrics such as the number of calls, bandwidth consumption, API errors and failed requests, and response time and latency. It also provides intuitive trend analysis such as top developers and top products to recognize individuals or determine product roadmaps.
User and group management	Administrators can add or import users and define groups to manage users. Consumers can request access through the developer portal and will get added as users once approved by the administrator.
Notifications	These allow an administrator to get updates on transactions and milestones for the published APIs. These can be subscription requests, application gallery requests, thresholds warnings, and issue tracking.

Feature	Description
Security	Administrators can define how secure APIs can be accessed. Multiple security options are available ranging from mere credentials to configuring an OAuth 2.0 authorization server such as Azure AD.
Customizing developer portal	Administrators can alter the look and feel of the developer portal using the options available in the publisher portal. Additionally, they can approve and publish consumer applications and add media content such as blogs and videos for the developer portal.

- **Developer portal**: API users use the developer portal for signing up and getting access to published APIs. They can access product documentation, API references, and code examples in multiple languages and open and discuss issues using the developer portal.

The following diagram describes how API publishers and consumers leverage Azure API Management:

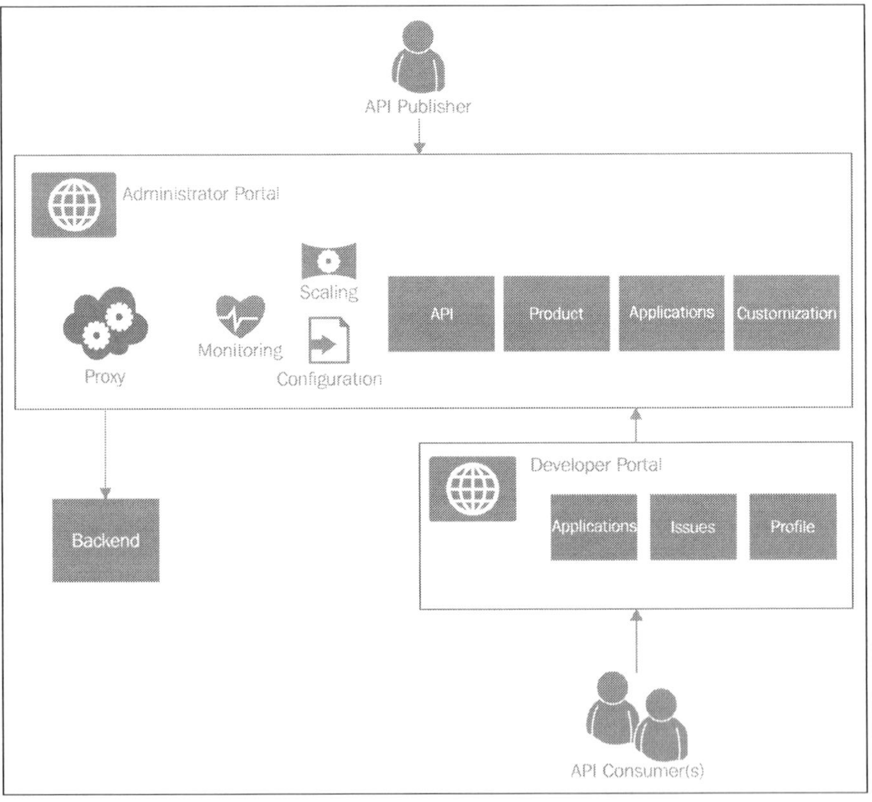

In the preceding diagram:

1. The API Publisher configures an existing Web API in the publisher portal. The API can be hosted to a public endpoint or on-premises.
2. The administrator defines the product, API, policies, and security required for the Web API.
3. The administrator can also customize the default view of the developer portal. The developer portal is available for consumers to access the Web API.
4. The consumers sign up to get access to the developer portal. They can then subscribe to products and use the tools in the portal to access and experiment with the Web API. They can also access documentation and API references available for the Web API and participate in discussing and logging issues.
5. Developers also register applications that will then be allowed to access the Web API through an API proxy.

Now that we have an understanding of the API management features let's leverage them to publish a Web API.

Managing a Web API

In this section, we will leverage Azure API Management to publish our existing Web API created in *Chapter 2, Extending the ASP.NET Web API*. The tasks performed in this section correlate to the activities performed in the publisher portal by an API publisher.

Creating an API Management service

The following steps show how to create a new Azure API Management service:

1. The first step is to create a new Azure API Management service. To create a new service, navigate to **New** | **App Services** | **API Management** in the Azure Portal.

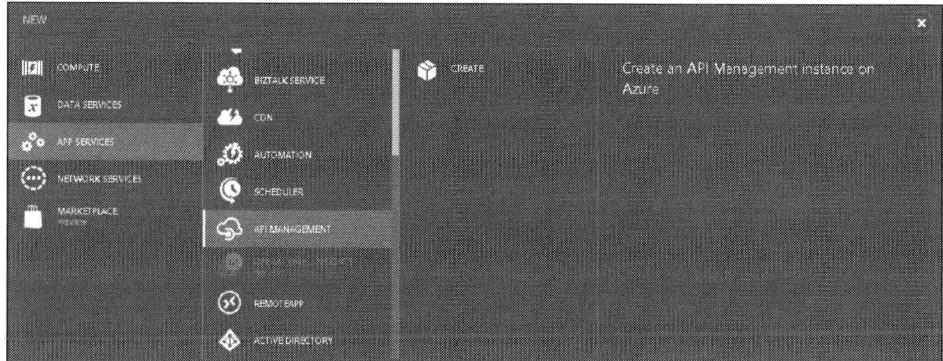

2. We then use the Create wizard in the Azure Management portal to create a new API Management instance.
    1. Provide a unique URL for the Management service. This URL will represent our Web API instance. In a production environment, we can map this URL to a custom domain name (for example, `http://mycustomapi.com`).
    2. Provide the Azure subscription and region for the Management service. The following screenshot shows a configured API Management Service:

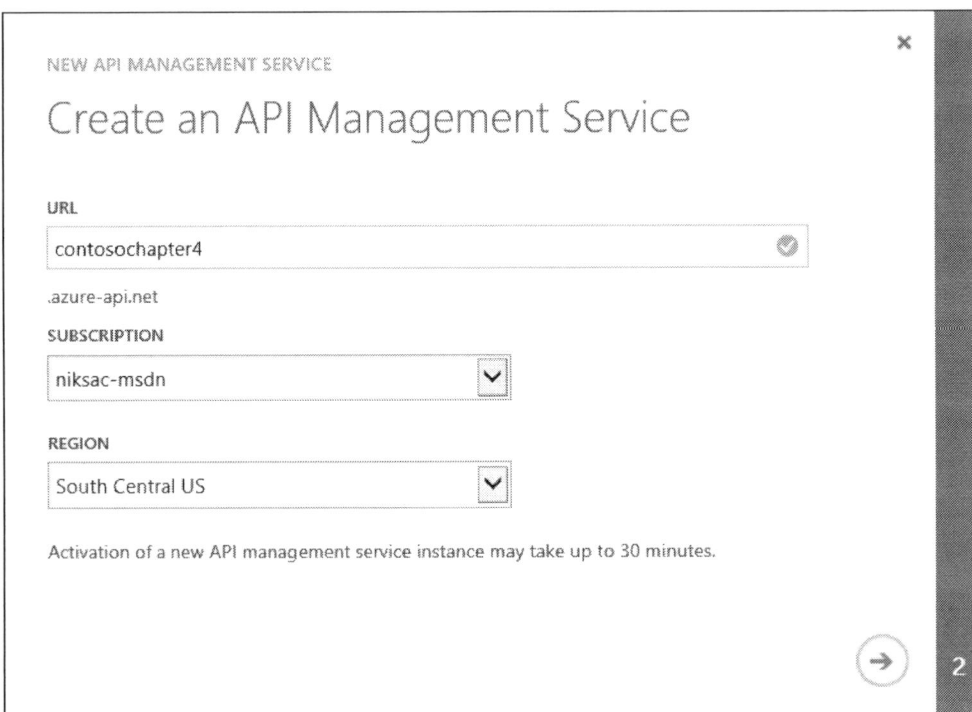

3. Next, we provide organization details that are used to display information in the developer portal and notifications to the administrator. There is also an **Advanced Setting** section that allows you to select additional configuration details such as pricing tiers. For this example, we will leverage the developer tier, which is available as the default option.

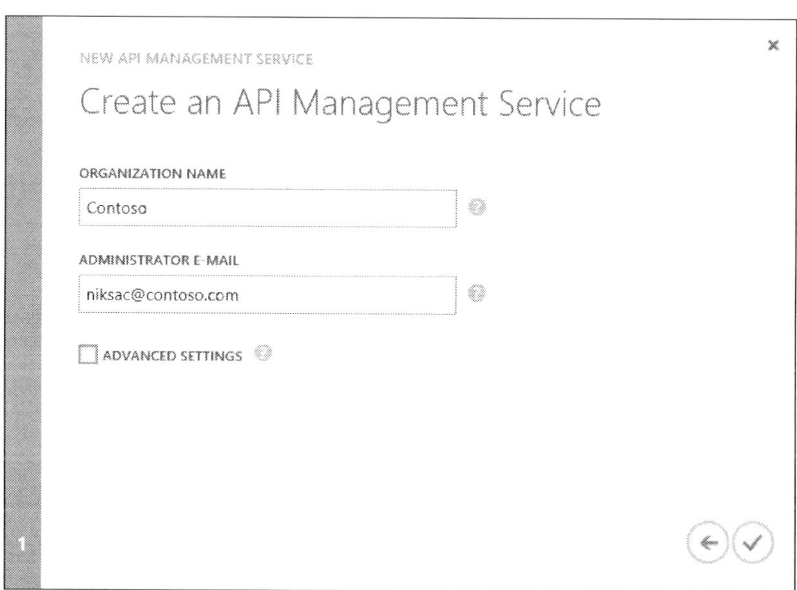

To know more about Azure API Management pricing tiers visit `http://azure.microsoft.com/en-us/pricing/details/api-management/`.

The creation of the Management API service instance takes some time (approx 5 to 15 minutes) depending upon the subscription and region selected.

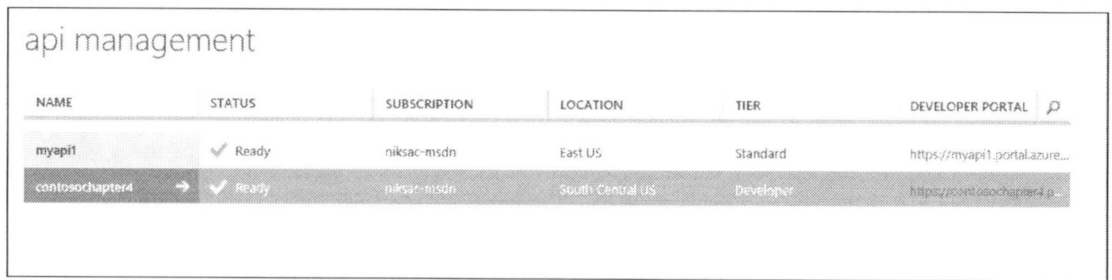

Our service is now ready, but we will need to configure it for our existing Web API; we do this in the next section.

Configuring the API Management service

In this section, we configure our API Management service instance to manage our existing Web API. The **Manage** button for the Management service allows us to access these operations.

Creating API operations

First, we define our API operations. These will represent the features we want to publish as part of our Web API. An API operation is defined within a container called API. The service provides two options to create API containers for our operations:

Option	Description
Add new API	Add a URL to an existing API
Import API	Import an existing API specification which is of the format is WADL or Swagger.

Web Application Description Language (**WADL**) allows you to represent the resources and association between the resources in a platform neutral way using XML. Organizations such as Yahoo expose their search APIs using WADL. For more information about WADL, please visit `http://www.w3.org/Submission/wadl/`.

Swagger is an open source initiative that provides an intuitive set of tools and frameworks for representing Web APIs. For more information on Swagger, please visit `http://swagger.io/`.

We will leverage the **Add new API** option from the APIs extension and specify the URL of the Web API we deployed in *Chapter 2, Extending the ASP.NET Web API*.

Add new API

Web API name

Package Tracker

Public name of the API as it would appear on the developer and admin portals.

Web service URL

https://contosochapter3.azurewebsites.net/api/package

A URL of the web service exposing the API. This URL will be used by Azure API Management only, and will not be made public.

Web API URL suffix

package

Last part of the API's public URL. This URL will be used by API consumers for sending requests to the web service.

Web API URL scheme

☐ HTTP ☑ HTTPs

This is what the URL is going to look like:

https://contosochapter4.azure-api.net/package

Save Cancel

The preceding screenshot shows the options available in the **Add new API** dialog. We specify a name and associate this API with the Web Service URL of our Web API. Additionally, a prefix for our Web API is provided to determine the path for the Web API representation. We can see this path at the bottom of the **Add new API** dialog. A recently added optional feature is to specify the product for the API, we leave this option blank for now. We will associate a product with our API is a later section.

Adding an operation

In this section we will define operations for our API, following the given steps:

1. Select the API we just created and click on the **Operations** tab to add a new operation for our API. This operation will be a representation of the request, parameters, and response of our Web API.

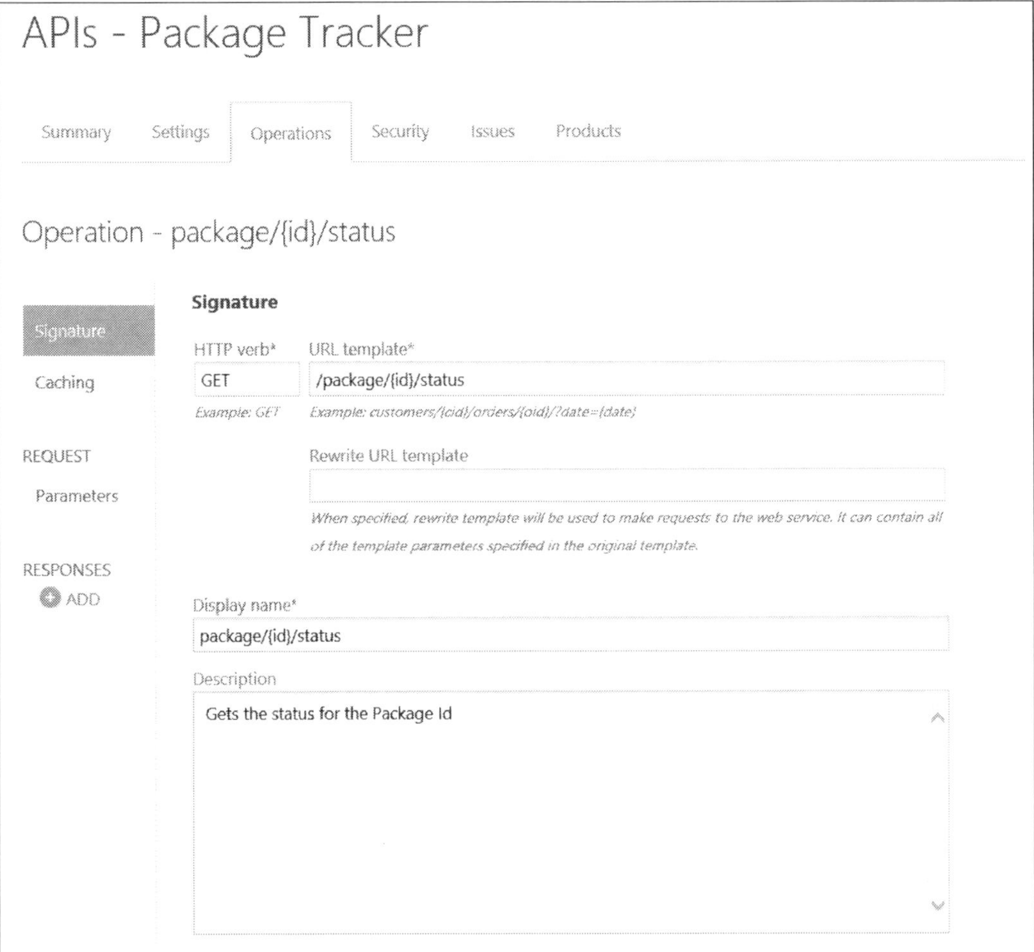

2. Additionally, we define a parameter for the API operation. In our case, the only parameter is the package identifier.

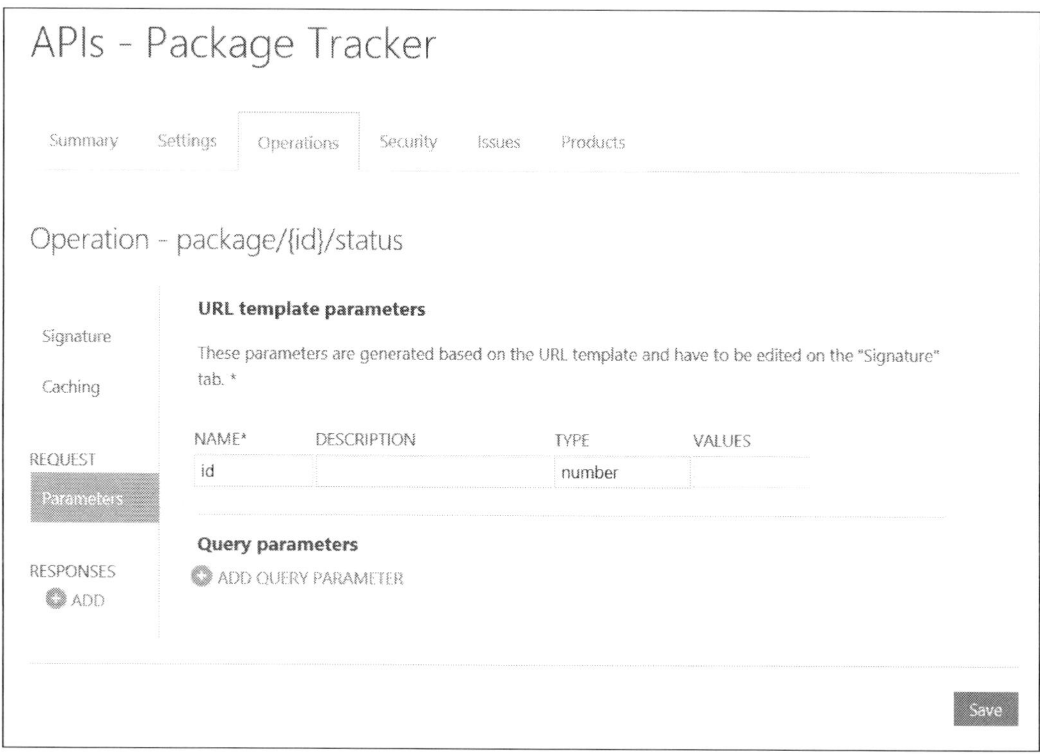

3. Finally, we define the response for the API operation. A response is useful when different clients expect the API to return various media formats. In this case, we only create an HTTP 200 response.

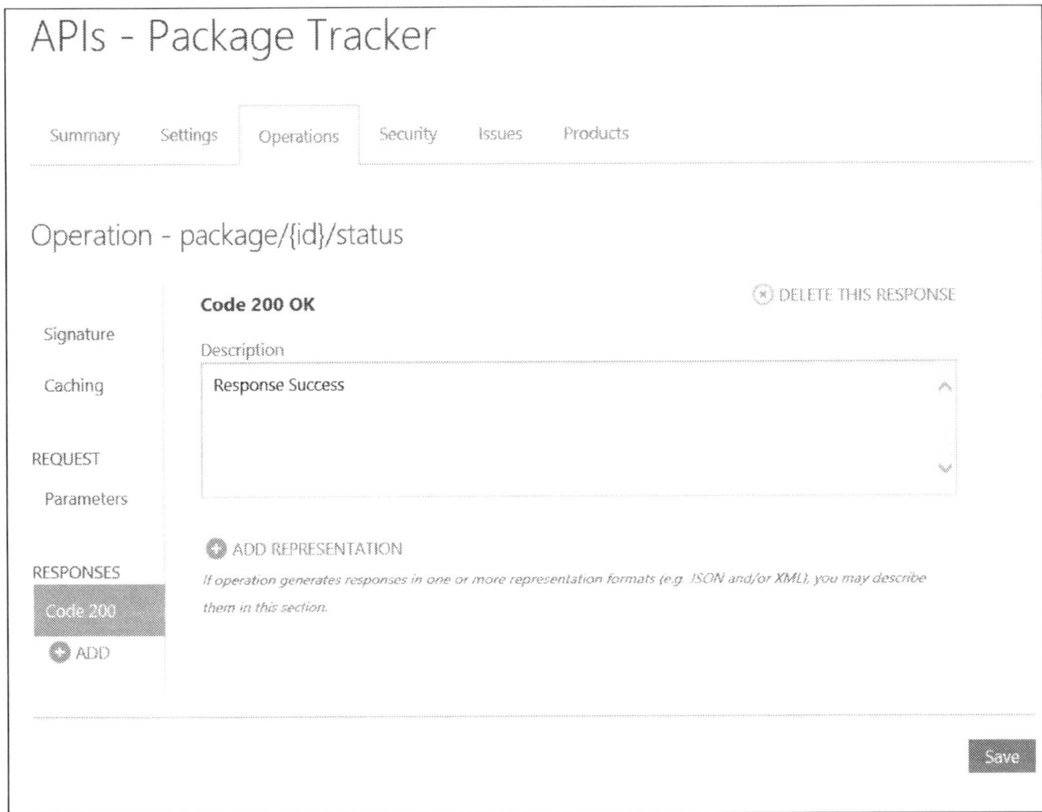

Adding an authorization server

Recall from *Chapter 2*, *Extending the ASP.NET Web API*, that we added Azure AD security to our Web API. In this section, we add an authorization server that can be leveraged to issue OAuth 2.0 tokens for API consumer calls to our API.

1. Access the **Security** extension in the **API Management** portal, select the **OAuth 2.0** tab, and click on **Add Authorization Server**.

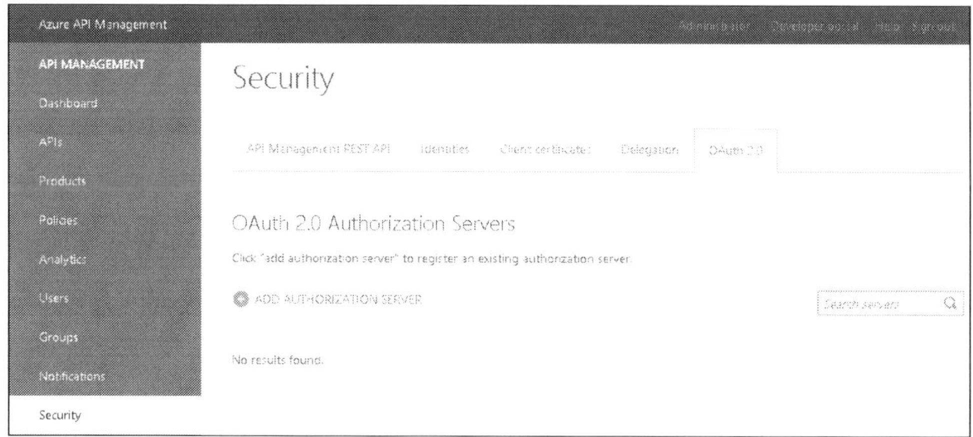

2. Enter the details of the OAuth 2.0 server to configure an authorization server that all APIs can access. The authorization server configuration will look like this:

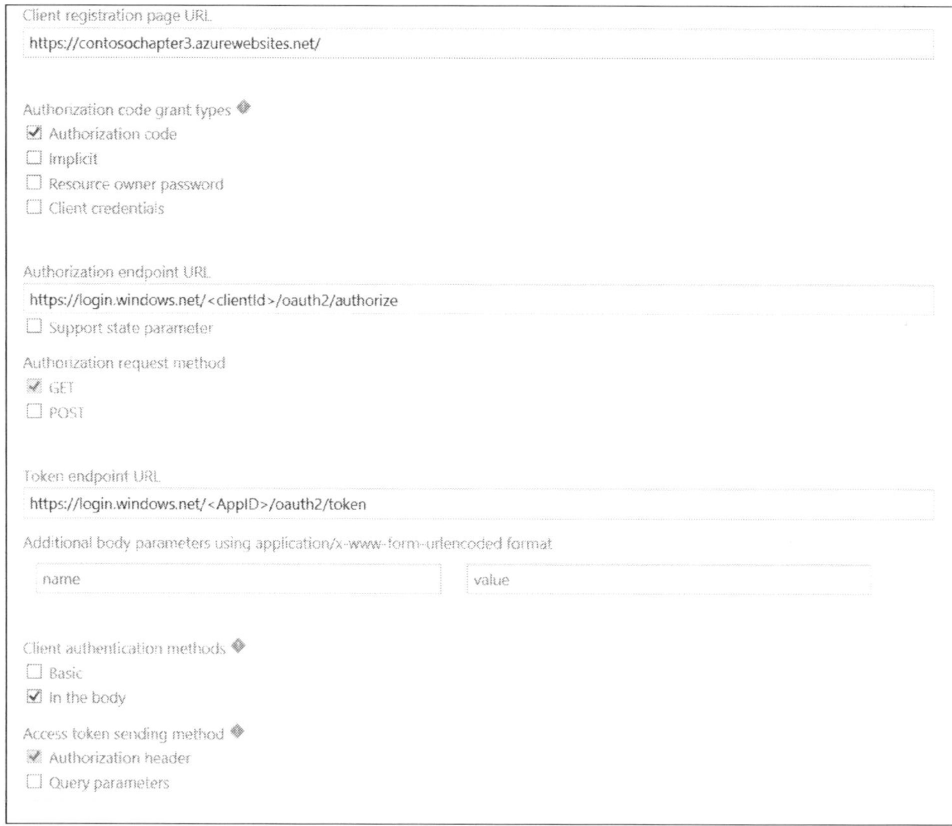

For more details on how to set up Azure AD as an authentication server for API Management, please visit http://azure.microsoft.com/en-us/documentation/articles/api-management-howto-oauth2.

We now have the authorization server configuration completed. Next, we will configure the API to leverage Azure AD as the authorization server.

Configuring an API with an authorization server

To configure security for our API, click on the **Security** tab on the **Package Tracker** API. In the user authorization, select the Azure AD authorization server we created in the previous section.

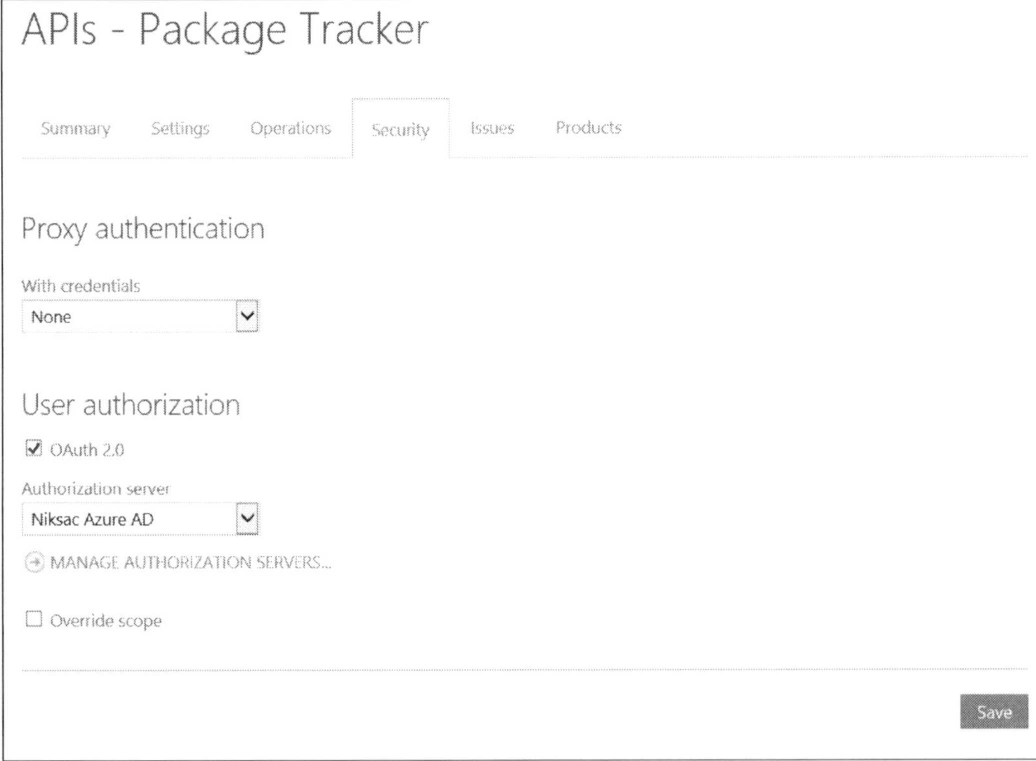

We have now created the API Management representation for our Web API and configured it for access to consumers. In the next section, we will add a product to publish our Web API.

Adding a product

In this section, we add a product to our API. Consumers will require subscribing to a product in order to make API calls to the operation created in the previous section. The following steps describe how to add a new product:

1. In the API Management portal, click on the products extension and then click on **Add Product**. The product definition page requests the following information:

Option	Description
Title	This requests the title for the product that is on the developer portal.
Description	This requests a description of the APIs exposed by this product and their functionality.
Require Subscription Approval	The administrator will have to approve subscription requests before granting approval. It is useful for validating consumer access to the APIs.
Allow multiple simultaneous subscriptions	Administrators can grant consumers access to multiple subscriptions for the same product.

The configuration for our packaging API looks like this:

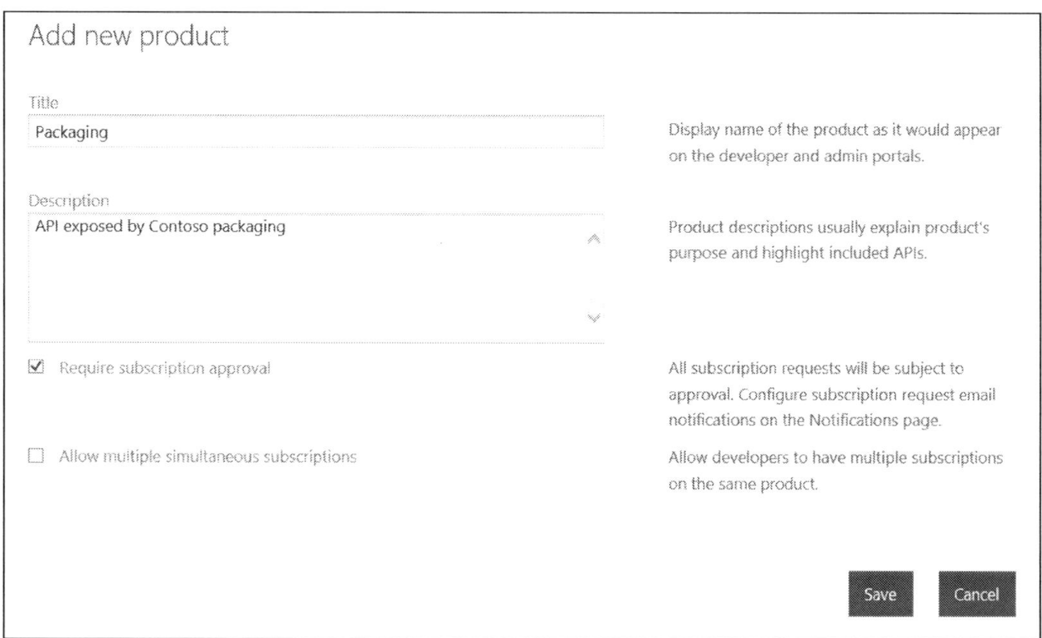

2. Next, we associate our API to the packaging product. From the product page, select the product we just created. In the summary page, click on **Add API to product** and select the **Package Tracker** API we created in the previous section.

3. In the **Summary** tab, click on **Publish** to publish the API for consumer access.

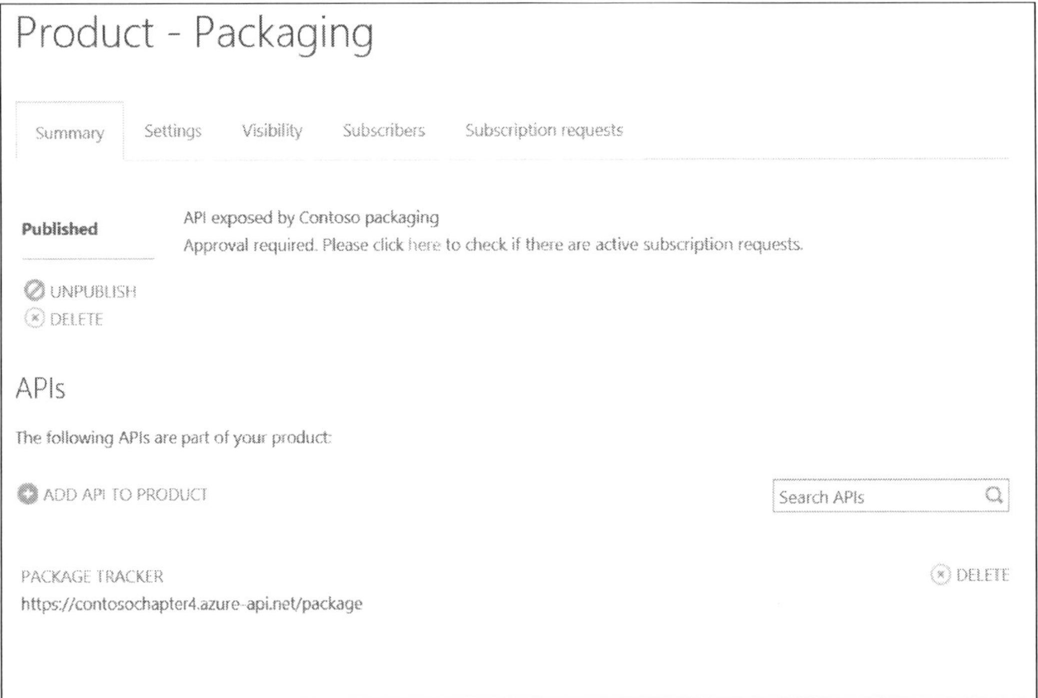

4. We now have a published product that allows access to our package tracker API. As a last step, we need to define who can access our Web API. API Management allows administrators to set visibility for a product using groups and user accounts. To ensure that a user can view the product, it must be part of one of these groups. We select the developer group for our API.

> API Management currently provides three built-in groups, namely, administrators, developers, and guests. Administrators can also create custom groups. For more information on groups and user accounts please visit `http://azure.microsoft.com/en-us/documentation/articles/api-management-howto-create-groups/`.

The following screenshot shows the **Visibility** options selected for our Web API:

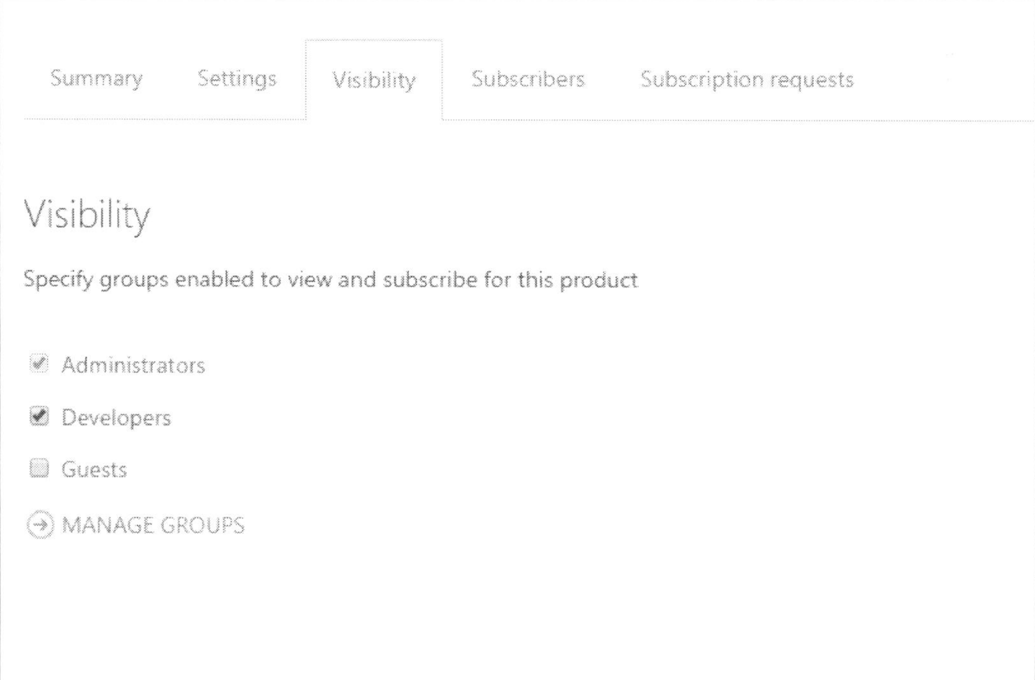

We now have an API published that is accessible to all users in the developer group. In the next section, we will consume this API using a developer account.

Here are some other actions that an administrator can perform using the API Management portal. Some of these actions include defining policies, user and group management, customizing the developer portal, and adding content, blogs, or media that can be displayed on the developer portal. We will skip these features for the scope of this book. For more information on configuring these features, please visit `http://azure.microsoft.com/en-us/documentation/services/api-management/`.

By default, two products are available as part of API Management: Starter and Unlimited. These can be used as a reference to create our products.

Consuming the Web API

Once our API is published, it can be accessed by developers for consumption. API Management provides a developer portal for developers to access the API and consume it in a client application.

The developer portal is the home from which consumers can access our Web APIs. Users sign up for access to the developer portal. Once approved, they can subscribe to products and then make calls to API operations and consume the results in their applications based on their access.

API Management provides a working portal with a default user experience for consumers to sign up and access the APIs. An API administrator can customize the developer portal to configure it with organization branding and styling guidelines.

The following steps describe how to access the developer portal for our Web API:

1. The developer portal can be accessed using the following URL: `HTTP://<yourAPIManagementServicename>.portal.azure-api.net/`.

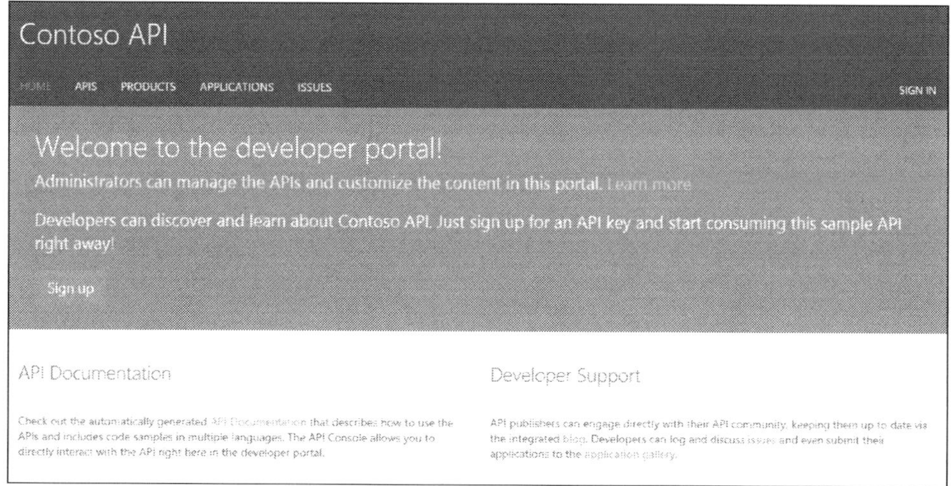

2. Consumers can then sign up for an account to access the developer portal.

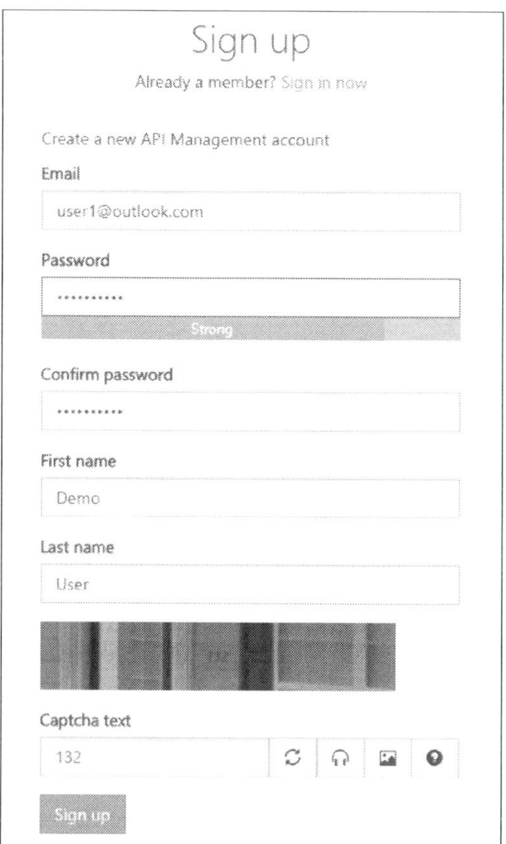

3. At this stage, developers are asked to verify their e-mail address. On successful activation, the user gets access to the published products:

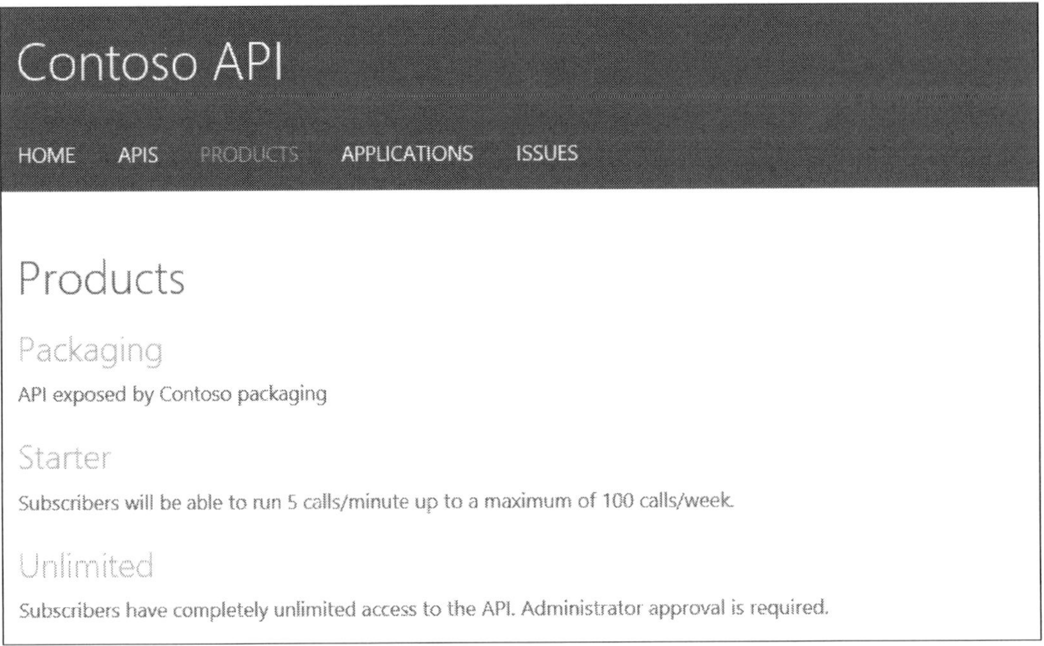

4. Once the user subscribes to a product, they can access the API using the subscription access keys generated by Azure API Management.

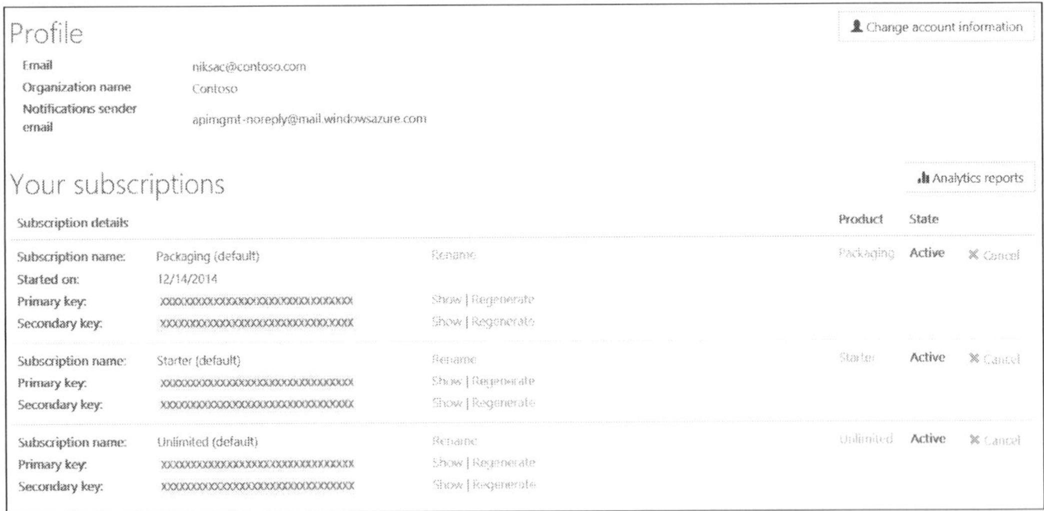

5. We can test our API using the console provided by the developer portal. The console is an intuitive way to verify our APIs before implementing them in the client application. Click on **Open Console** to open a window to test our API. We can edit our request before submitting it to the configured API.

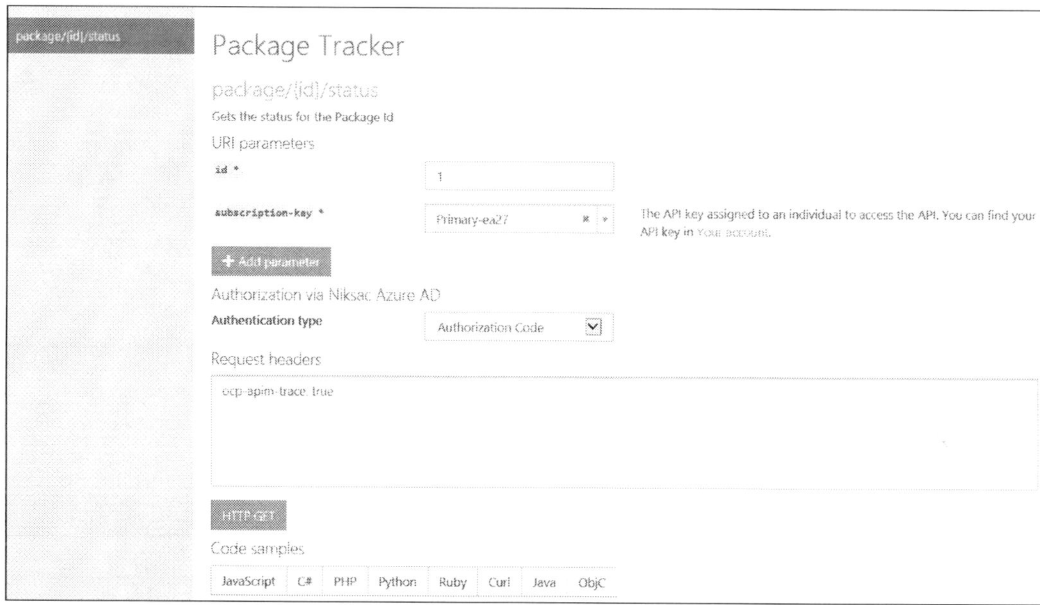

API Management now acts as a proxy to our Web API.

To integrate the Web API in client applications, we create an Application. An Application in the developer portal represents a custom client application that will consume the published API. The following steps describe how to create and configure an Application:

1. Add New Application and configure its properties.

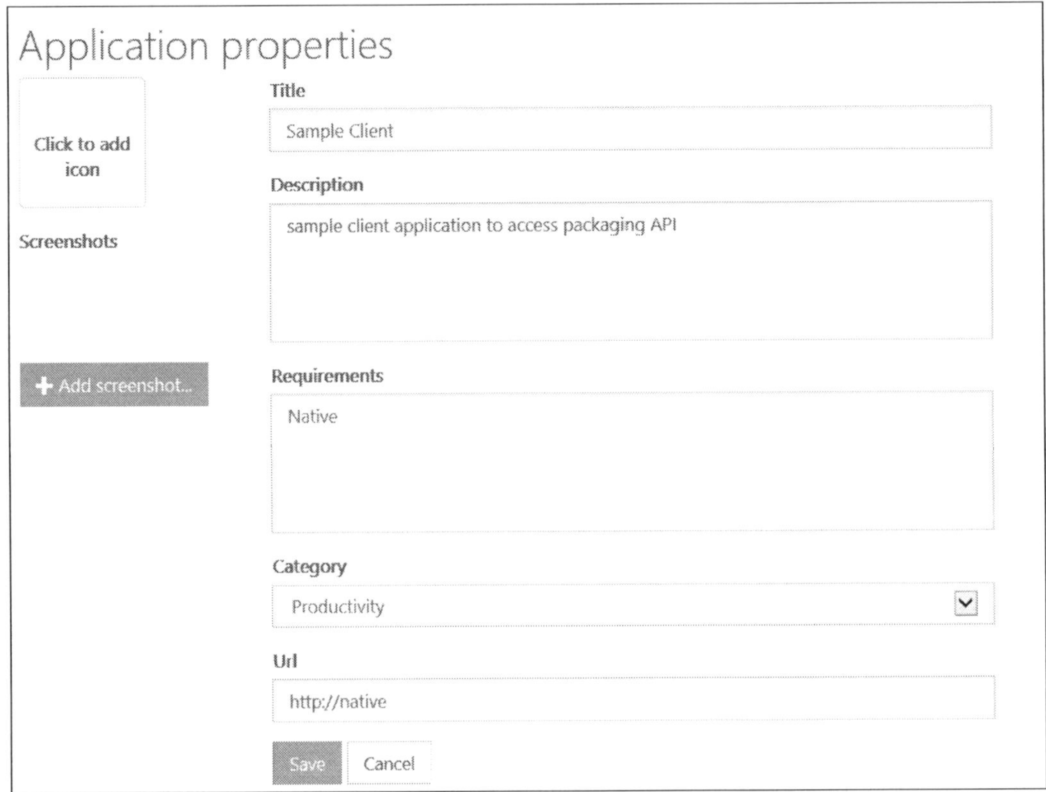

2. The application needs to be submitted for administrator's approval. Select **Submit for review** to submit the application for review and approval.

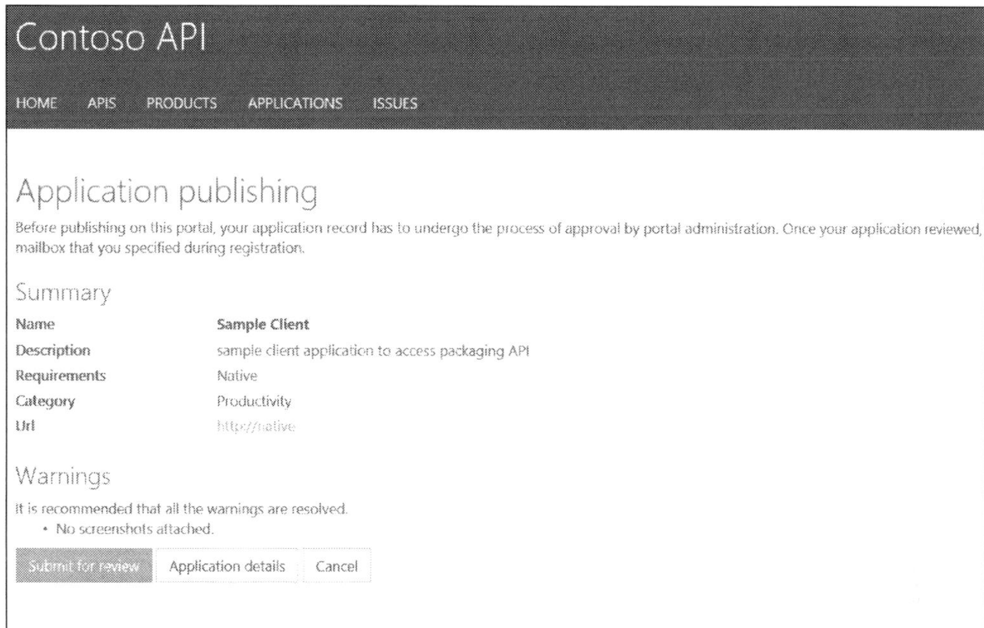

3. Once the application is approved, it will be in the published state. We can now use the keys generated by the subscription to access the Web API.

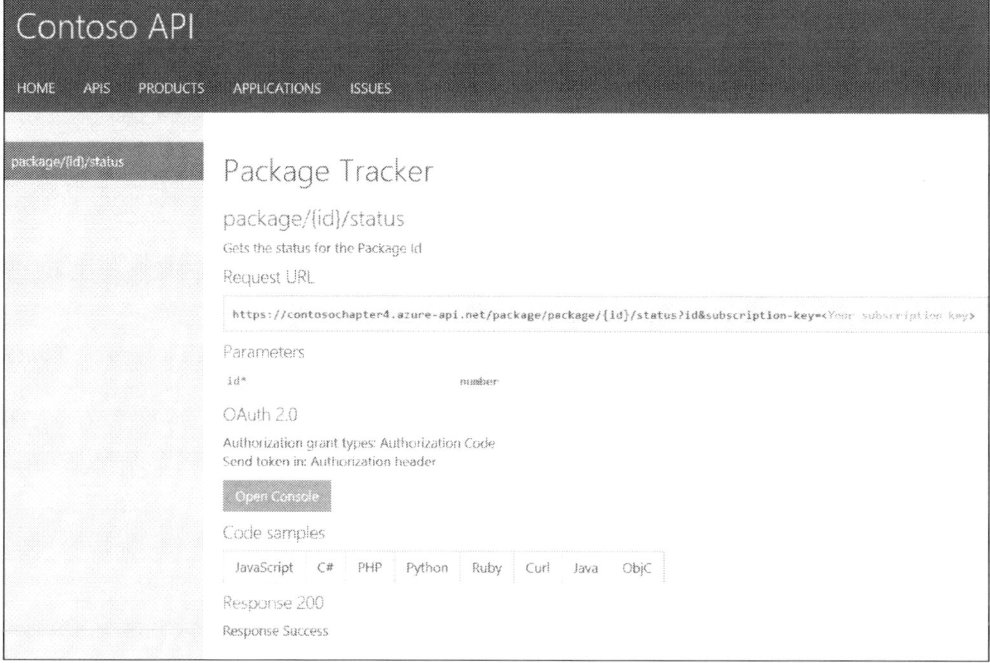

In this section, we demonstrated how we can consume an API published by Azure API Management in a console portal provided by the API Management infrastructure. Additionally, we looked at how client applications can be registered and provided with access to the API. The developer portal also offers a set of other features for reporting issues back to the API publishers. These are useful to start a discussion thread with the product owners and track issues when developing applications using the API.

Summary

In this chapter, we discussed Azure API Management, which provides features to publish and manage multiple APIs effectively. We discussed how to define APIs and API operation, and created products that allow packaging one of more APIs for consumer access. We then looked at the developer portal provided as part of Azure API Management and explored how a customer can request access and subscribe to products for consuming API within their client applications. In the next chapter, we will discuss how to leverage Azure Mobile Services to build and deploy scalable mobile applications.

4

Developing a Web API for Mobile Apps

In the previous chapters we saw how easy it is to create and deploy a Web API using Microsoft Azure Websites. While Azure Websites is an excellent platform to deploy and manage the Web API, Microsoft Azure provides, however, another alternative in the form of Azure Mobile Services, which targets mobile application developers. In this chapter, we delve into the capabilities of Azure Mobile Services and how it provides a quick and easy development ecosystem to develop Web APIs that support mobile apps.

Azure Mobile Services

Mobile programming constitutes a different breed of application developers; unlike the traditional development paradigms, these developers want to focus more on their ideas than on how the infrastructure is going to be set up behind the scenes. At the same time, releasing the mobile app in the market is also critical, the competition in the mobile app market is brutal and any delay in a release may drive customers away to a different app providing similar features. So does this make the backend services trivial? Well, it is the other way round. While mobile app development is typically popularized by ideating and realization through an intuitive UI and rich functionality, without a robust and scalable infrastructure backend, a successful mobile app will almost always remain an idea!

Azure Mobile Services acts as a bridge for mobile developers, relieving them from common backend tasks such as storage, authenticating users, sending notifications, and at the same time, providing rich tooling support for rapid development. It is complemented by the existing scalable infrastructure of Microsoft Azure along with its diagnostic and monitoring capabilities. The result is that mobile developers can now focus on enriching their functionality rather than worrying about infrastructure and technology concerns.

Mobile Services was recently renamed and is now part of Azure App Services. Mobile-based development is now referred to as mobile apps. For the scope of this book, we will focus on the existing service implementation. To learn more about App Services, please refer here: `http://azure.microsoft.com/en-us/services/app-service/`.

Features of Azure Mobile Services

There are a number of valuable features of Azure Mobile Services, which are as follows:

- The ability to create turnkey mobile app backend solutions in a quick and easy way. Mobile Services provides a jump start to mobile development by bundling some core services essential for any mobile app.
- Rich tooling support for multiple platforms and languages enable development in multiple platforms reducing the overall learning curve.

Azure Mobile Services also provides a free tier for initial prototyping and testing purposes. To get more information on Azure Mobile Services pricing visit `http://azure.microsoft.com/en-us/documentation/services/mobile-services/`.

- Mobile services are abstracted from the delivery platform of the mobile application. So, developing an app for iOS, Android, or Windows results in the same development effort at the backend.

As of writing of this book, iOS, Windows, Xamarin iOS, Xamarin Android, HTML, PhoneGap, Sencha, and Appcelerator can be used as the backend with Mobile Services. Additionally, we can write code either in .NET or in JavaScript on Node.js. Note that the Visual Studio 2013 templates for Mobile Services currently support creation of an ASP.NET Web API only.

- Mobile Services is a PaaS offering from Microsoft Azure, so all the goodies of Microsoft Azure as a platform are automatically inherited by Mobile Services.
- The deployment model for Mobile Services is flexible enough and it allows service upgrades without redeploying packages into Azure.

Core services

Under the hood, Mobile Services is an accumulation of existing Azure Services, which work together enabling end-to-end scenarios. Let's take a look at these Azure services:

Service	Description
Data	The data layer itself is based on Web API infrastructure and enables support for multiple data stores including Azure Database, SQL Server on-premise or hosted in Azure Virtual Machine, table storage, and MongoDB. Clients can leverage the auto mapper to convert legacy entity models into **Data Transfer Objects** (**DTO**) that allows abstraction at the Web API layer. Additionally, the client can use SyncDB for offline data synchronization.
Messaging	It leverages high scale Azure Notification Hubs for sending push notifications for various PNS such as Windows, iOS, and Android.
Connectivity	It provides support for real-time messaging using SignalR and WebSockets. Using Microsoft Hybrid connections, we can connect to the on-premise resources directly with Mobile Services (for example, an on-premise SQL server or a SOAP-based web service).
Identity	It supports multiple identity stores through easy configuration. As of writing of this book, providers such as Google, Facebook, Twitter, Microsoft, and Azure AD were supported.
Scheduling	Mobile Services also provides a scheduler service to schedule jobs. It provides configuration-based options to run jobs on demand or based on a frequency.
Server-side logic	It allows for quick and easy deployment of server-side logic. We can use .NET or Node.js for the server backend.

Using this information, we can architect a layered diagram for Mobile Services, as follows:

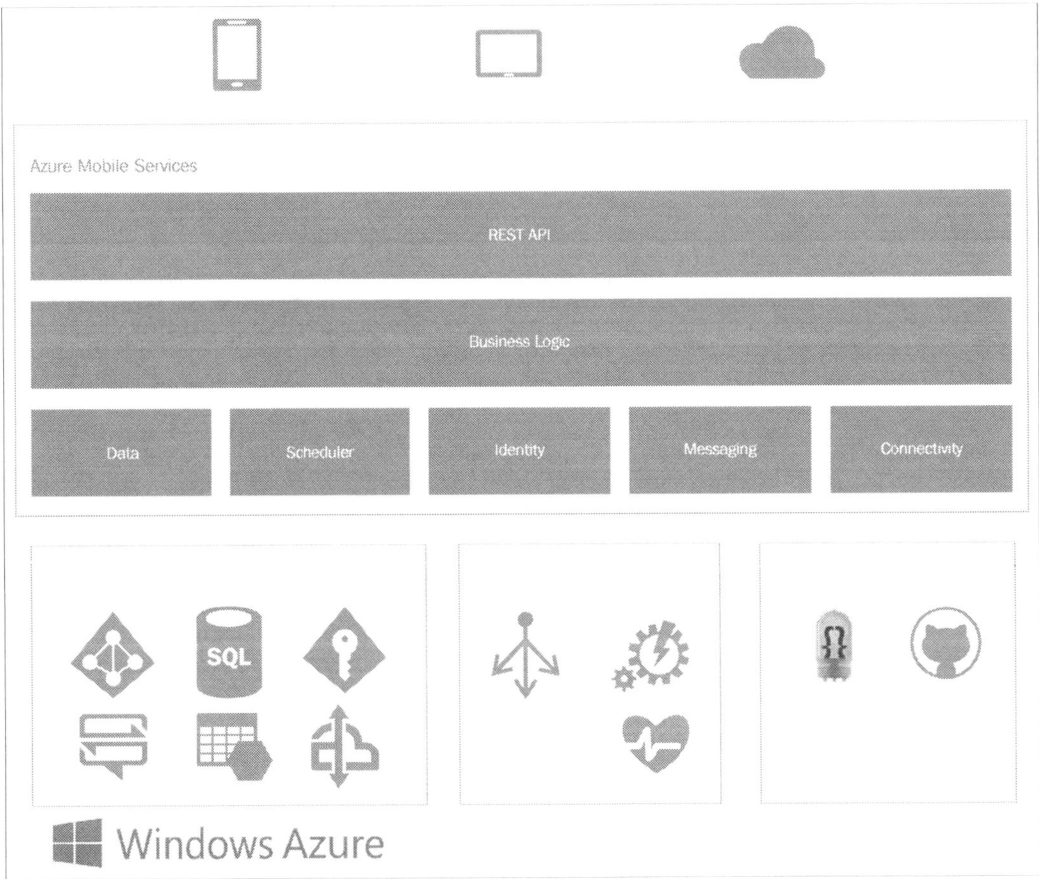

As we see from the preceding diagram, the foundation for Mobile Services is the robust and scalable Azure PaaS infrastructure. Mobile Services then provides a set of abstractions to simplify development and allow developers to add business logic, which can be a surface using REST-based endpoints to an array of disparate mobile clients.

The API of Azure Mobile Services

Azure Mobile Services provides a set of APIs that facilitate the development of Web API controllers and provide an abstraction to access data entities. These entities are referred to as controllers and domain managers. They allow consistent flow of data between the clients and the data sources. It is a pivotal abstraction since these take care of mapping existing entities into a common entity model and flattening the transformation between the clients and underlying data sources. We will discuss controllers and domain managers in the next sections.

In addition to providing a robust data and service abstraction, Mobile Services leverages the **Open Web Interface for .NET (OWIN)** platform and the Service Bus API to enable built-in identity and notification hubs' support.

OWIN provides the necessary middleware to abstract web applications from underlying web server bindings (for example, IIS). To know more about OWIN, please visit `http://owin.org/`.

The Service Bus API is the REST-based interface to access and manage Azure Service Bus. For more information about the Service Bus API, please visit `https://msdn.microsoft.com/en-us/library/azure/hh780717.aspx`.

The following diagram illustrates the Mobile Services API flow:

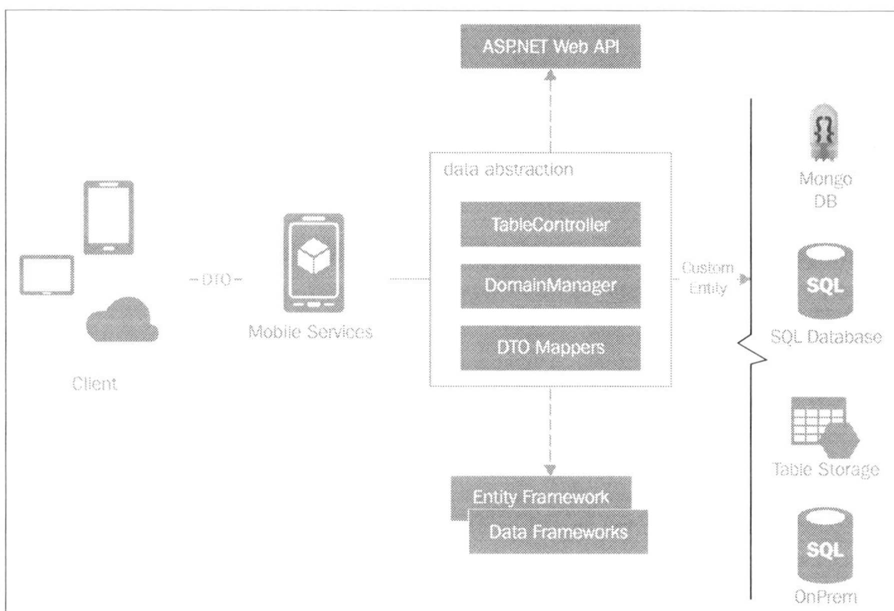

Mobile Services exposes a REST API endpoint that the client can connect to for performing backend operations. A request is typically targeted to `TableController`. `TableController` is similar to the ASP.NET Web API controller that we saw in *Chapter 1, Getting Started with the ASP.NET Web API*. It identifies the actions that need to be executed for the incoming request. Additionally, it also provides the necessary data bindings. Domain Managers provides a data abstraction over the underlying data sources and provides a consistent model for data retrieval and manipulation by the client. DTO mappers are object-relational mappers that allow the data source to client communication without understanding the underlying schema.

Let's look at some of these types in detail.

TableController

`TableController` provides the interfaces for clients to operate on the data models. The `TableController` type inherits from the ASP.NET Web API, `APIController`, and is primarily responsible for exposing data operations as HTTP methods. `TableController` can also be used to enable optimistic concurrency scenarios for offline sync capabilities. The abstract class has only one property—services, which represents the ApiServices associated with the controller. We will discuss Apiservice in the next section.

A variation of `TableController` is `TableController<TData>`. This type allows for generic abstraction for table entities and inherits from `TableController`. For more information on `TableController`, please visit `https://msdn.microsoft.com/en-us/library/microsoft.windowsazure.mobile.service.tables.tablecontroller.aspx`.

ApiServices

The `ApiServices` type enables a pattern in Mobile Services for attaching services to `TableController`. The design promotes Dependency Injection by hooking up service implementations when `TableController` is invoked. These services include standard mobile services such as Push Notifications, and other internal services such as logging and configuration. For more information on `ApiServices`, please visit `https://msdn.microsoft.com/en-us/library/microsoft.windowsazure.mobile.service.apiservices.aspx`.

EntityData

`EntityData` is the base type for all entities or **Data Transfer Objects** (**DTO**) created for a Mobile Services-enabled Web API. `EntityData` is just an extension of the Entity Framework and implements the `ITableData` interface. If we desire, we can skip this type altogether and create our implementation of `ITableData`. For more information on `ITableData`, please visit `https://msdn.microsoft.com/en-us/library/microsoft.windowsazure.mobile.service.tables.itabledata.aspx`.

Domain Manager

Domain Managers are primarily intended to map the operations exposed by `TableController` to the respective backend. Domain Manager provides the extension by which we interact with different data sources. All Domain Managers implement the `IDomainManager<TData>` interface, which provides the CRUD operation for managing custom entities.

Two Domain Managers are already available as part of the Mobile Services API:

- `EntityDomainManager`: This is the standard Domain Manager to manage SQL Azure tables; this represents the Entity Framework
- `MappedEntityDomainManager`: This manages SQL tables with entities not directly mapped to a table structure

For more information on `IDomainManager`, please refer to `https://msdn.microsoft.com/en-us/library/dn643358.aspx`.

Now that we have a basic understanding of Mobile Services' internals, let's leverage these types to create our first Web API using Azure Mobile Services.

Creating a Web API using Mobile Services

In this section, we will create a Mobile Services-enabled Web API using Visual Studio 2013. For our fictitious scenario, we will create an Uber-like service but for medical emergencies. In the case of a medical emergency, users will have the option to send a request using their mobile device. Additionally, third-party applications and services can integrate with the Web API to display doctor availability. All requests sent to the Web API will follow the following process flow:

1. The request will be persisted to a data store.

2. An algorithm will find a doctor that matches the incoming request based on availability and proximity.
3. Push Notifications will be sent to update the physician and patient.

Creating the project

Mobile Services provides two options to create a project:

- Using the Management portal, we can create a new Mobile Service and download a preassembled package that contains the Web API as well as the targeted mobile platform project
- Using Visual Studio templates

The Management portal approach is easier to implement and does give a jumpstart by creating and configuring the project. However, for the scope of this chapter, we will use the Visual Studio template approach. For more information on creating a Mobile Services Web API using the Azure Management Portal, please refer to `http://azure.microsoft.com/en-us/documentation/articles/mobile-services-dotnet-backend-windows-store-dotnet-get-started/`.

Azure Mobile Services provides a Visual Studio 2013 template to create a .NET Web API, we will use this template for our scenario.

Note that the Azure Mobile Services template is only available from Visual Studio 2013 update 2 and onward.

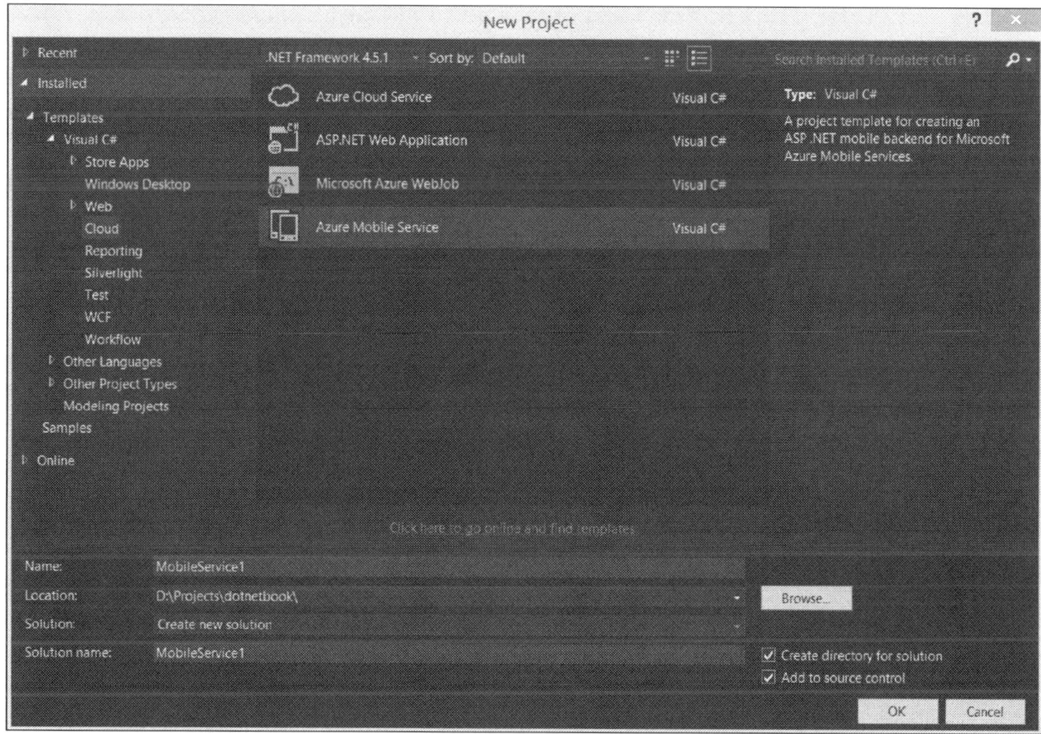

Creating a Mobile Service in Visual Studio 2013 requires the following steps:

1. Create a new Azure Mobile Service project and assign it a Name, Location, and Solution. Click **OK**.
2. In the next tab, we have a familiar ASP.NET project type dialog. However, we notice a few differences from the traditional ASP.NET dialog, which are as follows:
    - The **Web API** option is enabled by default and is the only choice available
    - The **Authentication** tab is disabled by default
    - The **Test project** option is disabled

- The **Host in the cloud** option automatically suggests **Mobile Services** and is currently the only choice

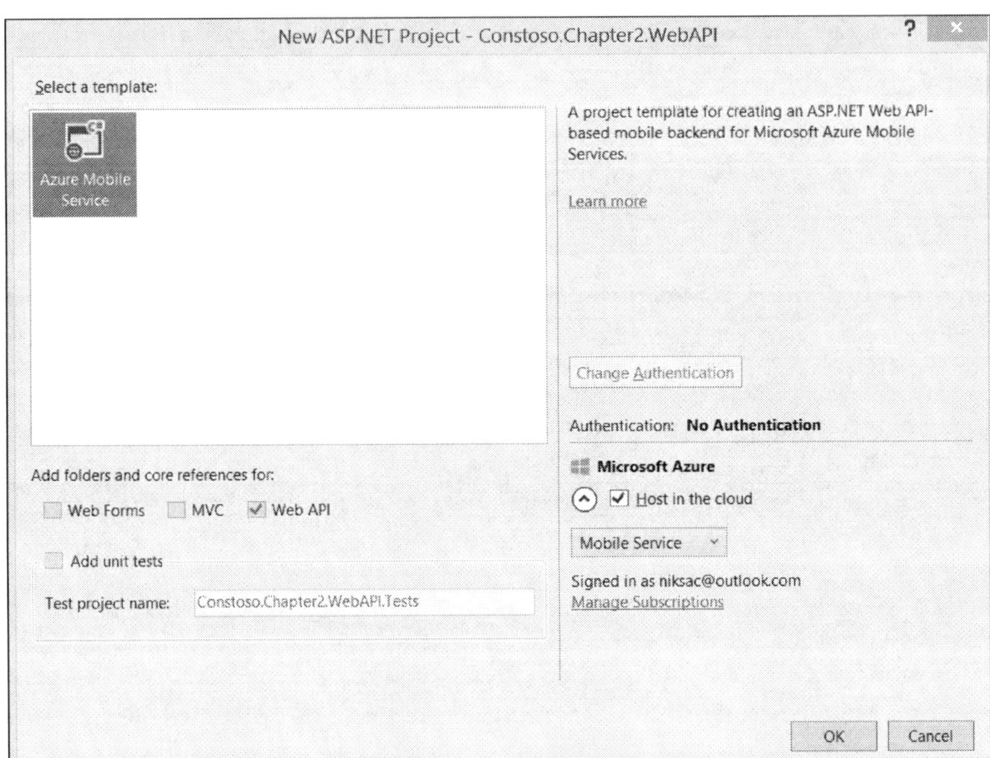

3. Select the default settings and click on **OK**.

   Visual Studio 2013 prompts developers to enter their Azure credentials in case they are not already logged in:

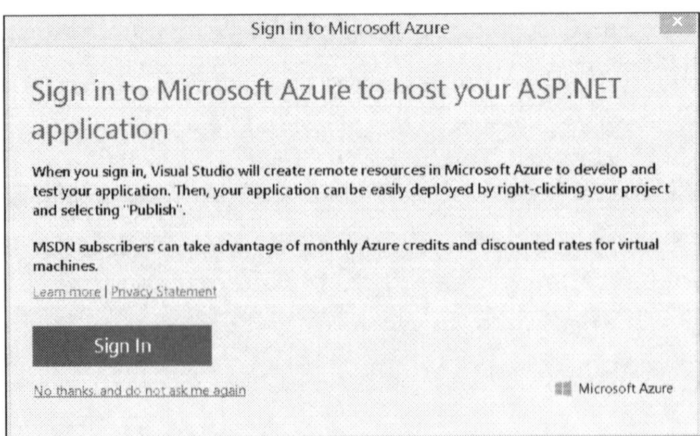

For more information on Azure tools for Visual Studio, please refer visit https://msdn.microsoft.com/en-us/library/azure/ee405484.aspx.

Since we are building a new Mobile Service, the next screen gathers information about how to configure the service. We can specify the existing Azure resources in our subscription or create new from within Visual Studio. Select the appropriate options and click on **Create**:

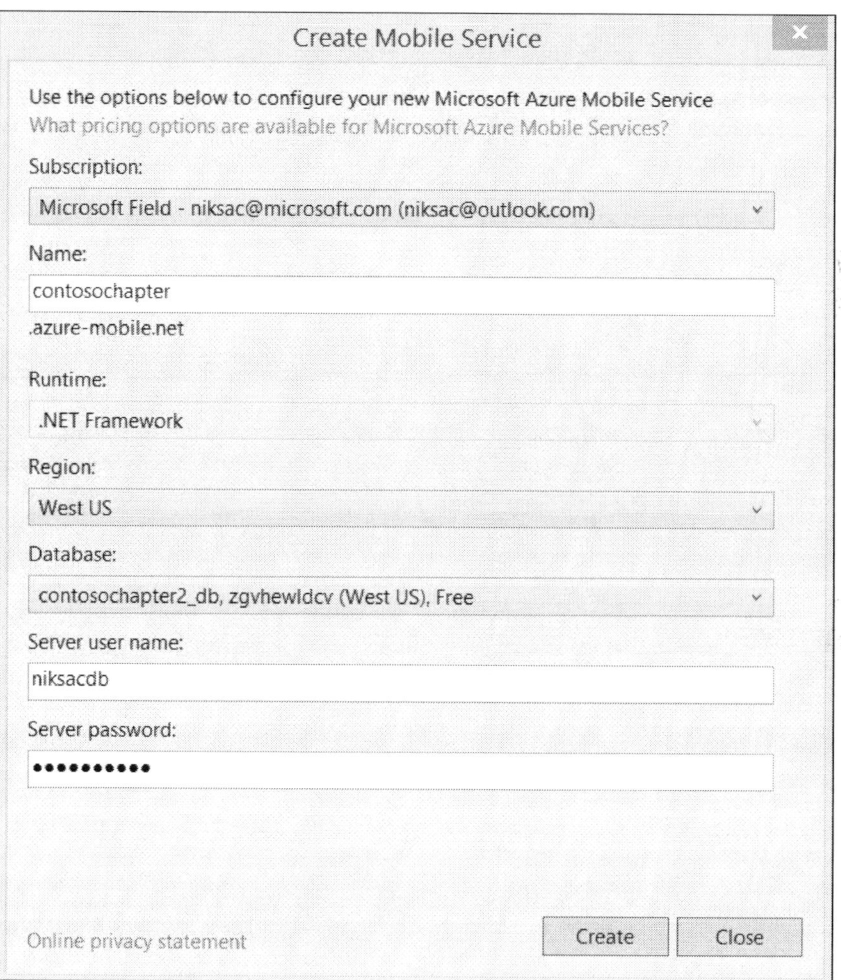

The options are described here:

Option	Description
Subscription	This lists the name of the Azure subscription where the service will be deployed. Select from the dropdown if multiple subscriptions are available.
Name	This is the name of the Mobile Services deployment, this will eventually become the root DNS URL for the mobile service unless a custom domain is specified. (For example, `contoso.azure-mobile.net`).
Runtime	This allows selection of runtime. Note that as of writing this book, only the .NET framework was supported in Visual Studio, so this option is currently prepopulated and disabled.
Region	Select the Azure data center where the Web API will be deployed. As of writing this book, Mobile Services is available in the following regions: West US, East US, North Europe, East Asia, and West Japan. For details on latest regional availability, please refer to `http://azure.microsoft.com/en-us/regions/#services`.
Database	By default, a SQL Azure database gets associated with every Mobile Services deployment. It comes in handy if SQL is being used as the data store. However, in scenarios where different data stores such as the table storage or Mongo DB may be used, we still create this SQL database. We can select from a free 20 MB SQL database or an existing paid standard SQL database. For more information about SQL tiers, please visit `http://azure.microsoft.com/en-us/pricing/details/sql-database`.
Server user name	Provide the server name for the Azure SQL database.
Server password	Provide a password for the Azure SQL database.

This process creates the required entities in the configured Azure subscription. Once completed, we have a new Web API project in the Visual Studio solution.

The following screenshot is the representation of a new Mobile Service project:

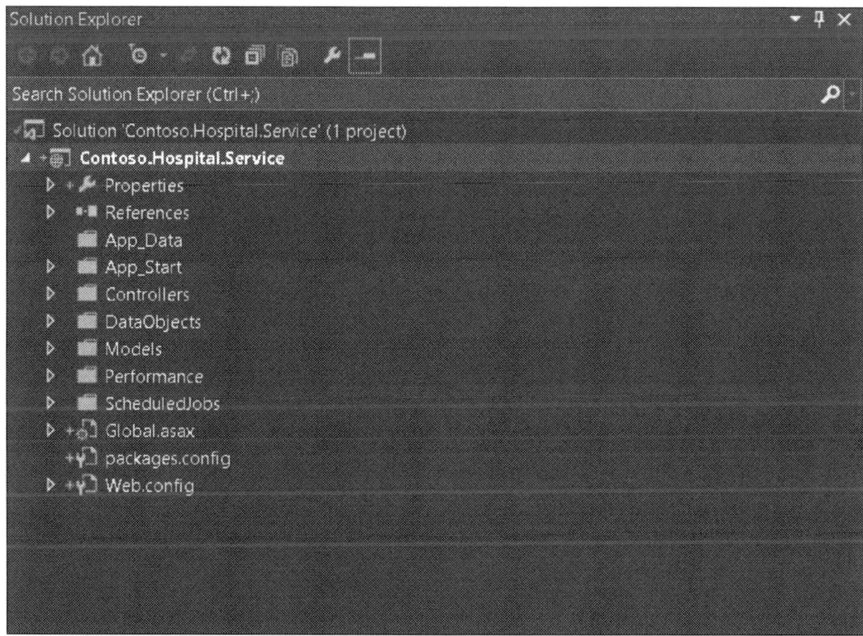

When we create a Mobile Service Web API project, the following NuGet packages are referenced in addition to the default ASP.NET Web API NuGet packages:

Package	Description
WindowsAzure MobileServices Backend	This package enables developers to build scalable and secure .NET mobile backend hosted in Microsoft Azure. We can also incorporate structured storage, user authentication, and push notifications. Assembly: Microsoft.WindowsAzure.Mobile.Service
Microsoft Azure Mobile Services .NET Backend Tables	This package contains the common infrastructure needed when exposing structured storage as part of the .NET mobile backend hosted in Microsoft Azure. Assembly: Microsoft.WindowsAzure.Mobile.Service.Tables
Microsoft Azure Mobile Services .NET Backend Entity Framework Extension	This package contains all types necessary to surface structured storage (using Entity Framework) as part of the .NET mobile backend hosted in Microsoft Azure. Assembly: Microsoft.WindowsAzure.Mobile.Service.Entity

Additionally, the following third-party packages are installed:

Package	**Description**
EntityFramework	Since Mobile Services provides a default SQL database, it leverages Entity Framework to provide an abstraction for the data entities.
AutoMapper	AutoMapper is a convention based object-to-object mapper. It is used to map legacy custom entities to DTO objects in Mobile Services.
OWIN Server and related assemblies	Mobile Services uses OWIN as the default hosting mechanism. The current template also adds: • Microsoft OWIN Katana packages to run the solution in IIS • Owin security packages for Google, Azure AD, Twitter, Facebook
Autofac	This is the favorite **Inversion of Control** (**IoC**) framework.
Azure Service Bus	Microsoft Azure Service Bus provides Notification Hub functionality.

We now have our Mobile Services Web API project created. The default project added by Visual Studio is not an empty project but a sample implementation of a Mobile Service-enabled Web API. In fact, a controller and Entity Data Model are already defined in the project. If we hit *F5* now, we can see a running sample in the local Dev environment:

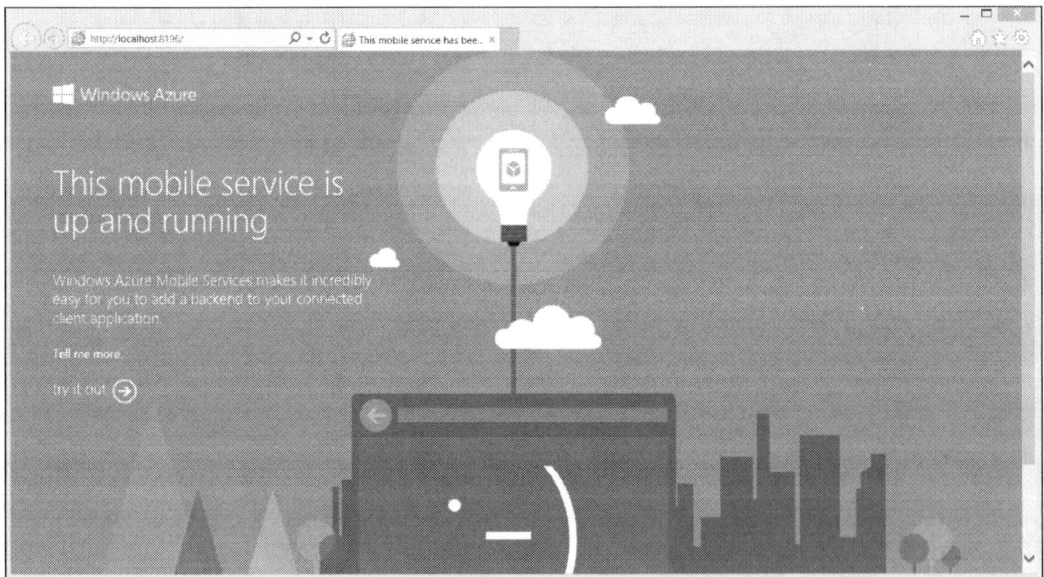

Note that Mobile Services modifies the `WebApiConfig` file under the `App_Start` folder to accommodate some initialization and configuration changes:

```
{
    ConfigOptions options = new ConfigOptions();

    HttpConfiguration config = ServiceConfig.Initialize
      (new ConfigBuilder(options));
}
```

In the preceding code, the `ServiceConfig.Initialize` method defined in the `Microsoft.WindowsAzure.Mobile.Service` assembly is called to load the hosting provider for our mobile service. It loads all assemblies from the current application domain and searches for types with `HostConfigProviderAttribute`. If it finds one, the custom host provider is loaded, or else the default host provider is used.

Let's extend the project to develop our scenario.

Defining the data model

We now create the required entities and data model. Note that while the entities have been kept simple for this chapter, in the real-world application, it is recommended to define a data architecture before creating any data entities.

For our scenario, we create two entities that inherit from Entity Data. These are described here.

Record

Record is an entity that represents data for the medical emergency. We use the `Record` entity when invoking CRUD operations using our controller. We also use this entity to update doctor allocation and status of the request as shown:

```
namespace Contoso.Hospital.Entities
{

    /// <summary>
    /// Emergency Record for the hospital
    /// </summary>
  public class Record : EntityData
    {
        public string PatientId { get; set; }

        public string InsuranceId { get; set; }
```

```
            public string DoctorId { get; set; }

            public string Emergency { get; set; }

            public string Description { get; set; }

            public string Location { get; set; }

            public string Status { get; set; }

        }
    }
```

Doctor

The `Doctor` entity represents the doctors that are registered practitioners in the area, the service will search for the availability of a doctor based on the properties of this entity. We will also assign the primary `DoctorId` to the `Record` type when a doctor is assigned to an emergency. The schema for the Doctor entity is as follows:

```
    amespace Contoso.Hospital.Entities
    {
        public class Doctor: EntityData
        {
            public string Speciality{ get; set; }

            public string Location { get; set; }

            public bool Availability{ get; set; }

        }
    }
```

We will look at how to create repositories and perform operations on these data models when we create the controller in the next section.

Creating the controller

We will now implement the Mobile Service controller. We will use the Microsoft Azure Mobile Services `TableController` template in Visual Studio since it provides inherent support for the Entity Framework. In case we want to develop against other data stores such as MongoDB, the Microsoft Azure Mobile Services custom controller can be used.

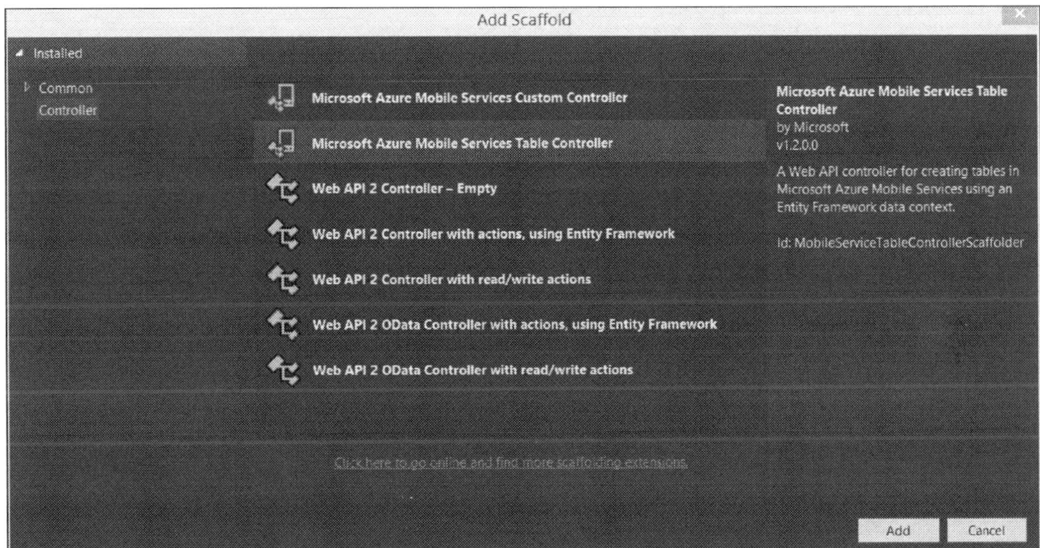

Next, we will provide information about the controller. Since this is `TableController`, we need to provide the relevant Entity Model and the database context to be used with the controller. We will use the doctor data model we created in the previous section.

We also create a new data context for the model. Click on the **+** sign in the **Data Context** section and enter the name for the data context as `ContosoContext`. Visual Studio will automatically scaffold a new data context type for the selected model class. The data context is inherited from the `DBContext` type in Entity Framework, which allows for the creation of a database repository. The repository will provide an abstraction between the entity models and the underlying data source. We will use the code-first technique to create the database context for our entities. The controller dialog should look similar to the below diagram:

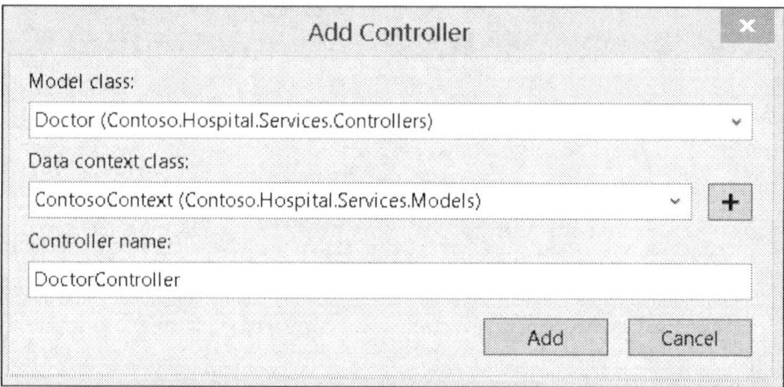

Entity Framework is a popular object mapper framework from Microsoft. To know more about Entity Framework, please visit `http://www.asp.net/entity-framework`. We discuss more about Entity Framework in the later part of this book.

The preceding step scaffolds a new controller that inherits from `TableController<Doctor>`.

There are a few important things to understand for the `DoctorController` type created:

- The controller inherits from `TableController<Doctor>`, so it now has a linkage to the `Doctor` entity we created earlier.
- The `Initialize` method registers our data context object (`ContosoContext`) to the Domain Manager of `TableController<Doctor>`. The Domain Manager will use this context for all data retrieval and data manipulation requests coming to the controller.
- The scaffolding also created a set of CRUD operations for performing operations on the `Doctor` entity.

We follow the same steps to create `RecordController`.

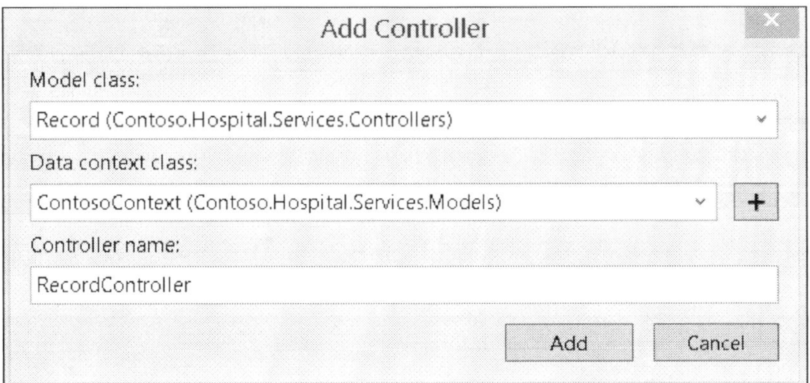

`RecordController` needs to perform additional tasks. It needs to fetch a doctor and associate it with the new patient request. We will modify our `RecordController` to incorporate these changes:

1. Move `ContosoContext` as a member variable, we use this in our `Post` method to fetch the doctor-state information:

```
MobileServiceContext context;
protected override void Initialize
  (HttpControllerContext controllerContext)
{
    base.Initialize(controllerContext);
    context = new MobileServiceContext();
    DomainManager = new EntityDomainManager<Record>
      (context, Request, Services);
}
```

2. Replace the `PostRecord` method with the following code:

```
public async Task<IHttpActionResult>
  PostRecord(Record item)
{
    // save record first
    var current = await InsertAsync(item);

    // record saved now randomly allocate a doctor to
      //the incoming request
    var recordPatch = new Delta<Record>();
    var doctorToAssign = this.context.Doctors.
      FirstOrDefault(doctor => doctor.Availability);
    if (doctorToAssign != null)
    {
```

```
                recordPatch.TrySetPropertyValue("DoctorId",
                  doctorToAssign.Id);

                // assign doctor to patient
                await this.UpdateAsync(current.Id, recordPatch);

                // block doctor
                doctorToAssign.Availability = false;
                this.context.Doctors.AddOrUpdate
                  (doctor => doctor.Id, doctorToAssign);
                await this.context.SaveChangesAsync();

                // TODO: send mobile notification
                //(broadcast only but you can add tags to target
                //a unique patient)
            }


            return this.CreatedAtRoute("Tables", new
              { id = current.Id }, current);

        }
```

The preceding code adds a new patient request. It then tries to find a doctor for the patient's request based on availability. Note that we use patch operations here to update the records; this improves performance and only the updated values are synced back with the existing objects in the database. Finally, we update the doctor's availability status to `Occupy` to ensure that the doctor is locked until he/she is finished with the current request.

> For the scope of this sample, we only modify the `Post` operation, however, we can similarly amend the `Patch` and `Put` operations with additional logic to make the solution more robust.

If we build our project, we will get the following error:

```
'System.Data.Entity.DbSet<Contoso.Hospital.Services.Controllers.
  Doctor>' does not contain a definition for 'AddOrUpdate'
  and no extension method 'AddOrUpdate' accepting a first
  argument of type 'System.Data.Entity.DbSet<Contoso.Hospital.
  Services.Controllers.Doctor>' could be found
  (are you missing a using directive or an assembly reference?)
```

`AddOrUpdate` is an extension method defined in the `System.Data.Entity.Migrations` namespace. We need to add a reference to this namespace to use this method. Add the following `using` statement to `RecordController`:

```
using System.Data.Entity.Migrations;
```

The `System.Data.Entity.Migrations` namespace provides a set of extension methods in the `IDbExtensions` type that augment the `IDbSet<T>` interface. For more information, please visit `https://msdn.microsoft.com/en-us/library/system.data.entity.migrations%28v=vs.113%29.aspx`.

Our project should now build without errors. We are only a few steps away from finishing our Mobile Service Controllers.

As the next step, update the connection strings for our Azure SQL database. The Mobile Services Visual Studio templates include some default application configuration settings in the `Web.Config` file of the project. The connection string setting is used in the database context created for the models. We will update these settings to provide the correct data source information:

```
<connectionStrings>
  <add name="MS_TableConnectionString"
    connectionString="Data Source=<yourserver.
    database.windows.net>;Initial Catalog
    =<yourdbname>;Persist Security Info=True;User
    ID=<username>;Pwd=<password>"
  providerName="System.Data.SqlClient" />
</connectionStrings>
```

The server name is the name of the SQL Azure Server Instance that was specified during the creation of the Mobile Service. Also, SQL Azure requires firewall rules to be enabled on the server before requests can be processed. As an additional step, add the local computer IP address as an allowed IP address to the SQL Azure Server configuration. For more information on configuring firewall rules in SQL Azure, visit `https://msdn.microsoft.com/en-us/library/azure/jj553530.aspx`.

The `MS_TableConnectionString` name is leveraged by `DbContext` created for the data models and should not be changed.

Our service is now ready. However, we need some prepopulated `Doctor` entities in the database so we can search for them. We will leverage the Entity Framework code first migrations approach to create a database initializer and register it during the service startup. The initializer for the `Doctor` type looks like this:

```
public class DoctorServiceInitializer : DropCreateDatabaseIfModelChang
es<ContosoContext>
{
    protected override void Seed(ContosoContext context)
    {
        var doctors = new List<Doctor>
        {
            new Doctor
            {
                Id = "1",
                Specialty = "PRI",
                Availability = true,
                Name = "John Smith."
            },
            new Doctor
            {
                Id = "2",
                Specialty = "GYNO",
                Availability = true,
                Name = "Ram Jaiswal."
            },
            new Doctor
            {
                Id = "3",
                Specialty = "ORTHO",
                Availability = true,
                Name = "Cassandra Stevens"
            }
        };

        foreach (var doctor in doctors)
        {
            context.Set<Doctor>().Add(doctor);
        }

        base.Seed(context);
    }
}
```

Additionally, we register the initializer to be invoked during our Web API startup. Add the following code in the `Register` method of `WebApiConfig` for our Web API.

```
Database.SetInitializer(new DoctorServiceInitializer());
```

We are done! In the next sections, we test our Web API functionality using a native browser and Windows 8.1 application.

Testing the mobile service

Since a mobile service is based on the ASP.NET Web API framework, testing a mobile service is no different from requesting resources for a Web API. However, Mobile Services provides some nice abstractions in the form of a client library, which we will explore in this section.

Testing in a browser

When testing a mobile service from a browser, since each action in a Web API controller represents a resource, we can just type the URL of the resource to fetch the results. The Visual Studio template also provides an intuitive user interface that can be used to test the mobile service. If we press *F5* now, we can see a page similar to this:

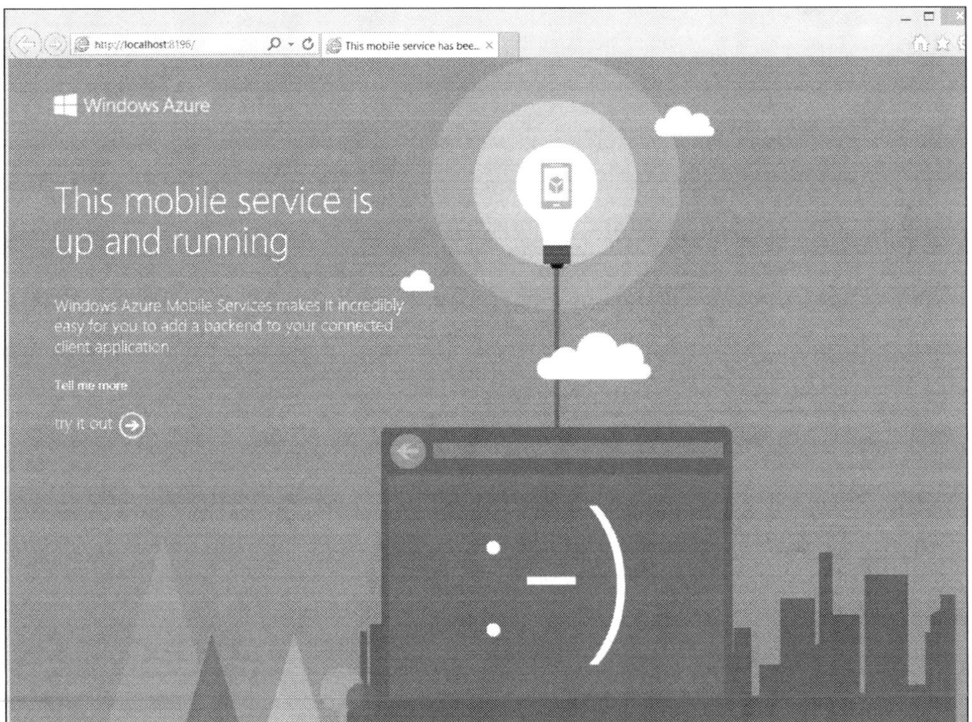

Click on **try it out** to view the operations exposed by the service, we can notice that all CRUD tasks for the entity are presented as actions here:

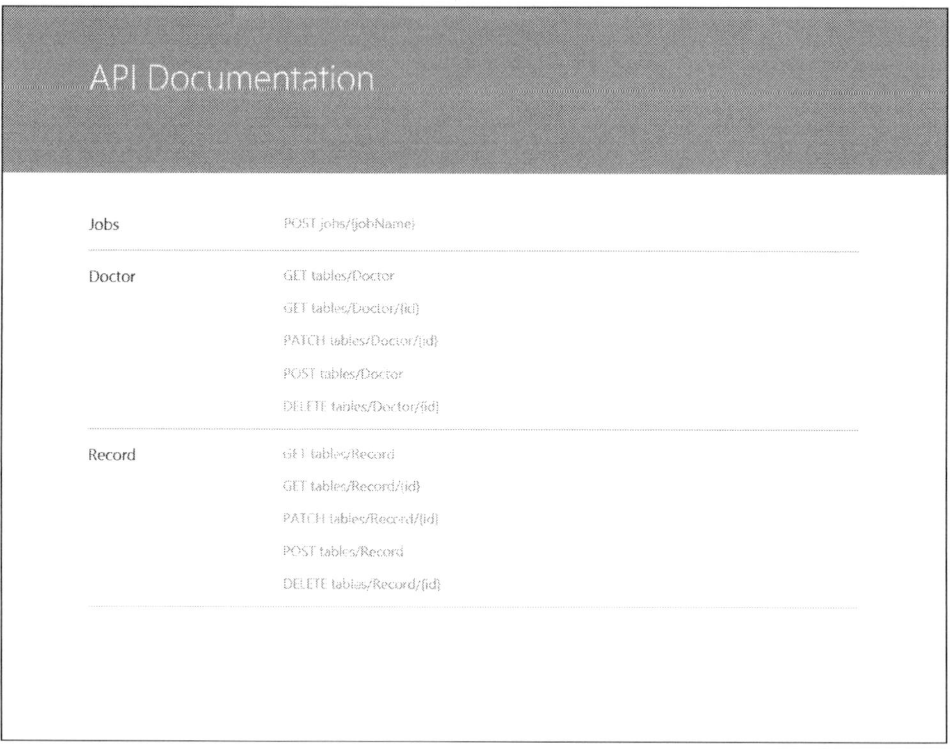

Clicking on any operation takes us to a test page where we can enter values in a test harness and execute the operation to return a response. We also have the option to add headers and body content for `POST` and `PUT` type of requests:

Here is the response for the preceding query, where we search for `Doctor` with ID `1`:

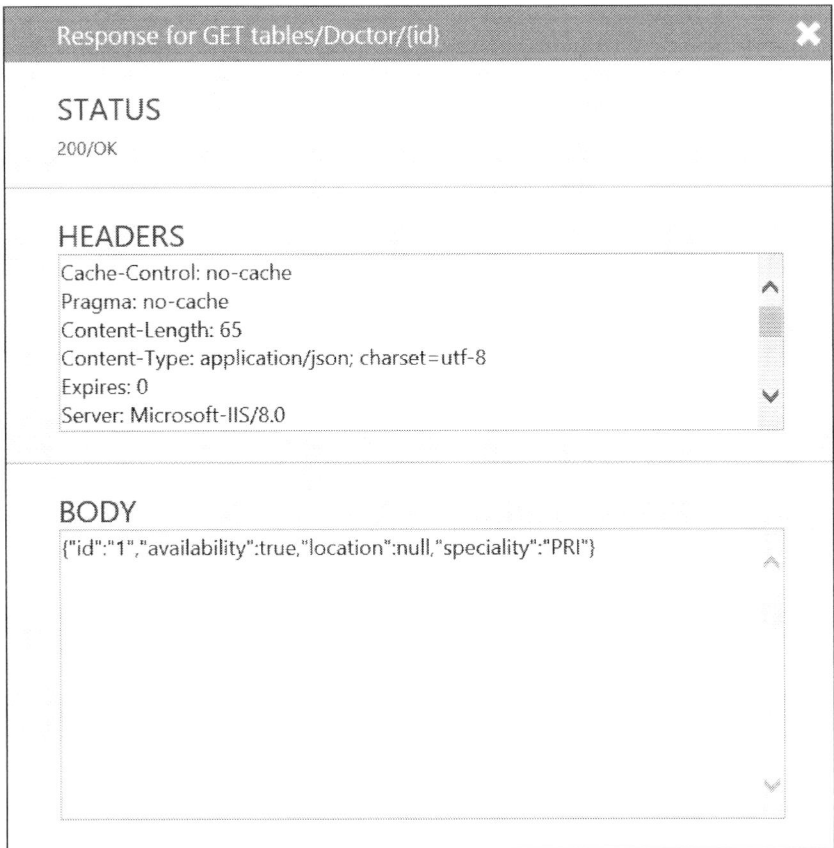

The preceding result is no different from manually executing a `GET` query in a browser using `http://<machine>:<port>/tables/doctor/1`.

Testing using a Windows 8.1 application

While testing the mobile service in a browser client is convenient, in most scenarios, we will access the service from a mobile application. In this section, we will create a Windows Store mobile application that will allow a patient to create an emergency record and then send a toast notification when a doctor is allocated to the patient. The following steps define the creation and configuration of the Windows 8.1 application:

> A Windows app developer license is required to execute this code. To obtain a license using an MSDN subscription, visit `http://msdn.microsoft.com/en-us/library/windows/apps/hh974578.aspx`.

1. We create a new Windows Store app in Visual Studio using the blank app template.

> For the scope of this book, we focus on a basic test Windows app. We do not discuss or implement any Windows app development patterns and best practices. To know more about Windows Store app development, please visit `https://dev.windows.com/develop`.

2. Next, we add the Windows Azure Mobile Services client library to the project using NuGet.
3. In the `App.xaml.cs` file, add the following code to create a client object and replace the URI with the mobile service deployment URI:

```
public App()
{
    // Create the mobile service client
    mobileServiceClient = new MobileServiceClient
      (new Uri("http://<machine>:<port>"));

    this.InitializeComponent();
    this.Suspending += OnSuspending;
}
```

4. Add three input controls to the screen and name them as:
    - `PatientId`
    - `InsuranceId`
    - `EmergencyType`

5. Add a button to the screen and name it `SubmitRequest`.
6. The screen should look like this:

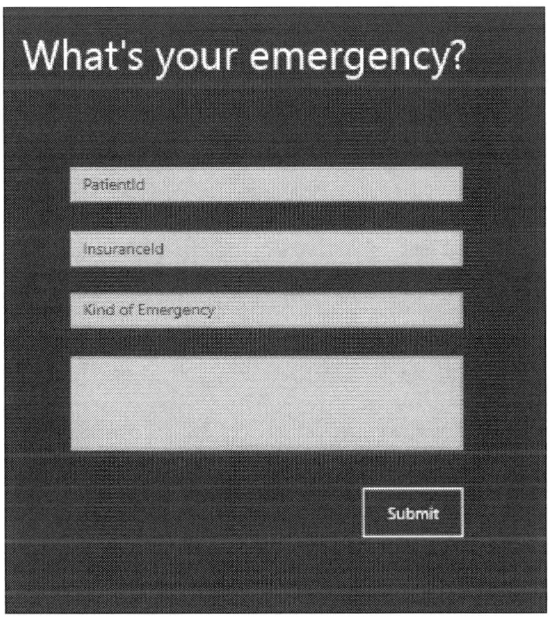

7. Add the following code on the click of the button:

```
private void SubmitRequest_Click
  (object sender, RoutedEventArgs e)
{
    var result = await this.PostToMobileServiceAsync();
    if (!result)
    {
        await new MessageDialog("Failure! call 911
          for emergency!!!").ShowAsync();
    }
}

private async Task<bool> PostToMobileServiceAsync()
{
    // create the model
    var record = new Record
    {
        Id = Guid.NewGuid().ToString(),
        PatientId = PatientId.Text,
        InsuranceId = InsuranceId.Text,
        Emergency = EmergencyType.Text
```

```
        };

        // insert the record using mobile services
        var table = App.mobileServiceClient.GetTable<Record>();
        await table.InsertAsync(record);
        return true;
    }
```

We now have a client that can submit requests in medical emergencies.

8. Next, we will add the Push Notifications capability to the Windows application so the patient gets a notification when a doctor is allocated. Right-click on the Windows Store app project and navigate to **Add | Push Notification** to start the notification wizard.
9. The wizard will require that we confirm the Windows Developer account details before proceeding. Once completed, we will enter an app name to reserve a name for the Windows Store application.
10. Finally, we select the mobile service we want to link to the Windows Store application. We can create a new service or can choose any existing mobile services available in the Azure subscription. The wizard will now finish adding the relevant code to connect our Windows app to our mobile service.
11. If all goes well, a confirmation page like the one shown here along with the next steps will be shown:

Push setup is almost complete...

Contoso.Chapter2.UI has been configured to receive push notifications. Complete the process by configuring your Mobile Service and client projects. After following the steps below, you'll be able to send push notifications with your Mobile Service.

Step 1: Create new Custom Controller

Create a new Custom Controller called "NotifyAllUsersController" in the Mobile Service project containing code for contososervice. In your Mobile Service project right-click on the Controllers folder, then click Add -> Controller. In the resulting dialog select "Windows Azure Mobile Services Custom Controller." then click Add.

Step 2: Insert snippet into Controller

Insert the following snippet in the "NotifyAllUsersController":

C#

```
// The following call is for illustration purpose only. The function
// body should be moved to a controller in your app where you want
// to send a notification.
public async Task<bool> Post(JObject data)
{
    try
    {
        string wnsToast = string.Format("<?xml version=\"1.0\" encoding=\"utf-8\"?><toast><visual><binding template=\"ToastText01\"><text id=\"1\">
{0}</text></binding></visual></toast>", data.GetValue("toast").Value<string>());
        WindowsPushMessage message = new WindowsPushMessage();
        message.XmlPayload = wnsToast;
        await Services.Push.SendAsync(message);
        return true;
    }
    catch (Exception e)
    {
        Services.Log.Error(e.ToString());
    }
    return false;
}
```

We will skip **Step 1** since we already created our controllers earlier; also remember that we skipped adding mobile notifications to our `RecordController` in the previous section, we will add those now.

12. To enable Push Notifications, we modify `RecordController` to include the code described in **Step 2** of the confirmation page:

```
private async Task<bool> PostAsync(JObject data)
{
    try
    {
        string wnsToast = string.Format
          ("<?xml version=\"1.0\" encoding=\
          "utf-8\"?><toast><visual><binding
          template=\"ToastText01\"><text
          id=\"1\">{0}</text></binding></visual>
          </toast>", data.GetValue("toast")
          .Value<string>());
        WindowsPushMessage message =
          new WindowsPushMessage();
        message.XmlPayload = wnsToast;
        await Services.Push.SendAsync(message);
        return true;
    }
    catch (Exception e)
    {
        Services.Log.Error(e.ToString());
    }
    return false;
}
```

Additionally, we need to reference the JSON.Net NuGet package to use the `JObject` type:

```
using Newtonsoft.Json.Linq;
```

13. Now, update the `PostRecord` method to send a Push Notification whenever the doctor gets allocated to a patient:

```
await this.Post(new JObject(new JProperty
  ("toast", string.Format("Dr. {0} is on its way!"
  , doctorToAssign.Name))));
```

14. Modify the Web API project `web.config` to include the values provided in step 3. Note that these values will be specific to the custom mobile service created, so it is recommended to copy these from the confirmation page directly. The modified `web.config` file looks like this:

```
<add name="MS_NotificationHubconnectionString"
  connectionString="<servicebusnamespace>" />
<add key="MS_NotificationHubName"
  value="<notificationhubname>" />
```

15. Step 4 allows the client to make calls to the mobile service-hosted Web API on a local machine.
16. Add the code in step 5 to register the client for receiving toast notifications.
17. Run the Windows Store application and add a new patient record.

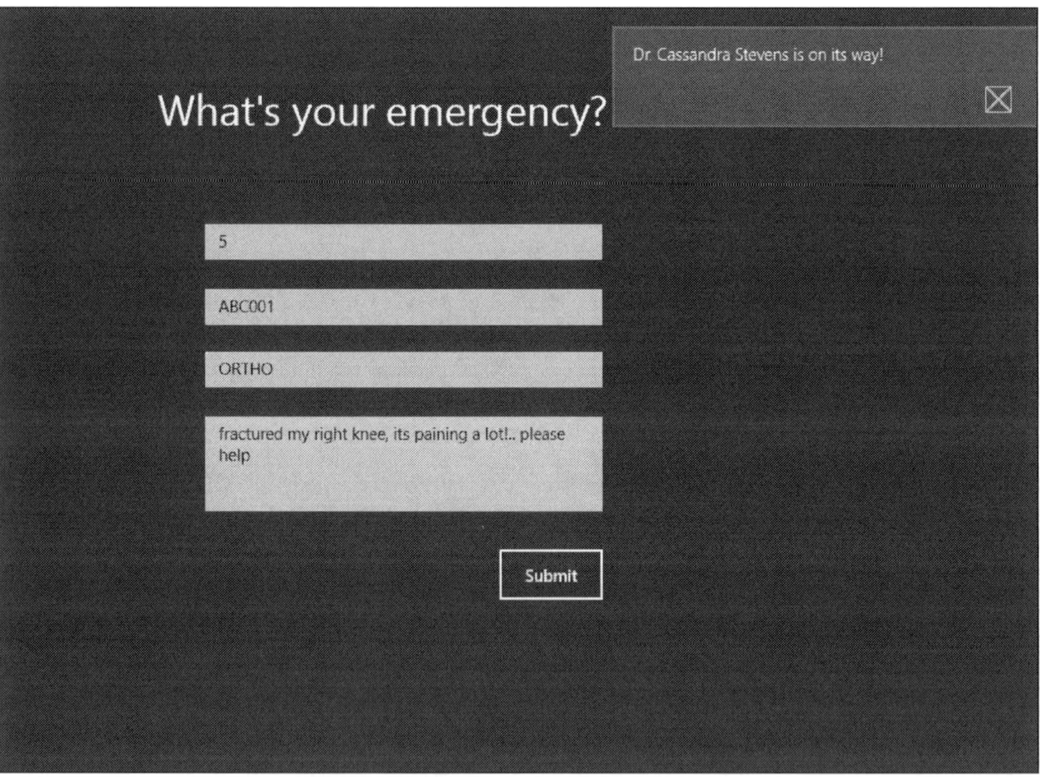

We will now see a toast notification in the Windows Store application for the doctor that is allocated to the patient.

Deploying to Azure Mobile Services

The final step is to publish the Web API to the mobile service that we already created:

1. Right-click on the Web API project and click on **Publish** to open the **Publish** wizard. Select **Microsoft Azure Mobile Services** as the publish target. It prompts the list of mobile services available in the Azure subscription. The dialog provides an option to create a new mobile service as well.
2. Select the mobile service that we created at the beginning of this chapter. It should populate the connection details about the Mobile Service.

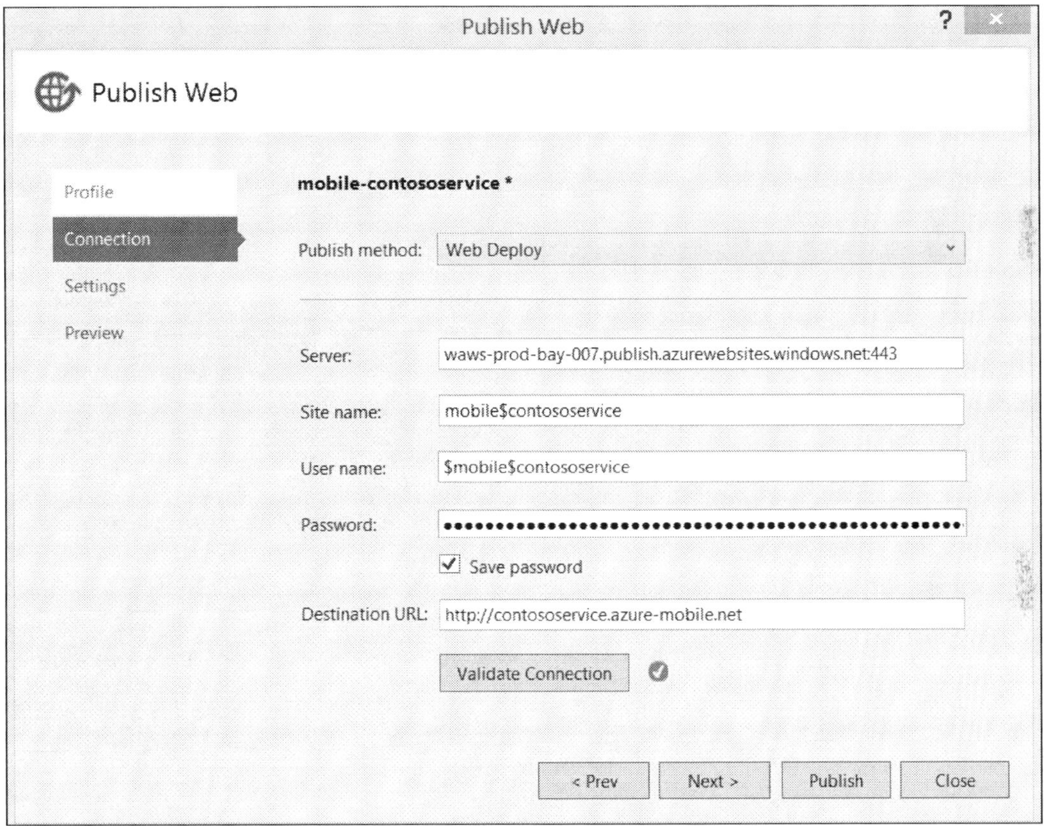

3. Click on **Validate Connection** to ensure that we can connect to the Mobile Service.
4. Once the deployment is completed (should not take more than a few seconds), we will have our mobile API running in the cloud.

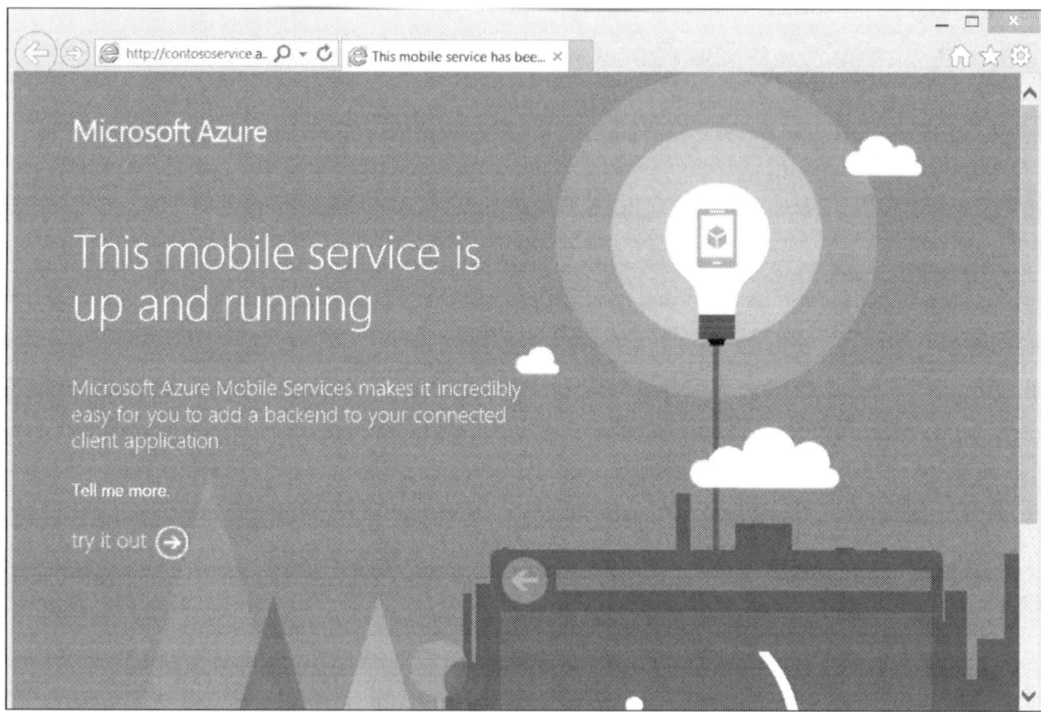

5. To point to the new deployment, just change `MobileServiceClient` in the Windows Store application to the URI deployed in Azure. Now when we run the client, it will connect to Azure instead of the local development machine.

6. Also, if we now browse to Azure Management portal and go to the Azure Mobile Service we created, we see how traffic is being monitored by the mobile service.

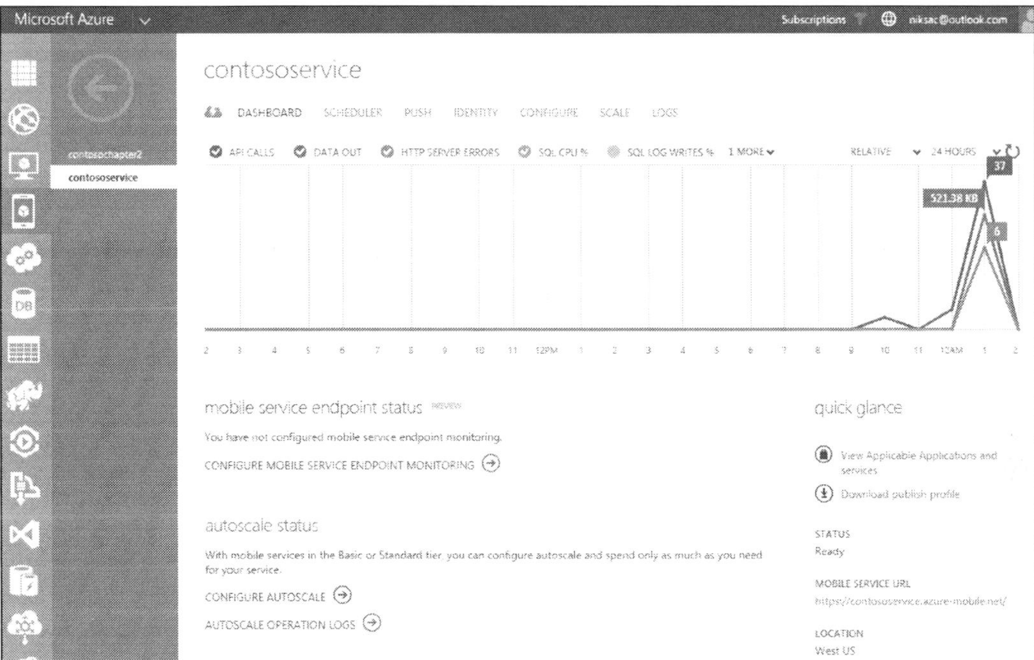

Leftovers

Although we cannot cover all aspects of Mobile Services as part of this chapter, it is worth mentioning some of the additional features that make Mobile Services a compelling solution for any mobile app development:

- **Identity**: Mobile Services provides an easy-to-use way of authenticating against multiple identity providers. While we did not delve into the topic in this chapter, there are some great examples available at `http://azure.microsoft.com`, which provide step-by-step instructions on how to incorporate authentication for disparate platforms and languages. These samples can be accessed at `http://azure.microsoft.com/en-us/documentation/articles/mobile-services-windows-store-dotnet-get-started-users/`.

- **Scheduling**: Mobile Services provides a scheduler engine that can be used to schedule recurring or time-based jobs for performing background tasks. To know more about job scheduler, please visit `http://azure.microsoft.com/en-us/documentation/articles/mobile-services-dotnet-backend-schedule-recurring-tasks/`.
- **Offline data Sync**: This is another essential feature of Mobile Services that allows caching data on the device for occasionally connected scenarios. It has built-in conflict resolution techniques and allows seamless persistence of data in offline mode giving the client an impression that they are online. More information is available at `http://azure.microsoft.com/en-us/documentation/articles/mobile-services-ios-get-started-offline-data/`.

> The Azure Mobile Services team's blog is an excellent resource for all frequent service updates and feature walkthroughs. The blogs can be accessed at `http://azure.microsoft.com/blog/topics/mobile/`.

Summary

In this chapter, we looked at a solution for developing a Web API that targets mobile developers. Azure Mobile Services provides an umbrella set of services that saves the developer from recurring tasks in mobile development, such as notifications and data operations. With seamless integration and tooling support in Visual Studio, Mobile Services can be quickly created and deployed for a variety of clients such as Windows, iOS, and Android.

The first two chapters were an introduction to the ASP.Web API and Microsoft Azure platform support for building and deploying scalable Web APIs. In the next chapter, we will look at advanced features of the ASP.NET Web API framework and how it provides first-class support for the HTTP protocol.

5

Connecting Applications with Microsoft Azure Service Bus

Up to this point in the book, we have focused on using ASP.NET for the frontend website and we have walked through the ASP.NET Web API for creating REST-based services. In this chapter, we will look at how to scale the application and provide elasticity, as well as provide loosely coupled connections between tiers of the application.

Azure Service Bus

We looked at how to create a web service, how to add functionality around notifications, integration with mobile services, deployment, and more. Now we will shift our focus to the middle tier of the solution architecture. In scalable systems, you would want to decouple direct connections between portions of your application. Just as when you created multi-tiered systems for use on-premises, we will do the same for our architecture in Azure. We want to divide the application components into separate features or areas of concern. By doing so we can create boundaries with low coupling, which leads to less feature overlap and more flexibility.

As such, you don't want to connect the web service directly to the database. There are many reasons for this. What happens if the database is inaccessible? What happens if there is processing that is needed on the incoming data? Azure provides components that we can utilize so that we don't connect components of our application together directly. Not only does this separation provide elasticity but also provides separate so that the system can continue to operate if we can't connect to the database.

In this chapter, we will plunge into the use of the Service Bus to provide the middle tier/business layer of our application architecture. The different tiers of a standard *n*-tier architecture can be seen in the following diagram:

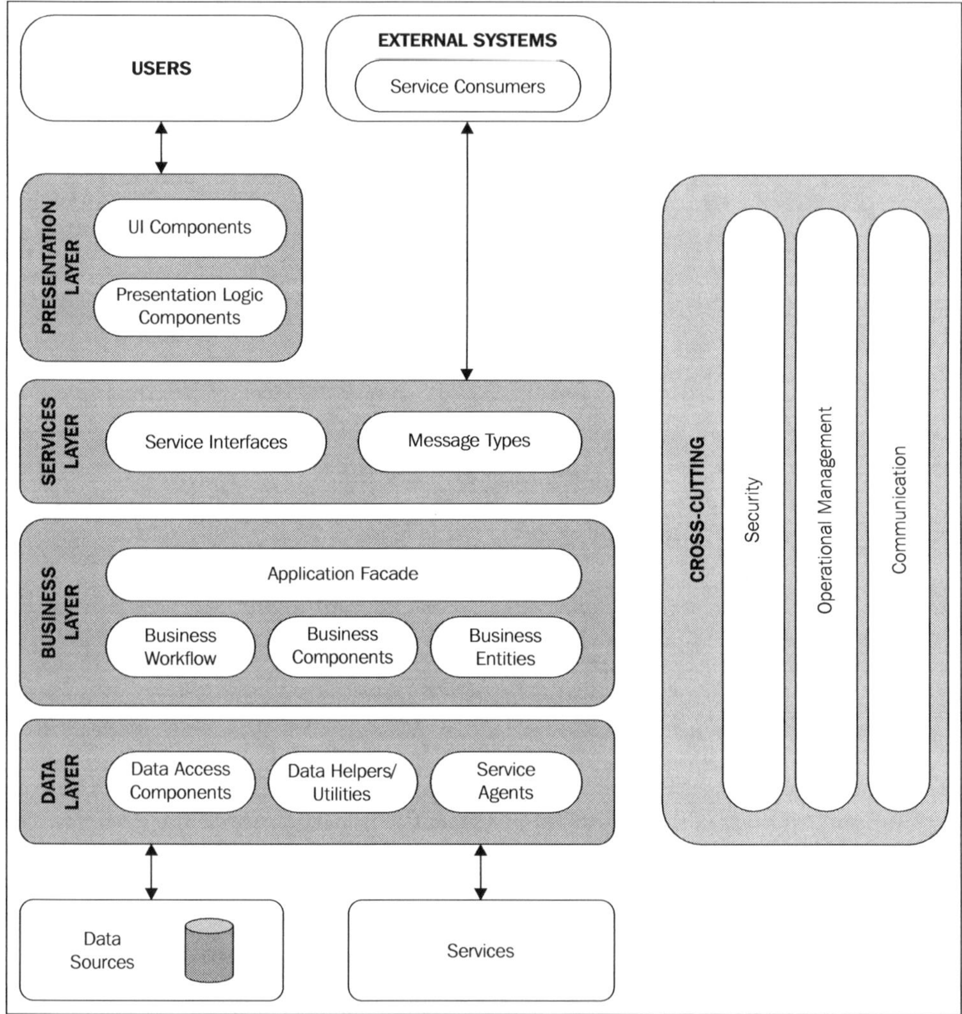

Standard architecture diagram from the Microsoft Application Architecture Guide

What is Azure Service Bus?

Azure Service Bus provides a cloud-based, loosely coupled message exchange system that we can utilize to connect the web service to the database (that we will create in later chapters). The Service Bus can provide communication between web and worker roles, websites, mobile services and the data store, or between external systems when creating a multi-tier application as well as between different components/tiers of a distributed system running in a hybrid configuration with portions of the application located on-premises and other portions located in Azure. The Service Bus also provides scalability, high availability, transaction support, security, and manageability. As we move through this chapter, we will focus on coding against the Service Bus in order to communicate between different tiers in our multi-tiered architecture. We will utilize the Service Bus so that we can scale out our application as required and also to enable more resiliency in our application.

Now that we know what the Service Bus is and how we will use it, let's look a bit deeper into what the Service Bus provides.

The Service Bus is made up of four different components: Queues, Topics, the relay service, and the event hub.

Service Bus Queues provide a **First In, First Out** (**FIFO**) message delivery system where a sender will submit a message to the Queue and a receiver will take the message off the Queue in the order submitted. The benefit is that the submitter doesn't have to wait for the downstream process to reply but continues to process and send additional messages. When using a Queue, there is only one receiver or message consumer per message. There can be many consumers to provide high availability but each message is consumed by one receiver. However, there can be multiple senders that can send message to a single Queue, as shown in the following figure:

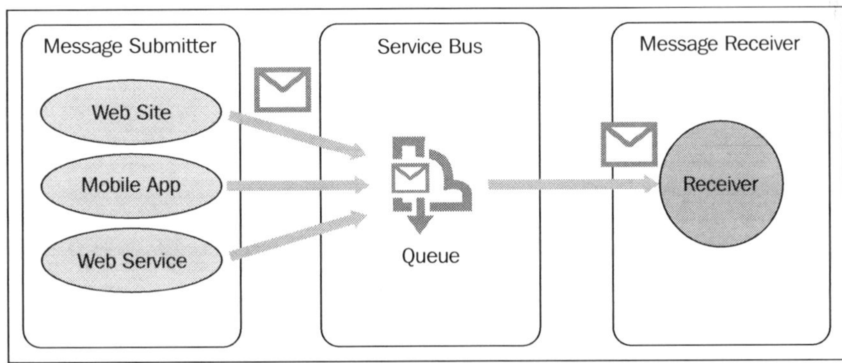

Service Bus Queue

Service Bus Topics provide a publish-and-subscribe message system where you can have multiple receivers and each can subscribe to a message. When utilizing Topics, each receiver can handle and process messages independently, and allows you to scale your system to process a very large number of messages across a very large number of application/receivers. As part of the Topic, you can provide filter rules for a Topic on a per-subscription basis, which allows you to filter or route messages to specific receivers as shown in the following figure:

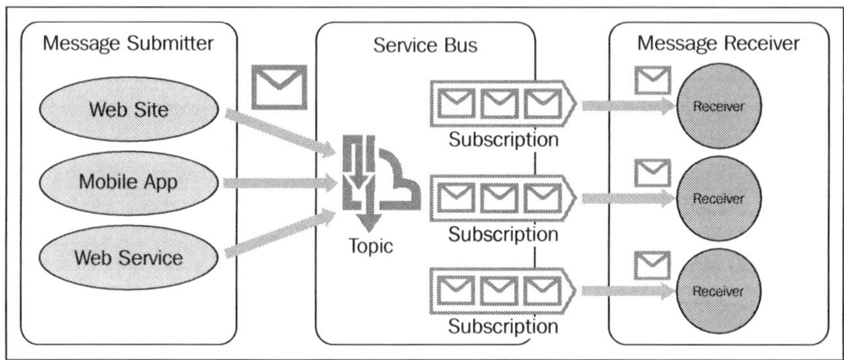

Service Bus Topic

Service Bus relay provides an interesting use case, in that it provides the ability to set up a hybrid architecture where web services are hosted on-premises, a proxy is created (the relay service) in Azure, and that proxy is securely accessible through the cloud by consumers outside the corporate firewall. This works by providing a communication pipe on top of existing WCF-based web services that are still hosted on-premises. There are no changes required to the corporate firewall or network and the communication pipe works with port `80` or `443`. The endpoint in Azure is then protected by **Azure Active Directory Access Control** to protect the end points from unauthorized access.

The Service Bus relay is one of the components that is available in Azure that lets you build hybrid systems as shown in the following figure. We are covering this topic in this chapter for completeness so that you know all of the components that make up the Service Bus. However, we will cover this in the next chapter as we talk about connecting to on-premises systems and creating hybrid systems.

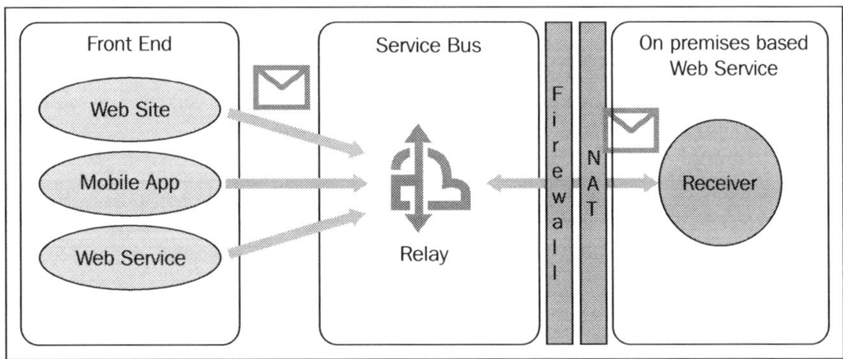

Service Bus relay

Lastly, event hubs provide the ability to collect streams of messages at very high throughput. This is the newest addition to Service Bus and it is a peer to Queues and Topics. One of the features of the event hub is that it isn't backed by the SQL Azure database, unlike Queues or Topics, which provides for very fast message processing. However, with this speed, there are things that we give up such as transaction support. Even with this, event hubs provide an important feature and are available for a wide variety of scenarios. These scenarios range from activity tracking in mobile apps, traffic information from web applications, in-game event capture or telemetry data flowing in from industrial machines to connected vehicles (as well as many other Internet of Things examples). The event hub acts as an event pipeline (event ingestor), which sits between the systems that produce the events and the consumers in order to decouple the systems.

Note that IoT is the next opportunity for the cloud. The cloud provides the scale and power that is needed to provide the foundation of what is needed for IoT scenarios. Imagine millions of devices/systems sending continuous streams of data without interruption. The servers must always respond and react to the requests to ensure that all of the telemetry data is captured and perform at adequate scale. Event hubs are targeted to solve these hyper-scale IoT scenarios and are specifically targeted towards ingestion of data from very few connected devices to millions of them.

One thing to note about the event hub is that it is tuned for high throughput and event processing scenarios through message stream handling. The event hub is not meant for traditional enterprise messaging where you need sequencing, transactions, and delivery assurance. If you need these features, then Topics is the pattern to utilize.

Now that we have an understanding of what the Service Bus is and what components make up the Service Bus, let's look at some patterns that can be implemented. Then we will dive deeper and write code.

Patterns

While there have been whole books dedicated to patterns and integration patterns, we will cover nine of the more frequently used patterns, get their description, and look at the implementation components in Azure with the Service Bus. We will cover patterns from both the messaging channel group of patterns as well as the message routing group of patterns. The first pattern we will cover is from the messaging channel group.

Publish/Subscribe

The publish and subscribe channel outlines the operation for a message or an event to be sent to a channel that will be delivered to each and every receiver, no matter how many receivers there are. Once the message has been received by each receiver, the message is deleted from the channel.

This is the primary functionality offered by Service Bus Topics.

The Topic allows applications that submit messages to send them to the Topic where many subscribers can be configured to listen to these submitted messages. Each of these subscribers can be individually managed. In addition, rules are created for these subscribers to determine which messages should be routed to the subscriber (depending on how the rule is written to each subscriber). When a message is routed to a subscriber, it will be stored until it is read by the receiver. If the receiver is not online, then the message is stored until the receiver retrieves it, or else the time to live expiry timeframe kicks in.

Messaging bridge

The Messaging bridge pattern provides a connection between different systems that have different messaging formats. This allows messages to be transmitted to a different system in order to connect two systems that were never programmed to communicate previously.

Both the Queue and the Topic can provide the functionality to implement this pattern. Either of these can be the intermediary with the receivers being programmed to communicate directly to the targeted system's end point. The Service Bus relay service can also be utilized if the source system is communicating through the cloud or located in the cloud, and the web service end points are located on-premises front ending system the located behind a firewall. Lastly, not covered in this book but included here for completeness, is the functionality of **BizTalk Service**. BizTalk Services provides additional functionality beyond that provided by the Service Bus to graphically define how a message transforms from one format or layout to another format or layout. BizTalk Services also includes a set of protocol adapters that can be set up as receivers from the Queue or the Topic and connected directly to the targeted system. BizTalk Services also provides functionality for EDI processing in the cloud.

Dead Letter Channel and Invalid Message Channel

Dead Letter Channel provides a means to hold messages that either can't be delivered/processed by the receiver or are of a format that can't be processed. This pattern is linked to Invalid Message Channel and both of these are the functionalities that are included in both Queue and Topic. Each provides the ability to designate a subqueue that is the dead letter Queue. You can either programmatically place a message into this subqueue, or the Service Bus infrastructure will place the message in the dead letter Queue. There are three occasions when the infrastructure will place a message in the dead letter Queue:

- When the maximum delivery count for a message is exceeded
- When a message expires and the dead-lettering for expired messages is set to `true`
- When a filter evaluation exception occurs and dead-lettering is enabled for that exception

> You can find out more about these patterns as well as the other patterns in the messaging channel grouping at `http://tinyurl.com/ServiceBusPatternsPart1`.

The next set of patterns we will look at are all in the message routing group.

Content Based Router and Recipient List

The Content Based Router and Recipient List patterns outline the operation for a message to be routed and directed based on data elements in the submitted message. The routing should be able to be based on different fields and the rules should be easily maintained since there can be frequent changes. The Recipient List is related in a way that this pattern provides for a means of sending a routed message to multiple receivers or a single receiver based on the rule expression.

Both of these patterns are implemented through the use of Topics. For the Content Based Router there are two parts that are implemented. The first is that you need to create the Topic and the subscription: one for every route/end point. The second is that a message (using the `BrokeredMessage` object described in more depth later in this chapter) needs to be created and specific properties need to be populated that can be utilized for the routing function. The Recipient List implements the functionality of what happens with the routing once a message has been submitted. The subscriptions that get created will utilize `SqlFilter` that will be used to route the messages to the appropriate recipients. An example of `SqlFilter` will look like this:

```
topic.AddSubscription("OtherMemberTypes", new SqlFilter("MemberType
LIKE '%Premium%'"));
```

When we create `BrokeredMessage` with the properties, it will utilize the properties object as shown:

```
message.Properties.Add("MemberType", "Premium");
```

This allows the client to set the properties and direct the routing as appropriate for the functionality required by the application. We will cover this in greater detail later in this chapter as this is a very common pattern and is used quite frequently.

Splitter and Aggregator

The Splitter and the Aggregator patterns outline the task of breaking apart messages and putting them back together again.

The Splitter pattern is useful when you have messages that comprise many subitems such as an order with many line items. Each line item may require a different receiver to receive the submessage and perform a task with it.

This pattern can be implemented with the Queue or Topic through sessions and by having the submitter break apart the message. The Queue or Topic needs to be set up with the `RequiresSession` property set. This pattern can also be utilized for messages that are larger than allowed (256 KB) to flow through the Topic or Queue. The message can be chunked into smaller message sizes and utilize the `SessionId` order to receive the entire message in the same session and then reassemble them.

The Aggregator pattern can utilize either the `SessionId` or `CorrelationId` properties of the `BrokeredMessage` object. When setting up the filter expression, you can utilize `CorrelationFilterExpressions` in order to receive all related messages. This can also be implemented within the functionality of the Topic using the `Session` feature. It will depend on what control you want as to which one makes the most sense. However, keep in mind that the use of the `CorrelationId` property provides exact match semantics and is better optimized for matching performance.

Resequencer

The Resequencer pattern outlines the task of putting messages back into a specific order. Because messages may be broken out for size reasons as well as business logic reasons, there may be times when messages are processed and resubmitted to the Queue or Topic out of order, and thus must be placed back in order again. The pattern outlines the use of a buffer (the Queue) and a receiver. It also outlines a requirement that the submitter places the value in the submitted message to indicate the order count. We will utilize the `MessageID` property in the `BrokeredMessage` object. Once the message has been submitted, the receiver will dequeue the first message and inspect the `MessageID` field. If it is not the first message, or the next in line, the receiver will call the `Defer()` method on the `QueueClient` object, which will put the message back into the Queue and return an ID that the receiver needs to keep. The ID will be used to recall that message when it is needed based on the order list. The receiver will need to keep an ordered list of the messages it has received as well as any messages it defers. When the receiver processes the messages, the receiver will process, and when needed recall, any deferred message when needed based on where they fit in the sequence.

[You can find out more about these patterns as well as the other patterns in the message routing grouping at `http://tinyurl.com/ServiceBusPatternsPart2`.]

Now that we have covered a group of patterns and how the Queue and Topics fit in, let's explore the Service Bus functionality in more depth.

The BrokeredMessage object

All interactions with the Service Bus happen by submitting a message that is contained in a `BrokeredMessage` object. The `BrokeredMessage` object holds system properties such as `TimeToLive`, `CorrelationID`, `Expiration`, `SessionId`, and the body. In addition, you can add custom properties to the object in the properties collection. By adding custom properties (in the form of a dictionary object), you can add custom items that are of relevance to your business process. These properties can be used to route on when utilizing Topics in the Service Bus. `BrokeredMessage` is the object that will flow between all of the layers of your application as well as any interactions between middle tier and integration services.

Creating `BrokeredMessage` can be as simple as:

```
BrokeredMessage msg = new BrokeredMessage ("Hello world!");
```

This will create the object with the text as the message body.

You can also create the `BrokeredMessage` objects with the body being created from serialized objects (using `DataContractSerializer`) or from streams.

If we want to create one using a serialized object, then we need to create the object that we will use for our body. In this case, let's create an order object:

```
public class CustomerOrder
  {
    public string Name { get; set; }
    public int ItemNumber { get; set; }
    public int Quantity { get; set; }
  }
```

Then we can instantiate that object and assign it to a new `BrokeredMessage` object:

```
CustomerOrder order = new CustomerOrder()
{
  Name = "Thumb Drive",
  ItemNumber = 1234,
  Quantity = 5
};

//We can create the object with the serialized class as the body.
//using either DataContractSerializer or XMLObjectSerializer
BrokeredMessage customerorderMsg = new BrokeredMessage (order);
```

Now that we have an object created, we can set properties. I mentioned these properties earlier but it is important we cover it in more depth. The properties are there for you to provide additional information to be used when evaluating the rules that will route your message. When routing messages, we shouldn't have to parse the body of the message when deciding how to route the message. This would not be efficient. In addition, the message body may be encrypted or even be in a binary format. Therefore, if we are going to route messages based on their content, we need to add data to the properties collection. This process is known as **property promotion**. When promoting properties, we will add the data to the built-in dictionary object that represents the `Properties` property.

We can take the `BrokeredMessage` object we already created earlier and start promoting properties as follows:

```
//Add the string-object property pairs to
  //the Properties collection
orderMsg.Properties.Add("region", "USA");
orderMsg.Properties.Add("memberType", "Lifetime");
```

Now we have a complete object that is ready to submit to either a Queue or a Topic. However, first, we need to create these items before we can send the message.

How do you create elements of the Service Bus?

Everything in Azure can be done either through the Azure Management portal or through an API. In this section, we will use the Azure Management portal to walk through the steps required to create the Service Bus components.

Creating a Service Bus Queue

To create a Queue, we will follow these steps:

1. Click on **New** on the bottom-left corner of the portal, click on **App Services**, and you should see **Service Bus** listed as shown in the following screenshot:

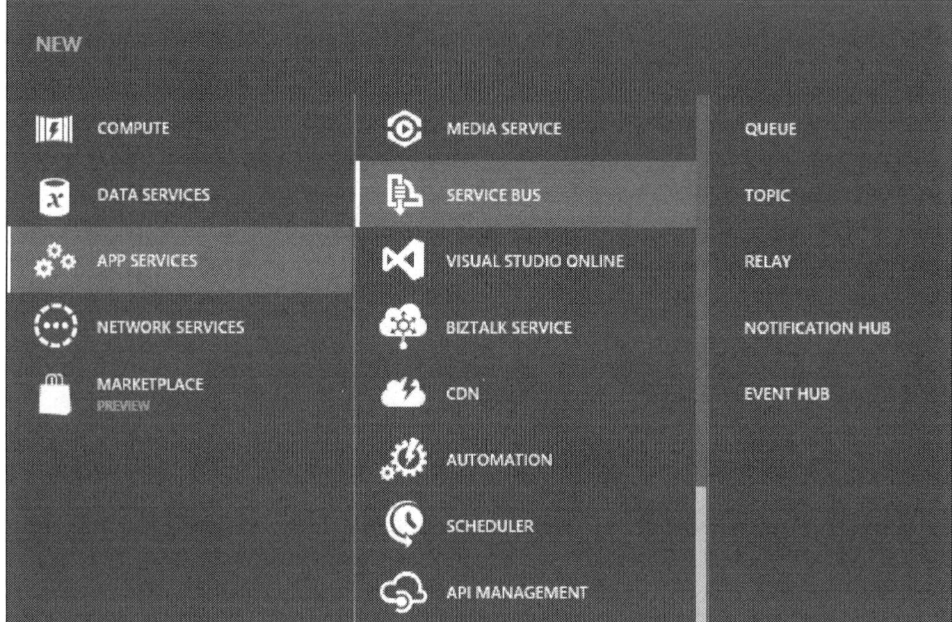

2. Select **Queue** and then select **Custom Create**.

Note that you can also click on **Quick Create**. This will provide you with the three required data elements—**Queue Name**, **Region**, and **Namespace**. After entering this data and clicking on the **Create A New Queue** button, a Queue will be created using the defaults for all options. However, we want to perform the custom create as outlined here.

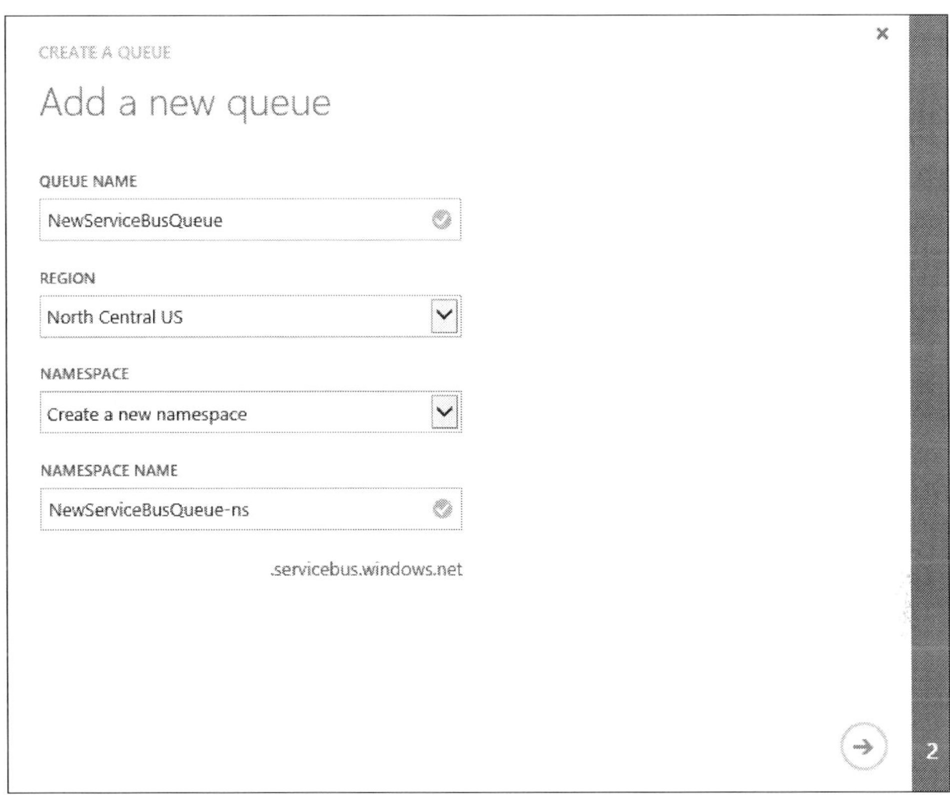

When the **Create a Queue** wizard appears, you will need to select the region in which you wish to create the Queue; choose whether you want to create a new namespace or create the Queue in an existing namespace. Lastly, the namespace will be created for you but you do have the option to modify it to meet your application infrastructure naming conventions.

3. Click on the right arrow to navigate to the next page of the wizard:

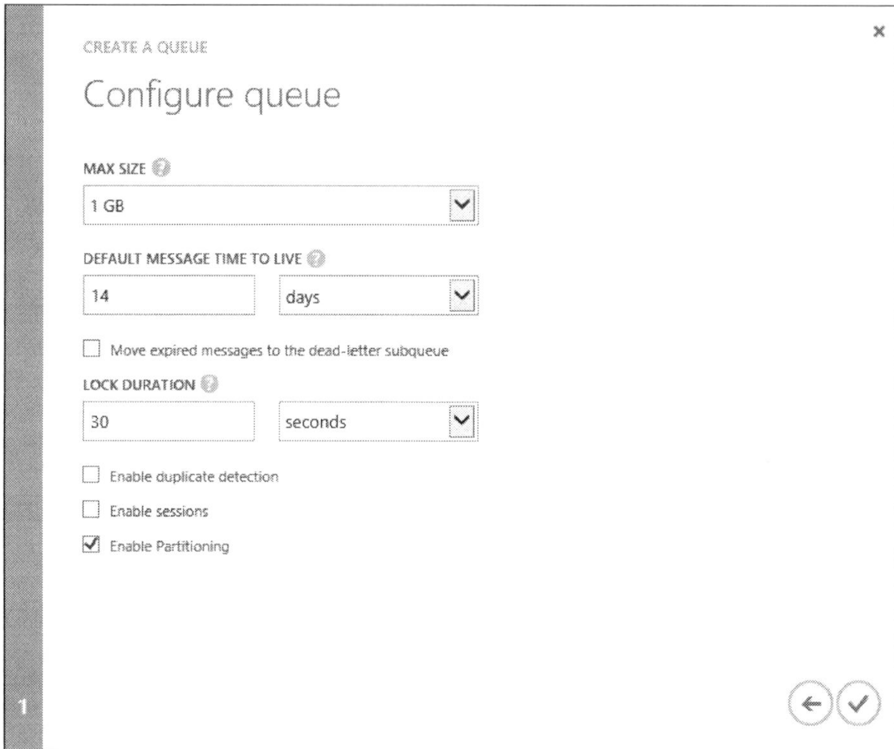

These are the options that we want to set and these wouldn't be available to us if we had selected the **Quick Create** option.

When configuring the Queue, there are a number of options that we can set:

- **Size of the Queue**: This is not the size of the messages that can be submitted to the Queue, instead, it is the size of the Queue and will determine how many messages the Queue can hold. The default is 1 GB and can be increased by 1 GB at a time up to a maximum of 5 GB.
- **Default time to live**: This determines the amount of time the message remains in the Queue before it expires. The time starts from the time the message is sent. The default is 14 days. However, it can be any number of seconds, minutes, hours, or days. In addition, you also have an option to move the messages to a dead letter Queue for action on the messages once they expire.
- **Lock duration:** The lock duration specifies the amount of time for a peek lock. This is the time that the message is locked for other receivers. This can be set as low as 5 seconds and as high as 5 minutes. The default is 30 seconds.

Lastly, we have three checkbox options:

- The first checkbox is to choose whether we want to enable duplicate detection. Duplicate detection will keep a list of messages that have been sent to the Queue and will remove the subsequent messages with the same `MessageID`. When you select this option, additional settings will appear that will allow you to select the amount of time that you want to keep a duplicate history for. The default is 10 minutes but you can set it for any number of seconds, minutes, hours, or days.
- The second checkbox is to choose whether we want to enable sessions. Sessions allow you to relate messages together that may be submitted by multiple submitters, or where there are many messages that are linked together and need to be processed by the same receiver in order to maintain state. Sessions also help if messages are submitted out of order or there are multiple receivers (competing consumers) and messages need to be processed together by one receiver. Lastly, when submitting the messages you must include a value in the `message.sessionid` attribute of the `BrokeredMessage` object.
- The third checkbox is to choose whether we want to enable partitioning. Partitioning is a feature that provides better availability and better performance. The Service Bus enables the Queue to be partitioned across a number of message brokers and message stores. This provides the ability to still process them even if there is a temporary outage. When the message is sent to the Queue you can include a partition key or if there is no partition key and you have enabled partitioning, the Service Bus will assign messages randomly. When the client receives a message it does not know that there is any partitioning occurring and the receiver is the same whether or not partitioning is used or not. One thing to keep in mind is that there is no additional overhead cost when sending or receiving from a partitioned Queue.

Note that there are some interactions between the checkboxes though. If you include a `SessionID` property value in `BrokeredMessage`, the Service Bus will use that as a partition key internally so that all the messages that belong to that same session are handled by the same message broker. However, if the message uses the `PartitionKey` property but doesn't set the `SessionId` property, then the Service Bus will use the `PartitionKey` property as the partition key. Moreover, if the `ParitionKey` and `SessionId` properties are both set, then both properties must be identical values. If they are different values, then you will receive an `InvalidOperationException` error.

When you are finished, click the check mark in the lower right-hand side corner of the wizard to create the new Topic.

Interacting with the Queue

Now that we have created the Queue we need to do something with it. Let's look at how to send messages and then how to receive messages.

Sending a message to the Queue

Create a console application and add the Service Bus NuGet package. Then, we need to include the using statement for the `Microsoft.ServiceBus` and `Microsoft.ServiceBus.Messaging` namespaces:

```
public static void Main()
    {
    //Create the URI
    Uri sbUri = ServiceBusEnvironment.CreateServiceUri
    ("sb", "<Service Bus Namespace>", string.Empty);

    //Create the message factory
    MessagingFactory factory = MessagingFactory.Create(sbUri,
    TokenProvider.CreateSharedAccessSignatureTokenProvider
    ("send_listen", "<Issuer Secret>"));

    //Create the queue client
    QueueClient queueClient =
    factory.CreateQueueClient("NewServiceBusQueue");
}
```

Looking at this code, we need to have our credentials and the URI. Once we have these, we can then create a `MessagingFactory` object, which will connect to Azure, and then we can create a `QueueClient` object from the factory, which will connect us to the Queue we want to interact with.

Next, we need to send something to the Queue. We just happen to have created a `BrokeredMessage` object earlier in this chapter that we will use as our message to send to the Queue. Our `BrokeredMessage` object `customerorderMsg` is what we created from our order object. To send our message to our Queue, we just need the following line of code:

```
//Send the order message to the queue.
queueClient.Send(customerorderMsg);
```

It sounds so simple. Just call the `Send` method. This is true but always follow defensive coding practices and ensure that you act on any exceptions that could be thrown. Microsoft has done a god job of providing many exceptions that can be caught and reacted to.

Receiving a message from the Queue

The next step is to receive the message from the Queue. In most circumstances, the application code that is sending the message to the Queue won't be the same application code that is receiving the messaging. Therefore, you will need to have the same code we used to create `TokenProvider` and the URI, and create `MessageFactory`. I won't show that code again here since we have seen it earlier.

However, when we receive a message, we need to have a `BrokeredMessage` object to place the received message into. Thus, our receive code block will look like this (ensure that `CustomerOrder` comes from the same namespace, otherwise there will be serialization exceptions):

```
//Receive a message from the queue
BrokeredMessage receivedOrderMessage = queueClient.Receive();

if (receivedOrderMessage != null)
{
    //Deserialize the message body back to our object type
    CustomerOrder orderOut =
      receivedOrderMessage.GetBody<CustomerOrder>();

    //Set the order message as completed
    receivedOrderMessage.Complete();
}
```

Lastly, ensure that you close out the `MessagingFactory` object. Connections are a limited resource and we also want to ensure that we clean up after ourselves. Closing the factory object will also close out the Queue client (placing the following code in a `finally` block):

```
//Close the MessagingFactory as well as everything it created
factory.Close();
```

Receiving different message types from a Queue

If you have a single submitting application sending a single type of message to one Queue, then it is as easy as calling the `GetBody` method to retrieve the body of the message just as we did earlier with the following line of code:

```
CustomerOrder orderOut =
  receivedOrderMessage.GetBody<CustomerOrder>();
```

This assumes that we know exactly what object is in the body of the message. We can take this one step further and read the body of the message regardless of what content is in it and place the body into a stream object through the following code:

```
Stream stream = receivedOrderMessage.GetBody<Stream>();
StreamReader reader = new StreamReader(stream);
string s = reader.ReadToEnd();
```

While this will read the body of the message, it is now up to another process to determine what was just read and what to do with it. This can be rather dangerous and while it is possible, it isn't always a recommended practice.

So, what do we do if we have multiple message types that will be placed in a `BrokeredMessage` object that will be put on a single Queue?

The sender can set the `ContentType` property of `BrokeredMessage` to the object type before sending the message to the Queue shown in the following code (you can choose whether you want a strongly typed message or JSON/XML):

```
BrokeredMessage customerorderMsg = new BrokeredMessage (order);
customerorderMsg.ContentType = order.GetType().FullName;
queueClient.Send(customerorderMsg);
```

Then on the receiving side, when we get the message from the Queue, we can inspect that property and based on the type, we can act on that specific object accordingly. This code shows how we can retrieve the message and assign it correctly:

```
var messageBodyType =
  Type.GetType(receivedOrderMessage.ContentType.ToString());
if (messageBodyType == null)
{
    //This should always be set before submitting the message
    Debug.WriteLine("This message does not have the ContentType
      property set for Message Id: {0}",
      receivedOrderMessage.MessageId);
    //Move the message to the Dead Letter queue so that we can
    //process the next message
    receivedOrderMessage.DeadLetter();
    return();
}

//read the body of the message
```

```
var method = typeof(BrokeredMessage).GetMethod("GetBody",
  new Type[] { });
var genericMethod = method.MakeGenericMethod(messageBodyType);
try
{
    var messageBody = genericMethod.Invoke
      (receivedOrderMessage, null);
    //Do something here with the data now that you have the body

    receivedOrderMessage.Complete();
}
catch (Exception e)
{
    Debug.WriteLine("Processing the body failed.
      Abandoning Message.");
    receivedOrderMessage.Abandon();
}
}
```

There are a couple of things to note about the code. First, if we don't have a value in the `ContentType` property, then we will move to the dead letter Queue so that we don't spend time dealing with the message. There can either be another process that acts on messages submitted to the dead letter Queue, or it can be a manual process to review what is in the dead letter Queue and act on them appropriately. Then if we get an exception, we call the `Abandon` method, which abandons the lock on a peek-locked message.

At this point, we have looked at how to create a message, how to send it, and multiple ways to receive it from the Queue. This works great for messages that have a direct connection between the sender and the receiver. Now, let's look at Topics and see how we can create a solution where we can have many receivers that subscribe to different messages based on rules acting on properties in the `BrokeredMessage` object.

Creating a Service Bus Topic

Now that we have looked at how to create a Queue, lets shift our attention to Topics. There are far more patterns that we can implement with Topics and we will focus more of our efforts around this area. Just as with Queues, we need to create the Topic infrastructure. We will look at creating the Topic in the Azure Portal next, and later in the chapter, we will look at other ways to create Topics outside the portal.

1. Click on **New** on the bottom-left corner of the portal, then click on **App Services** and you will see **Service Bus** listed, as shown in the following screenshot:

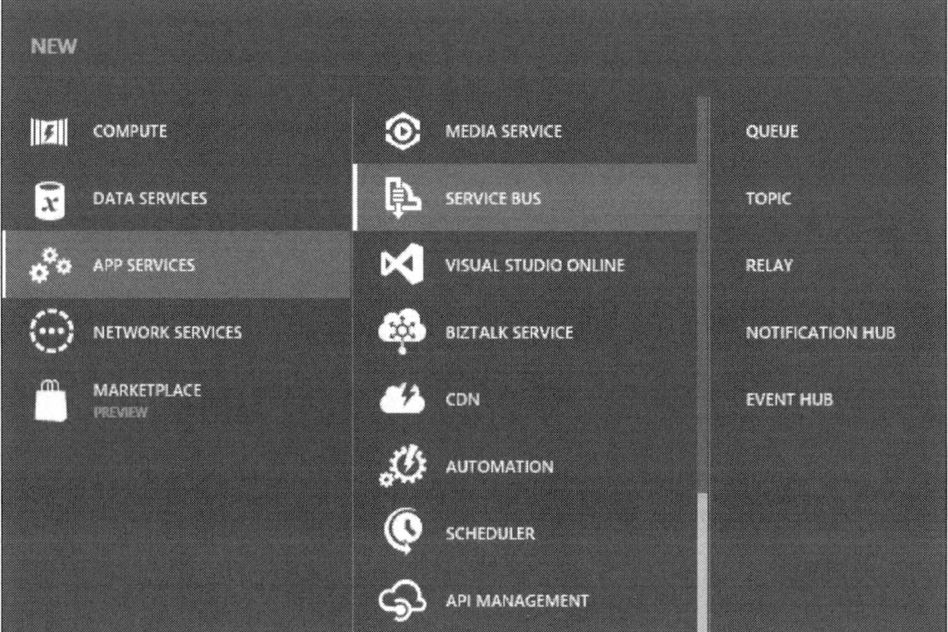

2. Select **Topic** and then select **Custom Create**:

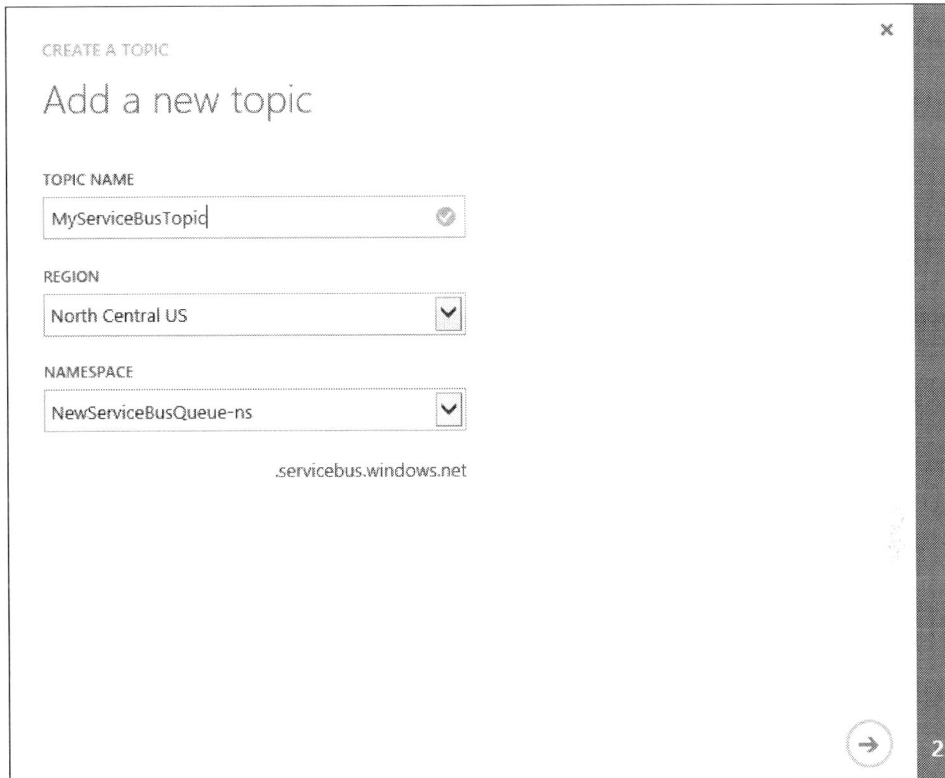

When the **Create a Topic** wizard appears, you will need to provide a Topic name as well as select the region in which you wish to create the Queue; select whether you want to create a new namespace or create the Queue in an existing namespace. If you select an existing namespace, then you can proceed to the next step.

3. Click the right arrow to navigate to the next page of the wizard:

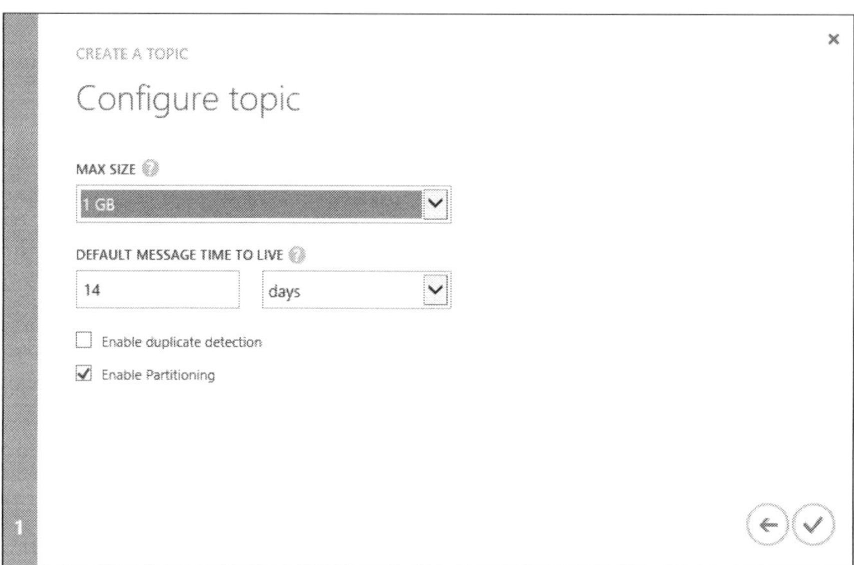

These are the options that we want to set and, just like when we created the Queue, they wouldn't be available if we had selected the **Quick Create** option.

When configuring the Topic, there are a number of options that we can set.

The first is the size of the Topic. This is not the size of the messages that can be submitted to the Queue. Instead, it is the size of the Topic and will determine how many messages the Topic can hold. The default is 1 GB and can be increased by 1 GB at a time up to a maximum of 5 GB.

Then, we can set the default time to live. This determines the amount of time the message remains in the Topic before it expires. The time starts from the time the message is sent. The default is 14 days. However, it can be any number of seconds, minutes, hours, or days. In addition, you also have an option to move the messages to a dead letter Queue for action on the message once it expires.

Lastly, we have two checkbox options. The first checkbox applies if we want to enable duplicate detection while the second allows us to enable partitioning. Both of these behave the same as the Queue, so I won't repeat the description here.

4. When you are finished, click on the check mark in the lower right-hand side corner of the wizard to create the new Queue.

We now have a Topic created. However, this is not the end. We need to do a few more things to get it configured and create subscriptions. In the portal, you will see the new Topic that we have created (if not, then navigate to **Service Bus Namespace** you created and click on **Topics** in the list of services along the top of the portal). You can double-click on the Topic option to provide additional information as well as options to modify the configuration.

The first thing that you will see is the **Dashboard** page. This provides a graph of statistics along the top of the page with usage and other statistics under it. You can also find the connection string, a sample solution to download, as well as the URL and settings. In addition to the **Dashboard** page, you will also have access to a **Monitor** page, a **Configure** page and a **Subscriptions** page.

The **Monitor** page provides additional statistics for the minimum, maximum, average, and total counts for items such as the number of incoming messages, failed requests, message sizes, successful requests, and internal server errors. You can also add additional metrics by clicking on **Add Metrics** at the bottom of the page.

The **Configure** page allows you to change the configuration options that you set when you created the Topic. It also lets you set the Topic state between **Enabled**, **Disabled**, or **Send Disabled (Receive Only)**. This will allow you to continue to receive messages into the Topic so that applications can continue to run even if the backend services aren't available. You can also set **Shared Access Policies** (refer to the section at the end of this chapter for more information) for the Topic and select the permissions between **Manage**, **Send**, or **Listen**.

Don't forget to hit **Save** at the bottom of the screen whenever you change something. This is the most forgotten activity when in the **Configure** page.

Lastly, the **Subscriptions** page is where we create and configure the subscribers that will receive messages from the Topic. This is one of the most important parts of configuring the Topic. You will create a subscription for each routing that you will need as part of the Topic. This is one of the main features that separate the Topic from the Queue. To create the subscription, you can either click on the Create icon at the bottom of the **Subscriptions** page or you can also create one on the **Dashboard** page. You can also create a subscription when you are in the list of all the Topics that are part of your namespace. Highlight the Topic that you want to create a subscription for and then hit the **Create Subscription** icon at the bottom of the screen. No matter which way you create the subscription, you will be presented with a wizard where you will be asked for a unique name on the first page.

Then, click the right arrow at the bottom to move to the second page:

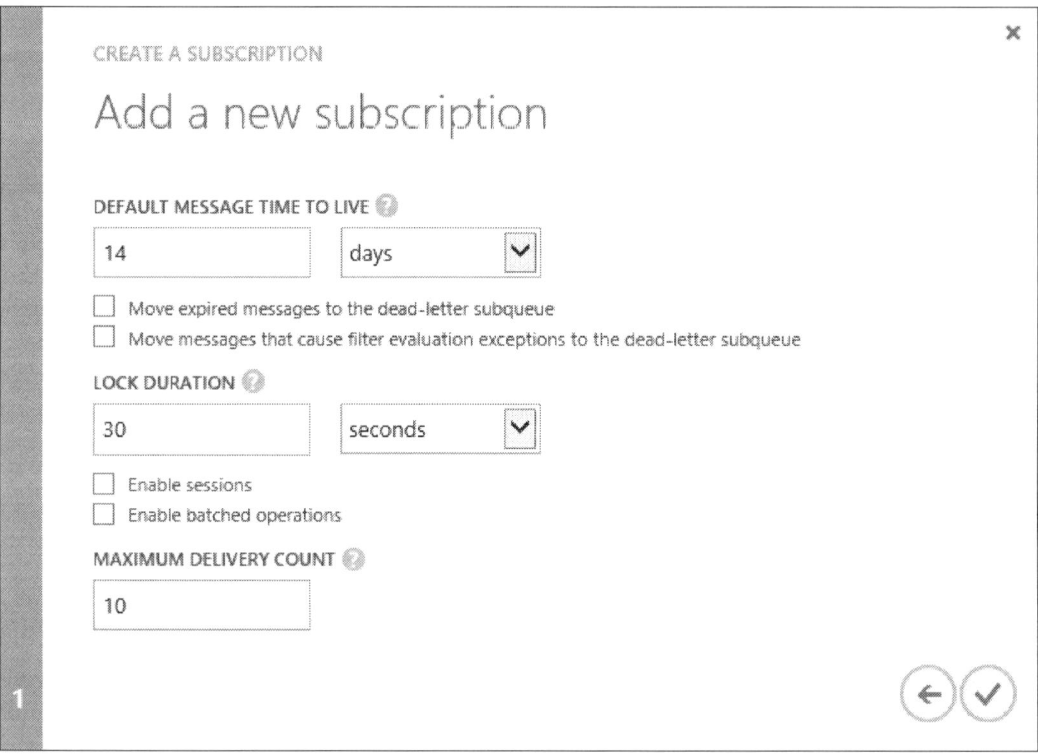

The settings on this page refer to the subscriber and we can set these to pertain specifically to each individual subscription. We can set **Default Message Time to Live**. The default is 14 days, but we can set it to any number of seconds, minutes, hours, or days. Next, we can decide what to do if the message times out. We can send the message to a dead-letter subqueue or move messages that cause filter evaluation exceptions to the dead-letter subqueue. Next, we can set the lock duration. The lock duration, just as with the Queue, is the duration of a peek lock in which the message is locked for other receivers. One thing to keep in mind though is that if you create multiple subscriptions that will be configured to receive the message, the message will be available to each subscriber and will be tracked so that every receiver receives it. The message is not duplicated for each receiver. Also, just as with the Queue, we can set attributes to **Enable Sessions** or batched operations. Lastly, we can set the delivery count. This is the number of times that the Service Bus will try to deliver the message before it places is in the dead-letter Queue. The default is 10 but you can set it all the way to 2000.

> Note that all of the settings that you select can be modified after you create the subscription.

Click on the check mark in the bottom-right corner of the wizard screen and the subscription will be created.

If you have been following along and walking through the process, you may have noticed something. Something is missing, something that we haven't done yet. How do we specify what the subscription will be listening to or what rules the subscription will execute to determine which messages are routed to it?

By default, every subscription created through the portal has the **Filter** property set to `1=1`, which means that every subscription created through the portal will receive every message sent to that Topic. Presumably, that isn't quite what you wanted.

The following screenshot from Visual Studio shows the default configuration of the subscription:

Action	
ActionType	Microsoft.ServiceBus.Messaging.EmptyRuleAction
CreatedAt	12/11/2014 4:42 AM
Filter	1=1
FilterRequirePreprocessing	False
FilterType	Microsoft.ServiceBus.Messaging.TrueFilter
Name	$Default

Creating a rule with Visual Studio's Server Explorer

One of the best things with Azure is that you always have options. You can create the subscription in the Azure portal and then configure the rules in Visual Studio. You can create the subscription or configure it through PowerShell scripts or code, or you can use a tool called the Service Bus Explorer (which you can download at `https://code.msdn.microsoft.com/windowsazure/Service-Bus-Explorer-f2abca5a`). The Service Bus Explorer is a very useful tool and there is a great tutorial on the site so we won't repeat the content here.

However, we will look at how we can implement this functionality using the tools built into Visual Studio as well as through code. First, we can interact with the Service Bus (as well as many more Azure services) directly from the Server Explorer in Visual Studio as shown here:

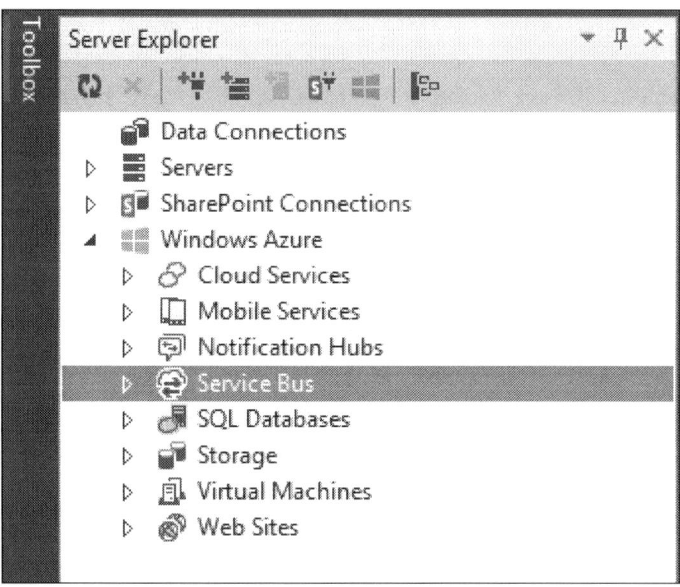

You can connect to Azure by right-clicking on the Windows Azure item in the tree and a pop-up menu will appear. Select **Connect to Windows Azure** and enter your credentials. Once you have successfully connected to Azure, you will be able to expand the tree view and see all of your Azure artefacts. You can use a subscription that you may have created using the portal or you can create a subscription by expanding the Service Bus node and continuing to expand the nodes until you get to your Topic. We will walk through creating a subscription in Visual Studio so that you can see the process and what options are available. Right-click and select **New Subscription**. The following dialog box appears:

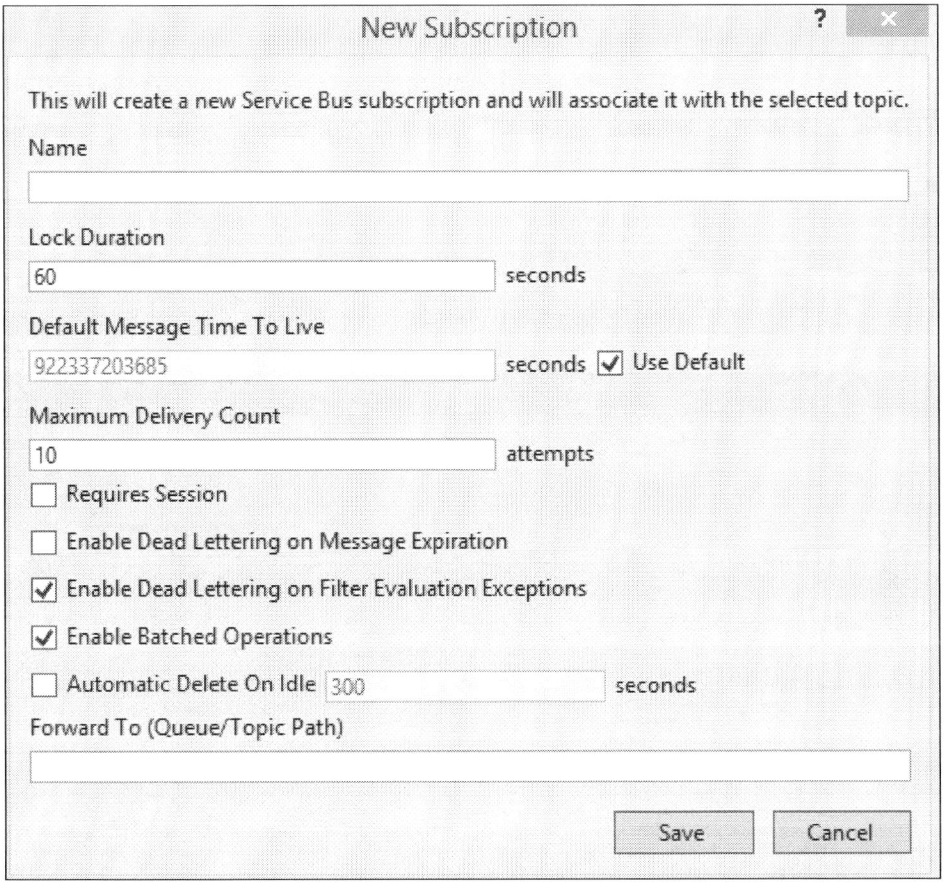

New Subscription

This will create a new Service Bus subscription and will associate it with the selected topic.

Name

Lock Duration

60 seconds

Default Message Time To Live

922337203685 seconds Use Default

Maximum Delivery Count

10 attempts

Requires Session

Enable Dead Lettering on Message Expiration

Enable Dead Lettering on Filter Evaluation Exceptions

Enable Batched Operations

Automatic Delete On Idle 300 seconds

Forward To (Queue/Topic Path)

Save Cancel

Enter all of the information as you would if you were going through the wizard in the portal. However, there is one thing that is included for configuration here that wasn't presented in the portal. We can set up chaining of Topics with auto-forwarding. Auto-forwarding allows you to chain a subscription or a Queue to another Queue or Topic within the same namespace, which allows you to scale out and overcome subscribing to one Topic limitation. The Service Bus will take out the message that is in the first Queue or subscription and put them in the destination Queue or subscription (the second Queue or subscription). Keep in mind that you can still send a message to the second Queue or subscription directly and you can't chain the dead-letter Queue. The full functionality of Chaining is outside the scope of this chapter, but it is well documented on MSDN at `http://msdn.microsoft.com/en-us/library/azure/jj687471.aspx`.

Now that we have created a subscription either through the portal or through the Server Explorer in Visual Studio, we can take the next step. In the Server Explorer in Visual Studio, expand the **Subscription** node and you will see a **Rules** node and a **$Default** node. We can't edit the default node so we will create new rules and will delete the **$Default** node. Start by right-clicking on the **Rules** node and selecting **Create New Rule** on the pop up menu. The following dialog box will appear:

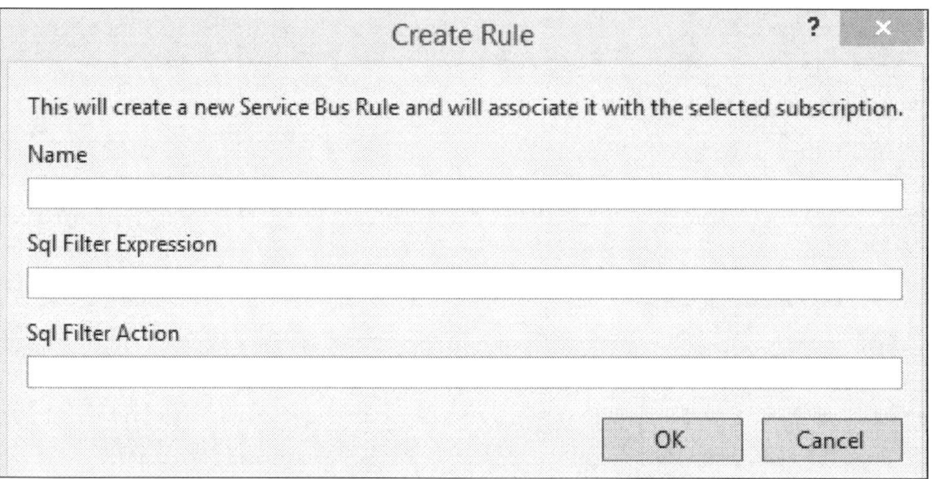

This is the first time that we will be able to create routing rules. In the preceding dialog box, create a name for the rule and then we can create the filter. For example, we may create three rules based on membership; one, for example, could be a regular member; the next could be a lifetime member and the third may be a yearly subscriber. We would create three separate rules and would name the first one `Lifetime`, and then we can set the SQL Filter Express and, if desired, the SQL Filter Action.

The Sql Filter Express is expressed as a subset of the SQL-92 syntax (you can find more about the syntax at `http://en.wikipedia.org/wiki/SQL-92`) and operates on the properties of the `BrokeredMessage` object. There are a number of properties already part of the object or you can add custom ones to the `Properties` property. When setting the Sql Filter Expression, we need to include the property so we will enter `Membership = 'Lifetime'`. Once a rule is matched through the Sql Filter Expression, you can also perform an action on the message. This also follows the SQL-92 syntax and allows you to modify an existing property in the submitted `BrokeredMessage` object such as setting a priority property. You will enter `SET priority = 1` in the Sql Filter Action expression.

[Note that you can also add a new property to a `BrokeredMessage` object by using the `SET` command.]

Creating a rule with code

We can create the rule through code and set the properties as shown here:

```
MessagingFactory factory = MessagingFactory.Create(
  ServiceBusEnvironment.CreateServiceUri("sb",
  <Service Bus Namespace>, String.Empty),
  TokenProvider.CreateSharedSecretTokenProvider("<Issuer Name>",
    "<Issuer Secret>"));

SubscriptionClient lifetimeClient =
  factory.CreateSubscriptionClient("MemberTopic",
  "LifetimeMemberMessages");

lifetimeClient.RemoveRule(RuleDescription.DefaultRuleName);

var lmPriority = new RuleDescription("LifetimeMember");
lmPriority.Filter = new SqlFilter("Priority = 1");
lmPriority.Action = new SqlRuleAction("SET <property>='<value>'");
lifetimeClient.AddRule(lmPriority);
```

Let's look at the code and get a better understanding. First, we need to create the `MessageFactory` object. The method parameters that we are utilizing require an address and a token provider. We will utilize the create method with the following signature:

```
public static MessagingFactory Create(
  IEnumerable<Uri> addresses,TokenProvider tokenProvider
)
```

Or

```
MessagingFactory.CreateFromConnectionString()
```

For the first method parameter, we will utilize the `CreateServiceUri` method on the `ServiceBusEvironment` class to create the address scheme. The method has the following signature:

```
public static Uri CreateServiceUri(
  string scheme, string serviceNamespace, string servicePath
)
```

The scheme parameter will be set to `sb`, `serviceNamespace` will be set to our namespace that we can retrieve from the portal and the `servicePath` (which follows the host name section of the URI) will be passed in as an empty string.

For the second parameter of the `Create` method, we will utilize the `CreateSharedSecretTokenProvider` method of the `TokenProvider` object. The method has the following signature:

```
public static TokenProvider CreateSharedSecretTokenProvider(
  string issuerName, string issuerSecret
)
```

Both of these parameters can be found in the portal and will be entered here. If this code were going to be placed into production, we wouldn't hardcode this here, instead, we would put it into the `config` file and access it from there.

We are now ready to create our subscription client. To do this, we will utilize the `CreateSubscriptionClient` method on our `MessagingFactory` object. The `CreateSubscriptionClient` method has the following signature:

```
public SubscriptionClient CreateSubscriptionClient(
  string topicPath, string name
)
```

The `topicPath` is the Topic path relative to the service namespace and the name parameter is the name of the subscription.

One thing to note is that using this signature will create a new object that points to an existing subscription. If you want to create a brand new subscription through code, then you need to use the following signature override:

```
public SubscriptionClient CreateSubscriptionClient(
  string topicPath,
  string name,
  ReceiveMode receiveMode
)
```

This signature will create a new subscription and will return the pointer to the subscription. The `ReceiveMode` parameter allows you to specify either `PeekLock` (the default value, which receives the message and keeps it locked until the receiver is finished with the message) or `ReceiveAndDelete` (which deletes the message after it is received).

In the next line of code you can see that we are removing the default rule. This is the rule that has the `filter` property set to `1=1`.

The last section of code is creating the new rule and setting properties. We will create a new `RuleDescription` object. We are using the following signature:

```
public RuleDescription(
  string name
)
```

This allows us to create the rule and specify the rule name. We will then set properties on this new object. The properties that we need to set are `filter` and we can decide whether we want to set the `action` property. After we set the properties, we will pass the new `RuleDescription` object to the `AddRule` method on our `SubscriptionClient` object.

We will repeat the creation of a new `RuleDescription` object for each filter we want to create for this subscription. We will create a new subscription and associate rules for each receiver that we want (that is, `Lifetime Member`, `Yearly Member`, and so on).

Interacting with the Topic

Now that we have created the Topic, subscribers, and rules for the subscribers, let's look at how to send messages and then how to receive them.

Sending a message to a Topic

One of the things that you may have noticed as you have been reading through this chapter is that we are doing similar things multiple ways. I want to show how these things can be done and provide different examples that you can take and use in your own code.

In the code examples in this section, we will look at how we can utilize the connection string that is stored in a config file either in a web config file for an Azure Website, or in the `*.csdef` and `*.cscfg` configuration file.

When sending a message to a Topic, we will use a `BrokeredMessage` object just as we did when sending a message to a Service Bus Queue. We will connect to the Topic and send the message through the `TopicClient` object instead of the `QueueClient` object. The rest of the code may look very similar.

However, we will do some defensive coding before we send a message to the Topic. Let's ensure that the Topic exists first:

```
var namespaceManager =
  NamespaceManager.CreateFromConnectionString
    (CloudConfigurationManager
    .GetSetting("ServiceBusConnectionString"));

if (namespaceManager.TopicExists("<Topic Name>"))
{
  //Now that we know the topic exists, let's get a connection
  //to the topic so that we can send a message
  TopicClient mytopicClient =
    TopicClient.CreateFromConnectionString(
  CloudConfigurationManager.GetSetting
    ("ServiceBusConnectionString"),
    "<Topic Name>" );

  //Alternatively you can use the TopicClient.Create if the
  //connection string is stored under the
  //default key name "Microsoft.ServiceBus.ConnectionString
  TopicClient mytopicClient = TopicClient.Create(<Topic Name>);

  mytopicClient.Send(customerorderMsg);

  mytopicClient.Close();
}
```

Now that we have seen the code that sends our message, let's focus on how to receive it.

Receiving a message from a Topic

When we receive a message from a Topic, we are actually receiving the message directly from a subscription. Remember from the earlier discussion, we created a subscription for each location that we wanted our messages routed, and then created the rule(s) for that subscription so that the Topic infrastructure could route the message to the correct location based on the SqlFilter that was used. So, when we want to retrieve a message we will create a receiver for each of the subscriptions that we have created and configured. The following code creates a receiver for the `LifetimeMemberMessages` subscriber that we created earlier when setting up our rules:

```
SubscriptionClient subscriptionClient =
SubscriptionClient.CreateFromConnectionString (
```

```
CloudConfigurationManager.GetSetting
  ("ServiceBusConnectionString"),
"MemberTopic","LifetimeMemberMessages");

subscriptionClient.Receive();
BrokeredMessage brokeredMessage = subscriptionClient.Receive();

if (brokeredMessage != null)
{
  try
  {
    //Do something with the message (i.e., get the message body)
    brokeredMessage.Complete();
  }
  catch (Exception)
  {
    brokeredMessage.Abandon();
  }
}
```

By default, this code will consume the message from the subscriber in the `PeekLock` mode. There is an override on `SubscriptionClient.CreateFromConnectionString` where we can add the `ReceiveMode` parameter and specify either `PeekLock` or `ReceiveAndDelete`. When using the `PeekLock` option, which represents a two-phase process, the message isn't removed from the subscription until the `Complete()` method is called. Therefore, if there is any problem or exception with the receiving code, the message will still be in the subscription in order to be processed after the error. If the `ReceiveAndDelete` option, which represents a single-phase process, is used, the message is automatically deleted as soon as the message is received by the receiving code. This can result in lost messages when there is an error.

While using the `PeekLock` option, during the lock time, the receiving application can set the message state to four different states.

- `Abandon`: This unlocks the message and it is available for the next read operation.
- `Complete`: This completes the process and the message is deleted from the subscription.

- `DeadLetter`: The message is moved to the dead-letter subqueue. The receiving application would set this if the processing failed because of bad content, missing message body, or other reasons that prevented the message from being successfully processed.
- `Defer`: The message stays in the subscription but it is put back for later processing. The message, however, is hidden from normal processing. When you defer a message, you are provided a unique message sequence ID. If you want to retrieve the message, you will need to do so using that supplied sequence ID. If you lose that sequence ID, the message is lost and there is no way to retrieve it again. Deferring can be utilized when you need to process out of order messages in a specific order as specified by a property in the `BrokeredMessage` object.

Creating an event hub

The event hub is different from the Topics and Queues in many ways. However, one of the biggest differences is that it doesn't utilize the `BrokeredMessage` object. It utilizes the `EventData` class instead. The `EventData` class represents the event data that is sent and received from an event hub stream. Like the `BrokeredMessage` object, it contains a body, some user-defined properties, and metadata describing the event. However, it is lightweight and doesn't have many of the properties that are contained in the `BrokeredMessage` object.

When sending events to the event hub, they are sent using either an HTTP post or via an AMQP connection. AMQP is useful when you have higher message volumes and require lower latency. AMQP provides a persistent messaging channel.

> Note that AMQP is an open standard application layer protocol for message-oriented middleware with implementations from different vendors that are interoperable. AMQP defines features including message orientation, queuing, routing (including point-to-point and publish-and-subscribe), reliability, and security. It was designed to balance efficiency, flexibility, and interoperability.

Sending data to an event hub

In order to create an event hub, we can use the `NamespaceManager` class and then call the `CreateEventHub()` method as shown:

```
var manager = new Microsoft.ServiceBus.NamespaceManager
  ("mynamespace.servicebus.windows.net");
var description = manager.CreateEventHub("MyEventHub");
```

The `EventHubDescription` class contains the details about the event hub including the authorization rules, message retention, partition IDs, status, and path. You can update the values in the class as needed for your solution.

Next, we need to create `EventHubClient`, which will utilize a connection string to connect to the event hub and allow us to send and receive messages:

```
var client = EventHubClient.Create(description.Path);
```

We can also create the client from a connection string so that we can use worker roles and store the connection string in the configuration file:

```
var client = EventHubClient.CreateFromConnectionString
  ("<your connection string>", "<path>");
```

You can also create the client from the `MessagingFactory` object. However, there are aspects that affect the throughput. When you create additional `EventHubClient` objects from the `MessagingFactory` instance, it will reuse the same TCP connection and the `Create` method uses a single messaging factory. If you need very high throughput from a single sender, then ensure that you create multiple message factories and have one `EventHubClient` per messaging factory.

Now we are almost ready to send a message to the event hub. However, we first need to create an `EventData` object. When we create this object, we can create it with a byte array, a stream, or an object with a supplied serializer for the message body. If you are using JSON, you can use `Encoding.UTF8.GetBytes()` to retrieve the byte array.

When we have the `EventData` object created, all we need to do is call the `Send()` method on the client object:

```
EventData ed = new EventData();
client.Send(ed);
```

Reading data from an event hub

The basic way to read from the event hub is to use the `EventHubReceiver` class. To create an instance of this class, you must use the `EventHubSconsumerGroup` class, as shown here:

```
EventHubConsumerGroup group = client.GetDefaultConsumerGroup();
var receiver = group.CreateReceiver(client.GetRuntimeInformation().
  PartitionIds[0]);
```

`CreateReceiver` has a number of overloads so that you can specify an offset as either a string or a timestamp as well as the ability to set whether you want the specific offset in the returned stream or to start after that. Once you create the receiver, you can start receiving events on the returned stream or start afterwards. The `Receive` method itself has four overloads that allow you to control the receive operation and include things such as batch size or wait time. Also, remember that there are asynchronous versions for increased throughput of a consumer. Let's look at the `Receive` code:

```
bool receive = true;
string theOffset;
while(receive)
{
  var message = receiver.Receive();
  theOffset = message.Offset;
  string msgBody = Encoding.UTF8.GetString(message.GetBytes());
  Console.WriteLine(String.Format("Received message at offset: {0} \
nbody: {1}", theOffset, msgBody));
}
```

Based on a specific partition, the messages are received in the order they arrive at the event hub. The offset is a string token that is used to specify a message in a partition.

Note that, at this time, a single partition within a consumer group cannot have more than five concurrent connected readers. As these readers connect and disconnect, it is possible that their sessions may stay active for a short time period before the service realizes that there has been a disconnect. Therefore, it is possible that during this time, trying to reconnect to a partition may result in a failure.

Also, when talking about receiving events from an event hub, any entity that reads event data from an event hub is an event consumer. Every event consumer reads the event stream through partitions in a consumer group and when writing your code, each partition should only have one reader at a time. Every event hub consumer connects through an AMQP session where the events are delivered as they arrive. The event consumer does not need to poll for data availability.

Now that we have gone through the process to understand how to read data from the event hub, let's look at a helper library that was created to more efficiently read from the stream. The Microsoft team created `EventProcessorHost`.

> Note that `EventProcessorHost` can be downloaded from NuGet at `https://www.nuget.org/packages/Microsoft.Azure.ServiceBus.EventProcessorHost/0.3.1`. `EventProcessorHost` is not part of the ServiceBus NuGet package so you will need to add it separately.

As you read this section, it is apparent that building distributed, load balanced, fault-handling consumers can be a difficult task. `EventProcessorHost` was created to help with this task and provides the ability to distribute the partitions across workers equally. In addition, it will load balance the partitions and detect if errors occur in the workers or if the worker terminates for any reason.

`EventProcessorHost` implements an `IEventProcessor` interface that contains three methods: `OpenAsync`, `CloseAsync`, and `ProcessEventsAsync`.

Once you create your derived class implementation, you will need to register and unregister it using the `RegisterEventProcessorAsync` and `UnregisterEventProcessorAsync` methods.

As your code starts to process messages, they will acquire a lease for each partition in the event hub. These leases last for a specific amount of time and then need to be renewed. As each processor acquires a new lease, the load will shift and there will be a balance. The event hub provides a massive scale. Part of that scale is through partitions but the other part is out of the message processors.

While event hubs may not be utilized in every one of your enterprise applications, event hubs enable you to build distributed applications that require durable collections of event streams at a very high throughput with low latency and originating from a variety of sources, services, and devices. One of the most important scenarios that event hubs provide services for is that of the Internet of Things. This scenario is fast becoming one of the hottest trends in the industry and you may find yourself in need of services to build an IoT application yourself.

Service Bus Security

The last topic of this chapter will focus on securing the Azure Service Bus. Now that we have an understanding of the different parts of the Service Bus and have looked at creating and accessing the different components, we need to ensure that we can secure the different aspects. This section will be an overview to provide a base foundation but it isn't a complete in-depth look at security. It will specifically focus on the Service Bus. There are entire books related to security in Azure.

The Service Bus utilizes Shared Access Signatures in order to secure the components. Shared Access Signatures provide the ability to fine tune access to the different resources. SAS authentication works through the use of a cryptographic key along with associated rights for the specific resource. When a client tries to access the Service Bus component, they need to present a SAS token. You can create different tokens for different levels of access including `Manage`, `Send`, and `Listen`. This token contains the resource URI to be accessed as well as an expiration entry signed with the configured key. You can apply a SAS rule on the Service Bus namespace, a Queue, or a Topic. However, as of writing this, you cannot configure the SAS rule on the subscription level. When assigning the SAS rule to a namespace, all entities in the namespace inherit the SAS rule.

Now with that said, by default, when you create a Topic, Queue, or event hub, an authorization token is configured with all rights and is assigned to that namespace. This way you will be able to perform all actions on the Service Bus directly after creation. While this works nicely for testing, it is not the way we want security configured in a production environment. I will also note that you can include the Shared Access in the connection string. In fact, the default connection string the Service Bus NuGet package uses looks like this:

```
<add key="Microsoft.ServiceBus.ConnectionString"value="Endpoint=sb://
[your namespace].servicebus.windows.net;SharedAccessKeyName=RootManage
SharedAccessKey;SharedAccessKey=[your secret]" />
```

What happened here is that this connection string contains permissions to listen, send, and manage for the entire namespace. Never use this for anything more than development. If you put this policy into your applications, then you are acting almost as though there were no security. Instead, use the `SharedAccessAuthorizationRule` object. The Shared Access Security's `SharedAccessAuthorizationRule` object provides the ability to set three different claims: `Manage`, `Send`, and `Listen`. Since you can apply multiple authorization rules to an artefact, you can manage the end user rights individually even if they have rights to the same Queue or Topic. This allows you to have quite a bit of flexibility in managing user access.

Let's take a look at some code and see how we can implement different rights for a Queue or Topic:

```
// Create a QueueDescription object so that we can add our security
rules
QueueDescription targetQueueDescription = new QueueDescription("Targe
tQueue");

// Create the authorization rule key name
```

```
string targetQueueSendKeyName = "TargetQueueSendKey";

string targetQueueSendKey = SharedAccessAuthorizationRule.
GenerateRandomKey();

// Create a rule for send rights and add it to the queue descriptions
SharedAccessAuthorizationRule targetQueueSendRule = new SharedAccessA
uthorizationRule(targetQueueSendKeyName, targetQueueSendKey, new[] {
AccessRights.Send });
targetQueueDescription.Authorization.Add(targetQueueSendRule);

// Create the queue with the security permissions that we added
QueueDescription targetQueue = namespaceManager.CreateQueue(targetQueu
eDescription);
```

While I have demonstrated the way to secure a Queue, the security for a Topic follows the same pattern but utilizes a `TopicDescription` object that also has an `Authorization.Add` method that accepts `SharedAccessAuthorizationRule`.

Before we end this section, there is one more aspect to cover; that of managing the namespace access key. Think about how, and the frequency that, you may regenerate or revoke the keys used for SAS rules. Microsoft recommends that you periodically regenerate the keys that were used in the SAS Rule.

Applications should use the primary key to generate the SAS token. Then, when you go to regenerate, replace the secondary key with the old primary key and generate a new key as the primary key. This will allow you to continue using tokens for authorization that were issued with the old primary key that haven't expired.

> Note that you can configure SAS rules on Service Bus Queues, Topics, and the event hub. Service Bus Relay support will be added in the future.

Summary

In this chapter, we discussed how we can utilize the Service Bus to disconnect our application components and communicate between the different tiers of our application. We discussed how we can create and send messages through Service Bus Queues and Topics and when we would use each. Lastly, we discussed patterns for the use of these Azure components.

In the next chapter we will discuss how to create hybrid applications where the frontend of the application runs in the Azure cloud while line-of-business or database systems remain and run on-premises.

6
Creating Hybrid Services

In this chapter we will cover services that provide the ability for us to create a hybrid solution. A hybrid solution is based on applications that connect to data and services across a mix of data centers that can either be in the cloud or on-premises. This provides you with the ability to move your applications to the cloud in your own timeframe and in a manner that best fits the business situation. It also allows systems that are subject to regulations to keep part of the application (that is, the data tier) on-premises while still taking advantage of what the cloud provides for other tiers of the application. To do this, you need a solution that can adapt to how you design and develop your application.

While designing an application that will utilize both the corporate network and the cloud, you can create your hybrid connected configuration at either the network layer or the application layer. While connecting the data centers at the network layer, you can utilize Azure's virtual network to create logically isolated networks in Azure and connect them securely to your on-premises data center; you can do this either over the Internet or through the **ExpressRoute** private network connection. This lets your Azure subscription be connected to your corporate network. This in turn allows your application components to connect to the components on the corporate network as though they are in the same physical location. While this may sound like the perfect solution, there are many reasons why you may not want, or need, to connect the two networks (such as separation of concerns, security barriers, or a physical separation between modern applications and legacy on-premises systems).

That leaves us with connecting the data centers at the application layer, which will be the focus of this chapter. The good news is that we have a number of options available to us that provide flexibility and different features.

Now, you must be wondering why you can't just open the firewall on your data center and provide access to the on-premises systems from your application in Azure. Alternatively, you may consider creating a set of data services that sit on top of the data source and opening access to these services from the internet. Both these options might not make it past your security reviews. Plus, the security team may demand that you put in place a reverse proxy, which would mean extra expenses, time, and management efforts. What if there were an easier way?

In the previous chapter we started with an overview of everything in Service Bus and then delved deeper into a number of areas. What wasn't covered was Relay Service. Relay Service is one service that can be used to create a hybrid solution. The other service is BizTalk Hybrid Connect Service. Let's look at Relay Service of Service Bus first.

Service Bus Relay Service

Does your on-premises system already include **Windows Communication Foundation** (**WCF**) services, SOAP services, or REST services that utilize HTTP(s) or TCP? If so, you can utilize Service Bus Relay Service to create externally accessible endpoints in the cloud that will serve as a proxy for your on-premises services.

Service Bus Relay allows you to host WCF services within your corporate network. Relay Service provides a function by which it becomes a communication agent listening for incoming sessions and service requests for these WCF services. This allows you to securely expose the end points to the cloud without needing to open up a firewall connection, placing the services in a DMZ, or creating a reverse proxy setup.

Relay Service has one of the harder jobs among all the Service Bus components. It has to deal with making very advanced communication scenarios easy. Internet connectivity is difficult. We throw all sorts of barriers into the mix. We have load balancers, dynamic addressing, non-routing addresses, firewalls, and other security mechanisms. So, how does Relay Service deal with all of this and still provide the communication that is needed across these different protected networks?

Relay Service works as a perimeter network hosted in Azure that provides a single place to manage the client and service credentials and provides the security to encapsulate and segregate the service by obscuring its identity and location. The location (the actual endpoint of your service) is never made available to clients. The client is bound to the Service Bus endpoint, which is a virtual address, thus allowing you to move your service or service address (of course, you have to make sure that it is registered with Service Bus). Service Bus and the use of the virtual address provide an extra layer to help keep away malicious activities and things such as DDOS attacks.

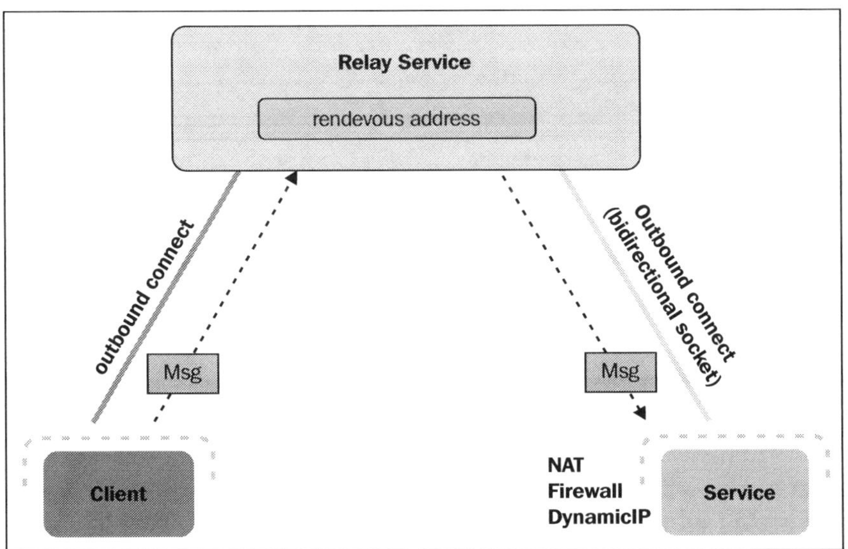

In the preceding figure, we can see that both the client and the service initiate an outbound connection. The client must perform an additional step of authenticating against Relay Service. Relay Service is able to broker the two-way communication by having the application code establish the outbound connection, which remains open. By having the communication occur outbound to Relay Service, the firewall allows the applications to communicate through the firewall without having to open any new ports. And because the communication end points are consistent, there are no NAT issues to deal with.

Relay Service connects to WCF services and therefore will be utilizing WCF bindings. As such, there are WCF bindings that are specifically utilized for Relay Service (outlined in the following *Bindings* section). For example, if you are using the `netTcpRelayBinding` class with the direct mode, Relay Service will communicate as shown in the preceding figure. However, once the client connects and authenticates itself to Relay Service, Relay Service will "promote" the connection to a direct connection between the client and the service. Once this occurs, the client will interact with the service directly. If a direct connection between the client and the service is possible, Relay Service will promote the connection to direct. If not, it will stay as a relayed connection. This promotion can be accomplished without any loss of data. One thing to keep in mind though is that for this to work, the service needs to open port `819` on its server.

Note: Your service must be up and running to communicate with Relay Service. This means that you must start your WCF host before it receives a request. However, **Windows Activation Services** (**WAS**) isn't enough since it launches your host after the first request is received (which won't occur since the host wouldn't have connected to the Service Bus to register itself). However, if you are still utilizing `AppFabric` on top of IIS, you can take advantage of the feature to auto start your service (but be aware that `AppFabric` is almost at the end of support). Another option is to have an out-of-band mechanism to call the service after a restart in order to provide the first request.

While looking at the functionality with a WCF service versus a Relay Service-enabled WCF service, the only difference is in the bindings. You can still retain any existing bindings that may have been used by on-premises applications to communicate with these services, but you will need to add a new binding for the Service Bus Relay Service to communicate through. One of the things that Microsoft provided was **binding** that match the existing binding offerings so that you would still be able to retain features such as sync/async, callbacks, and transactions, while implementing the specific Relay bindings.

One thing to note is that your WCF service doesn't have to be in Azure. It can be in any environment that has a connection to the Internet. This is one of the benefits of Relay Service, that it allows you to overcome many network issues and makes it so you don't have to deal with setting IP address, changing or opening ports, and many of the other tedious error-prone tasks that come up.

Bindings

Those who have been working with WCF for a while will be familiar with bindings. They separate the implementation of the service from the manner in which a service communicates. If you have existing WCF services, all that is needed is to add a Service Bus Relay endpoint in addition to any other existing endpoint, and our service will be exposed to the cloud. The Service Bus supports both HTTP and TCP and provides the following bindings:

- HTTP:
  - `BasicHttpRelayBinding` for SOAP
  - `WebHttpRelayBinding` for REST
  - `WS2007HttpRelayBinding` for SOAP utilizing `WS-*` functionality

- TCP:
    - `NetOnewayRelayBinding` for one-way messaging using SOAP over TCP
    - `NetEventRelayBinding` for forwarding messages to subscribed addresses
    - `NetTcpRelayBinding` for two-way messaging using binary encoded SOAP over TCP

There will be different uses for the different bindings; however, the TCP relay binding provides the best performance and minimizes overhead. It supports request replay, one way operation, and duplex callbacks. There are more ports that need to be opened where the TCP relay binding uses `808` or `828` when using transport security (most of them are usually open, but you need to ensure that they haven't been closed). While this binding is fast and provides low overhead, it does use binary encoding and therefore is not interoperable. The calling application therefore also needs to utilize the TCP relay binding in order to communicate.

Let's look at how we can configure the Service Bus Relay functionality.

Creating Relay Service in Azure

1. Click on **New** in the bottom-left corner of the portal, and click on **App Services**. You should see Service Bus listed as shown in the following screenshot:

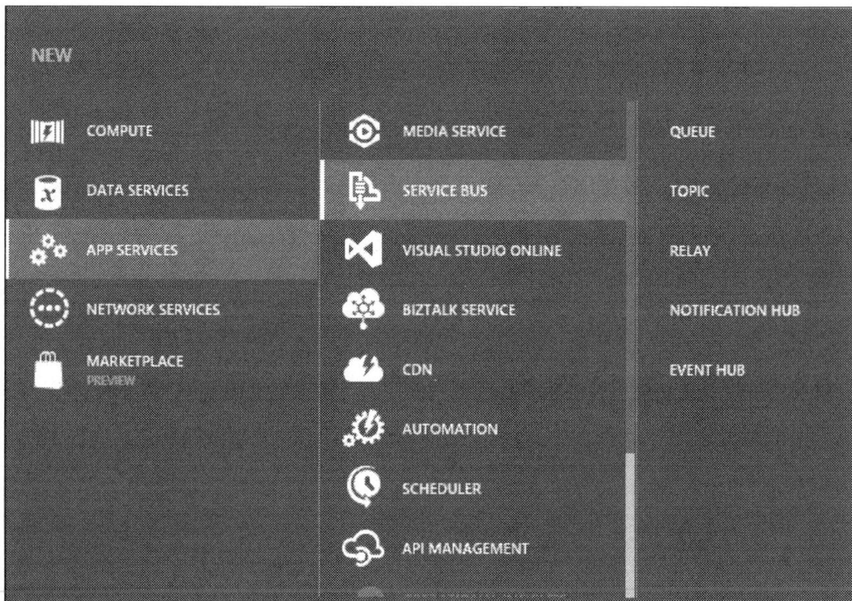

2. Select **Relay** and then select **Quick Create**.

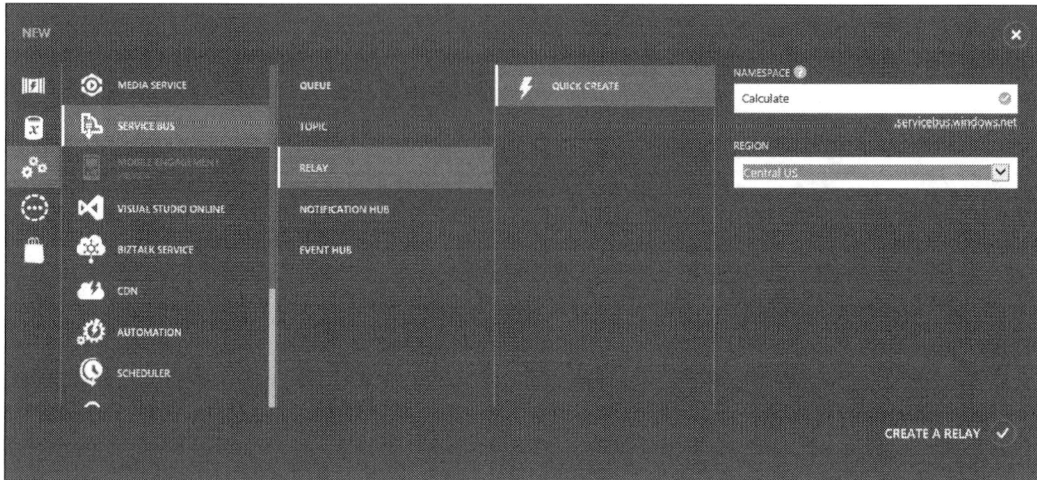

When you select the region make sure that it matches the location that you will use to deploy your application. It doesn't make sense to introduce the additional latency that will occur if the relay is in a different region from your application or further away from your data center.

3. Click on the **Create a Relay** arrow to create the relay.

That is all that there is to do in the portal. You need to create the WCF service and client and have them register before you can see anything else in the portal. Once they have been registered and you open the **Relay** page in the portal, you will see the service names, the listener type (binding), and the number of listeners registered for each service.

Creating the WCF service

There are many books on writing WCF services so we aren't going to focus on how to write the service. Instead, we are going to look at a simple example and highlight what is needed to get the WCF service to interact with Azure Relay Service. We will use the classic calculator example, but we will only implement one operation.

The first thing that we will need to create is the service contract. You can create a WCF service application in Visual Studio or you can self-host in a console application as shown:

```
[ServiceContract(Namespace="http://servicebus/relay/")]
public interface ICalculateService
{
    [OperationContract]
    int Multiply(int number1, int number2);
}
```

Then we can implement the service based on the contract:

```
[ServiceBehavior]
public class CalculateService : ICalculateService
{
    public int Multiply(int number1, int number2)
      { return (number1 * number2);}
}
```

So far, this is all standard WCF. Now let's host our service, and we can see through code what the bindings would look like and how we can use `NetTcpBinding`. Place the following code in the `Main` method and use the NuGet package manager to include the Microsoft Azure Service Bus library in your project:

```
ServiceHost sh = new ServiceHost(typeof(CalculateService));

sh.AddServiceEndpoint(typeof(ICalculateService),
  new NetTcpRelayBinding(),
ServiceBusEnvironment.CreateServiceUri("sb", "namespace",
"calculate"))
    .Behaviors.Add(new TransportClientEndpointBehavior {
        TokenProvider = TokenProvider.
          CreateSharedAccessSignatureTokenProvider(
            "RootManageSharedAccessKey", "putyourkeyhere")}
        );

sh.Open();

Console.WriteLine("Press ENTER to exit");
Console.ReadLine();

sh.Close();
```

By putting this code in the `Main` function of a service application, you can host this service. When you customize the namespace to your namespace, `CreateServiceURI` will create a fully qualified URI in the form of `sb://[your namespace].servicebus.windows.net/calculate` and will utilize TCP as the protocol. I have put the binding information in the following code to show how you can configure everything in code. However, if you want to utilize a config file, you need to remove the `sh.AddServiceEndpoint` code and place the binding in the config file as follows:

```
<services>
    <service name="Service.Calculate">
    <endpoint contract="Service.ICalculateService"
      binding="netTcpRelayBinding"
      address="sb://namespace.servicebus.windows.net/calculate"
      behaviorConfiguration="sbTokenProvider"/>
    </service>
</services>
<behaviors>
    <endpointBehaviors>
        <behavior name="sbTokenProvider">
        <transportClientEndpointBehavior>
        <tokenProvider>
        <sharedAccessSignature keyName=
          "RootManageSharedAccessKey" key="putyourkeyhere" />
        </tokenProvider>
        </transportClientEndpointBehavior>
        </behavior>
    </endpointBehaviors>
</behaviors>
```

Run the service that you have just created on-premises. This will create and register the Service Bus Relay endpoint in Azure; you should be able to log into the portal and see that there is now a service registered under the **Relays** tab.

The next step is to create a client to connect to our new endpoint in the cloud.

Creating the client

Our client will be a simple service application that will pass two values to the multiply operation on our service. Replace the generated code in the `Main` method with the following code:

```
var cf = new ChannelFactory<ICalculateServiceChannel>(
    new NetTcpRelayBinding(),
```

```
        new EndpointAddress(ServiceBusEnvironment.
          CreateServiceUri("sb", "namespace", "calculate")));

    cf.Endpoint.Behaviors.Add(new TransportClientEndpointBehavior
            { TokenProvider = TokenProvider.CreateShared
              AccessSignatureTokenProvider
              ("RootManageSharedAccessKey","putyourkeyhere") });

    using (var ch = cf.CreateChannel())
    {
        Console.WriteLine(ch.Multiply(9, 11));
    }
```

Keep in mind that you will need to have the interface that was created earlier when we created the WCF service. The preceding code will utilize the `ChannelFactory` object, call our service, invoke the operation, and return our multiplied value.

Or, if you want to utilize the configuration file, modify the code as follows (remember that you can implement binding in code or through config but it only needs to be done in one location):

```
var cf = new ChannelFactory<ICalculateServiceChannel>("calculate");
using (var ch = cf.CreateChannel())
{
    Console.WriteLine(ch.Multiply(9, 11));
}
With the configuration file setup as follows:
  <client>
    <endpoint name="calculate" contract="Service.ICalculate"
              binding="netTcpRelayBinding"
              address="sb://namespace.servicebus.windows.net/
calculate"
              behaviorConfiguration="sbTokenProvider"/>
  </client>
  <behaviors>
    <endpointBehaviors>
      <behavior name="sbTokenProvider">
        <transportClientEndpointBehavior>
          <tokenProvider>
            <sharedAccessSignature
              keyName="RootManageSharedAccessKey"
              key="putyourkeyhere" />
          </tokenProvider>
        </transportClientEndpointBehavior>
      </behavior>
    </endpointBehaviors>
  </behaviors>
```

Make sure that you modify the entries to match your naming and you are ready to run the client. When you compile and run the code, the client will reach out to Service Bus, connect through to the WCF Service, and return the answer to our multiply call. Remember that your WCF doesn't have to be in Azure. It can be in any environment that has a connection to the Internet.

BizTalk Hybrid Connect

The other technology available in Azure that enables the creation of hybrid applications is BizTalk Hybrid Connect. The Hybrid Connect technology allows you to connect Azure Websites and Azure Mobile Services to your on-premises resources as if they were local. In fact, you can make calls through the Hybrid Connect tunnel without needing to set up or create an external access point. The Hybrid Connect feature is different from the Service Bus Relay Service in that you do not need a web services layer residing in your on-premises network to communicate with.

There are two parts that you need to configure while setting up the Hybrid Connect feature. The first is registration in the Azure Portal and the second is an on-premises agent.

Here is what we need to do to set up the configuration in the Azure Portal.

First, click on **New** in the bottom-left corner of the portal and click on **App Services**; you should see BizTalk Services listed as shown in the following screenshot:

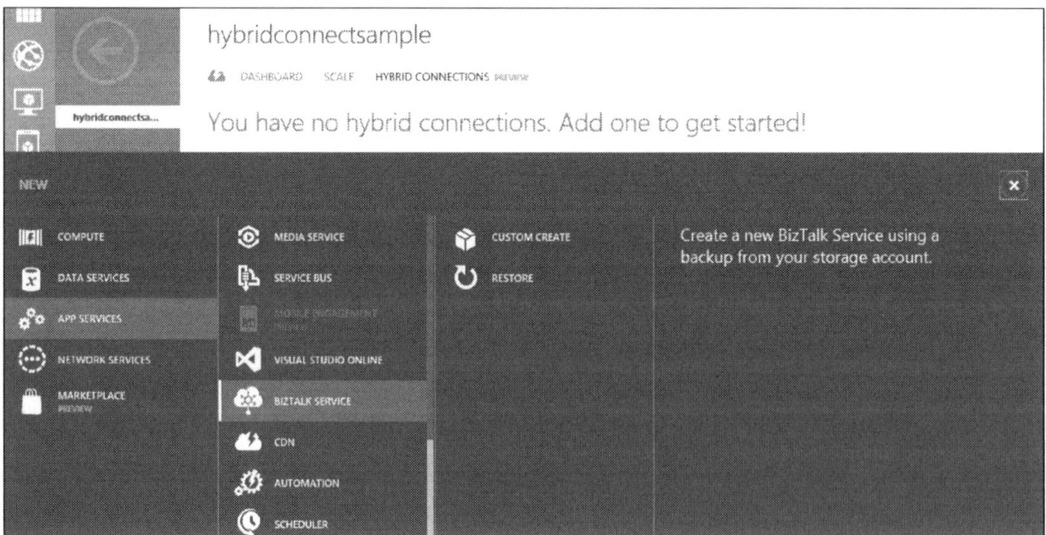

Select **Custom Create** and then provide a name for your hybrid connection in the BizTalk Service **Name** field. Select **Free** under the **Edition** drop down and select a region.

Once the hybrid connection has been created, click on the **Hybrid Connections** tab in the portal and click on **Create a Hybrid Connection**. The following screen will appear:

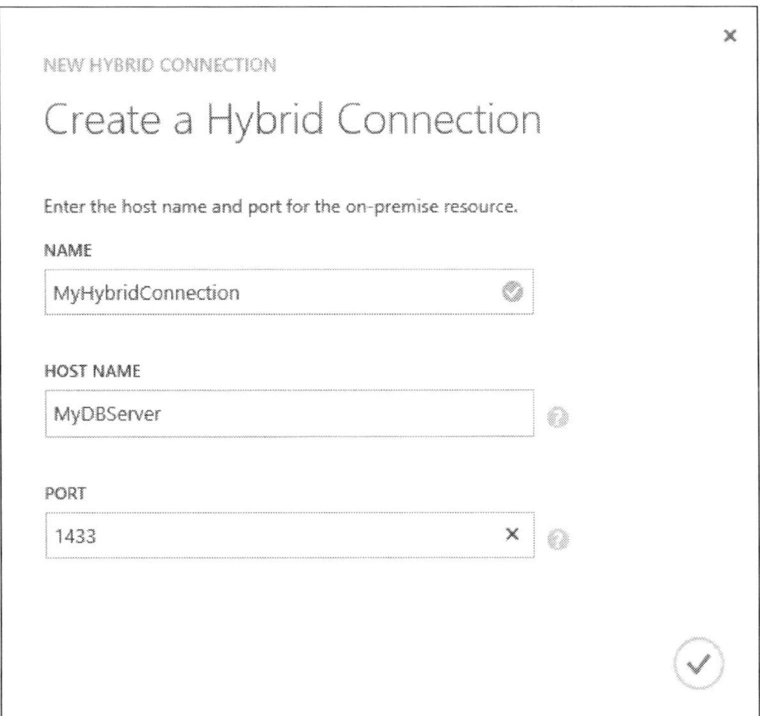

The **Name** field needs to be either a fully qualified name or an IPv4 address. Provide the name of the host system and the port that you will be using for communication. In this example, we are using a SQL Server database and it is configured for the default `1433` port. Once you click **OK**, your connection configuration is finished and you will see the registration in the portal as shown in the following screenshot:

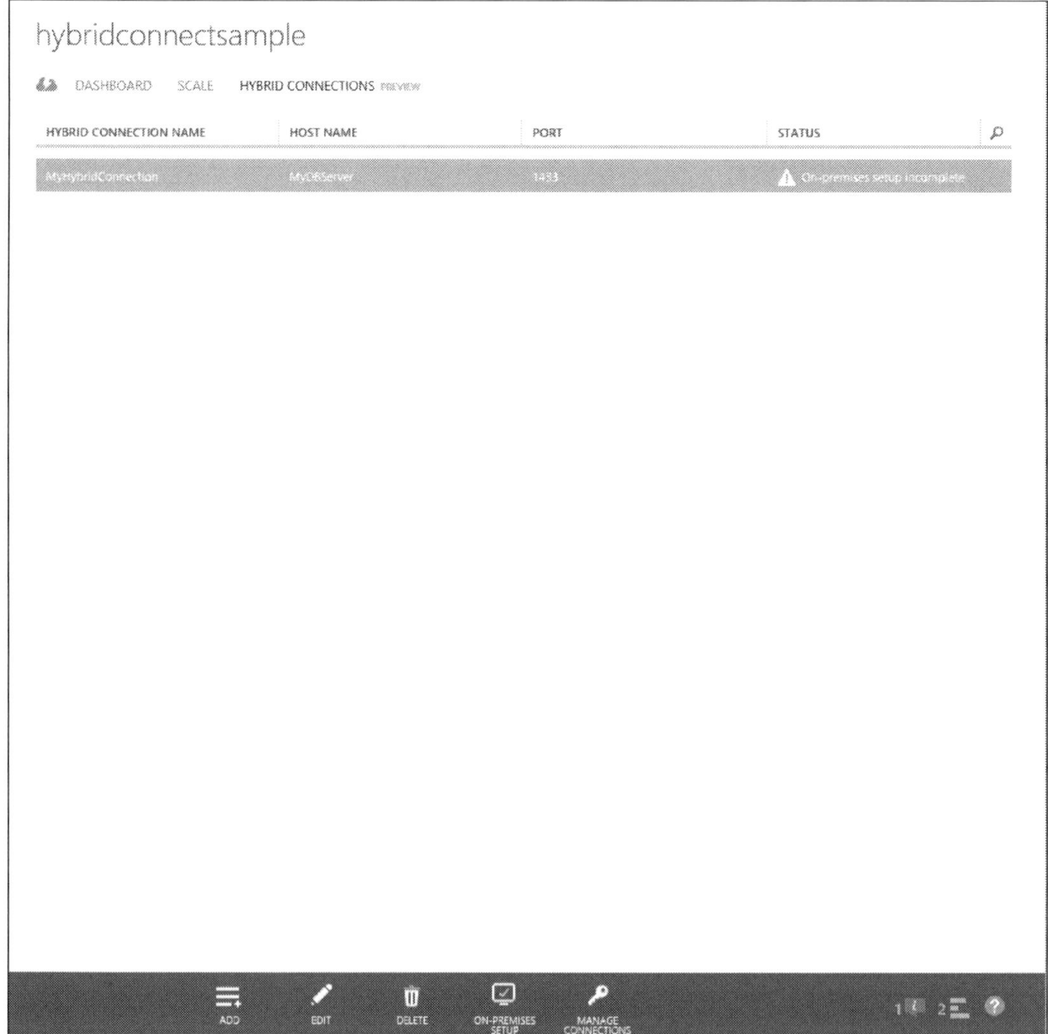

Now that we have registered the connection, we can see that there are different options available to us at the bottom of the portal. We can edit or delete the registration as well as manage connections and perform the on-premises setup. We will do the on-premises setup in the next section. But before we go to that let's talk about the **Manage Connection** option. When you click on this, it will bring up the screen shown in the following screenshot. In this dialog, we can manage the connection strings. You can regenerate the connection strings in order to update the security settings. However, when you do that, you need to remember to update your application to use the new connection string and must also rerun the on-premises agent. While doing this, it will pick up the new connection string and connectivity will be up.

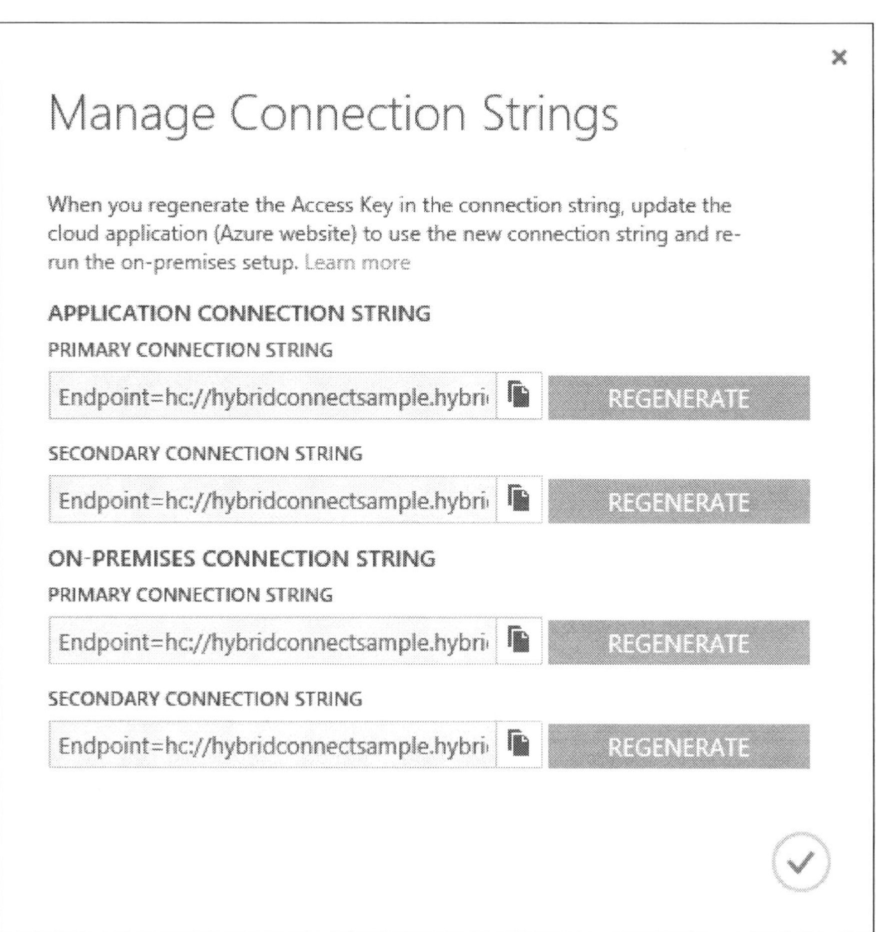

Now that we have the Azure-based configuration accomplished, we need to install the on-premises agent. The on-premises agent is what is used to connect to the on-premises data sources (whether they be a SQL Server database, a MySQL database, HTTP Web APIs, or Http(s) Web Services) and must be installed on a machine somewhere in the on-premises network. It does not have to be installed on the database server but must be installed on a machine that has connectivity and access to the database server since most database administrators won't let other software run on the database server. In addition, no security changes or changes to the network, firewall, or ports are required.

Once the agent is installed, your application in the cloud will connect to the database using a connection with a similar configuration to what you would have used on-premises. However, the connection is routed via the hybrid connection to the agent over port `80` or `443` (for HTTP) or `5671` and `9352` (for TCP), at which point the agent converts the incoming message to the standard SQL Server request and modifies the connection to connect to the database using the standard port.

Let's look at what we need to do to get the agent installed. In the portal, click on **On-Premises Setup** at the bottom. The following dialog box will appear:

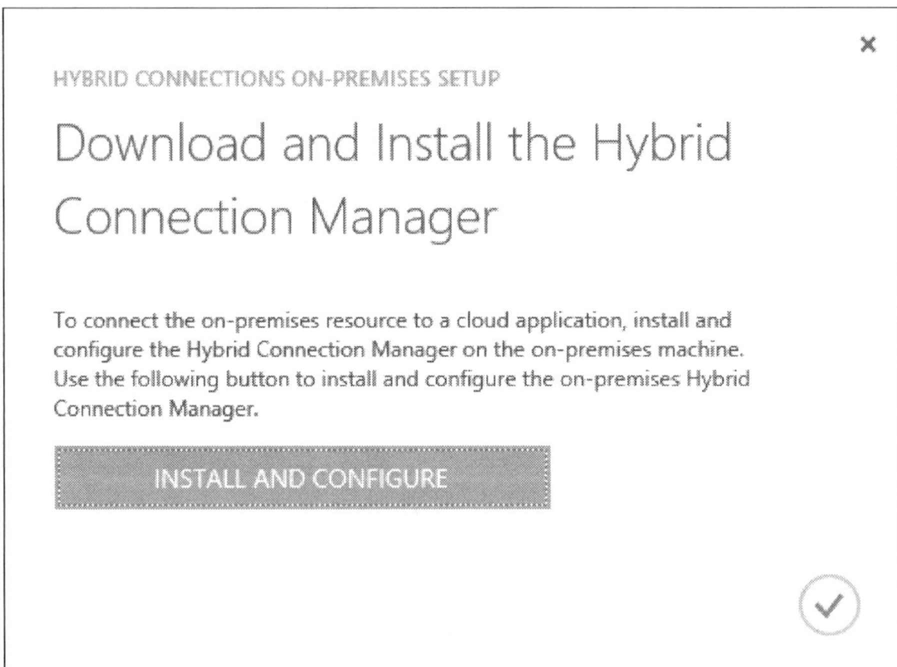

When you click on **Install and Configure**, the installation will begin. The following is a screenshot of the installation in progress:

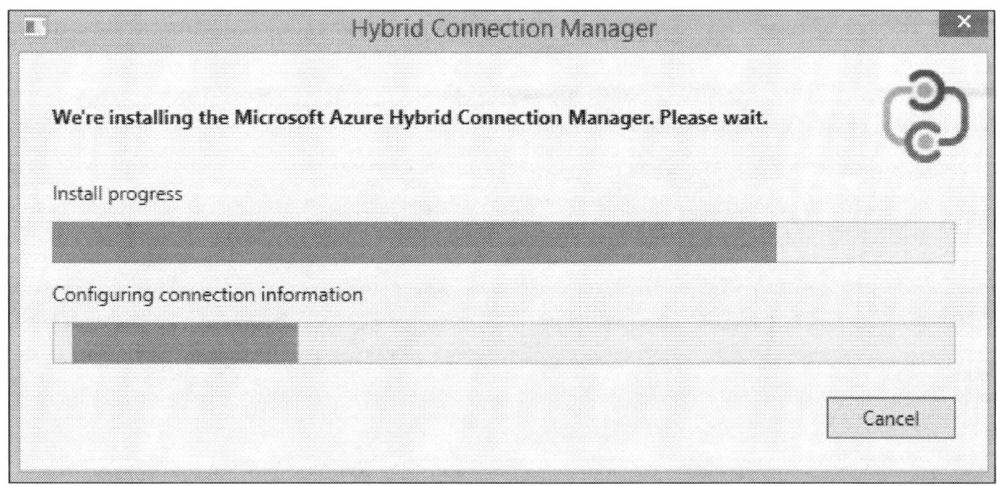

When the installation process is complete, you will see the following dialog box (which includes the path that was just created):

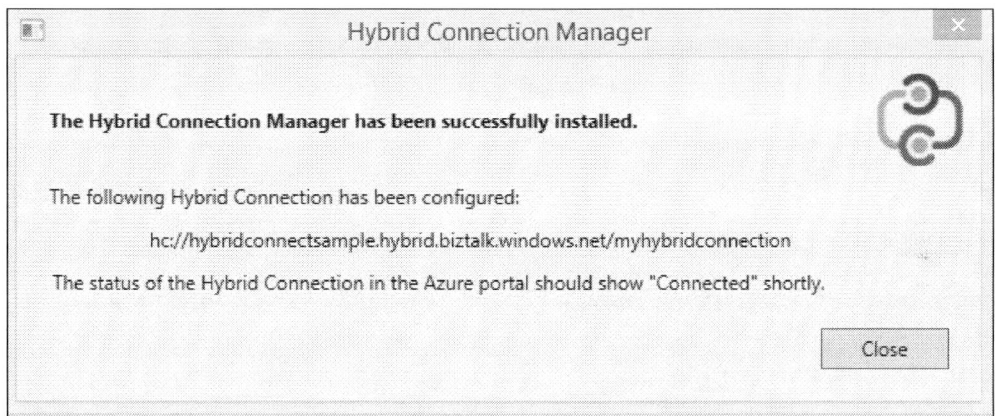

Note: You will need to have `Newtonsoft.Json.dll v5.4.0.0` installed on the machine, and it will be need to be registered in the global assembly cache. If it is not present, you will receive a `CmdletInvocationException` stating that it could not load the file or assembly. You can find more information on loading DLLs in the GAC at `https://msdn.microsoft.com/en-us/library/dkkx7f79(v=vs.110).aspx`.

Once you have the agent installed, log back into the portal. You should see that you now have a completely configured connection. As you can tell by the following screenshot, you can see how many connections you have configured and how much data has been flowing through the connection. In addition, you can click on the **Operations log** hyperlink on the right-hand side and you will be to see the activity as well as what operations have been performed.

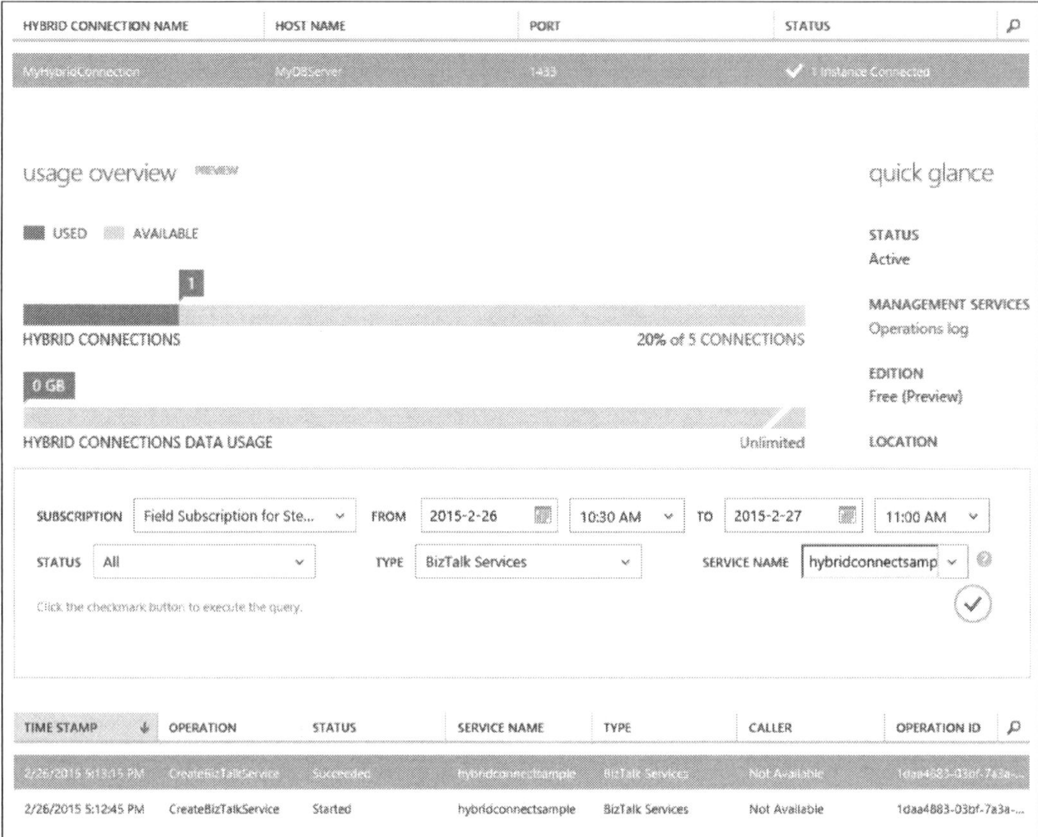

You now have a completely configured connection and your application is ready to communicate to your on-premises host system.

There are, however, a couple of things that we should recap and understand about the hybrid connect functionality.

First, when you configure and create the connection, the end point is created in the cloud and is available before the agent is listening. This provides the ability to have development take place against the end point even if connectivity is not yet established. This is different from Relay Service, where the endpoint in the cloud doesn't exist until the on-premises WCF service comes online.

Next, the hybrid connect is currently only available to be used with Azure Websites and Azure Mobile Services. Relay Service can be utilized by any service and can also be utilized by resources outside Azure.

Lastly, while neither technology requires changes to the on-premises network, configuration, or firewall, the hybrid connection function does require that an agent be installed somewhere in the on-premises network. Contrastingly, Relay Service requires that you have a WCF service on premises to communicate through and requires you to add an additional binding in your configuration file.

Hybrid Connect security

Shared access security authorization is utilized to secure the hybrid connect connections from both the Azure application and Hybrid Connection Manager on premises. There are separate keys that get created for the application and the Hybrid Connection Manager on-premises. Just as with any SAS keys, these can be refreshed or revoked and this can be done independently.

Summary

In this chapter we looked at how we can create hybrid applications that allow parts of our application to run in Azure and parts to remain on a corporate or on-premises network. We looked at how we can utilize the Service Bus Relay Service to connect to on-premises WCF services that can sit on top of systems that will remain in the corporate network. We did all this while keeping those connections secure and proxied so that clients don't connect directly to the on-premises service endpoint. Lastly, we discussed how we can utilize the BizTalk Hybrid Connect functionality to connect directly to data sources for situations where we don't have a service layer built out.

7
Data Services in the Cloud – an Overview of ADO.NET and Entity Framework

Every application that is dependent on data should have storage that will be used for that data. It can be memory storage, a file on the local or remote disk, or a database. Each storage type has its own characteristics; for example, if we use memory or a local disk, we are merging two different application layers—the data access layer and the store itself—and we don't have a really effective way of managing the fault tolerance of our solution as it is limited to local storage. Sometimes this is good—for example, when we are developing an application that will be or should be small and fault-tolerant. If we want to develop an application that is fault-tolerant (for example, if one server does not respond, the user would still have access to his information) and have code that is easy to maintain, we have to split application layers.

In this chapter we will go through an overview of layers that are common to distributed systems. We will describe these in detail and with examples and will be technology-agnostic at that time. Further, we will move to an overview of the data access technologies (ADO.NET and Entity Framework). Finally, we will go through the process of modifying our existing Web API application with the technologies described in the chapter. To do this, we will leverage Visual Studio 2013, Entity Framework 6.1.1, and cloud Microsoft Azure SQL Azure databases.

Key layers of distributed applications

In this section, we will describe key layers of distributed applications. Every application that is going to be used by end users should be designed appropriately as users are expecting to process information from various data sources that might be geographically distributed. They are also expecting this information to be up-to-date and capable of being inflected very fast. Designing such applications is not an easy task and involves integration among different groups of components. Let's review the layers that form a typical distributed application.

The responsibilities in a distributed system can be divided into four layers:

- The data layer
- The business logic layer
- The server layer
- The user interface layer

The data layer

The data layer is responsible for storing and accessing data and for querying, updating, or deleting this data. This layer includes the logic of data access and store performance that can be a complicated task, especially dealing with a large volume of data distributed among different data sources.

The business logic layer

The business logic layer is responsible for the crucial part of the application: logic that is executed between the client and data layers. Basically, the business logic layer contains the logic of the application. It is the "brain" that coordinates the integration between the data layer that is used for reading and storing the data and the user interface layer that interacts with the client.

The server layer

The server layer is sometimes called a services layer, and that is an accurate term as well. The server layer is responsible for exposing some of the capabilities of the application that can be consumed by other services and used as a data source, for example. This layer works as the interface between our application and the world of other services, which is different from that of the end users. The server layer is an extremely important part of every distributed application; its proper design can impact the overall performance of the system as it is responsible for the defining of the collaboration principles between parts of applications and the distribution of load and data. It contains security mechanisms that validate requests as well.

The user interface layer

The user interface layer is the layer that is used by clients interacting with the application. This layer must contain only that part of the system that is responsible for rendering the interface consisting of the data, user interface components, and other things important in the process of interacting between the user and the application. This layer also has the logic that can be used in the process of adapting the application user interface layer for different form factors, people, cultures, interfaces (such as touchscreens), screen sizes, and resolutions. At the same time, it must be simple and effective and must provide a smooth user experience. Properly designed user interface design is important; if the user interface is not friendly and experience is not smooth or if the user does not understand how the system works and how it should be used, the application will not be used.

Data and data access technologies

We did an overview of the characteristics and requirements of different layers of distributed applications. Now we will go through the most crucial layer of any distributed application, the data layer. In this part, you will be introduced to various database technologies, along with .NET-related technologies.

Data can be stored in a wide range of data sources such as relational databases, files on the local filesystems, on the distributed filesystems, in a caching system, in storage located on the cloud, and in memory.

- **Relational databases** (**SQL server**): This is the traditional data source that is designed to store and retrieve data. Queries are written in languages such as T-SQL-utilized **Create, Retrieve, Update, and Delete** (**CRUD**) operations model. We will have an overview of the SQL server and its use with Entity Framework in this chapter.
- **The filesystem**: The filesystem is used to store and retrieve unstructured data on the local disk system in the files. One of the simplest options to store and retrieve data, it has many functional limits and is not distributed by its nature.
- **The Distributed File System** (**DFS**): The DFS is the next level of file system that solves the size and other limitations introduced by local disks. In a nutshell, DFS is a pool of networked computers that store data files.

- **NoSQL databases**: NoSQL databases are a new way of storing data in a non-relational fashion. Often, NoSQL databases are used to store large or very large volumes of data, and the biggest difference between these databases and relational database is that NoSQL data stores are schema-free. However, data can be organized by one or more different models, such as key-value stores and document stores, among others. We will cover some NoSQL options available in the Microsoft Azure cloud offering in the final chapter.
- **Cloud storage**: Any infrastructure located on the cloud solves many issues, such as security, reliability, resilience, and maintenance. Cloud offerings such as Microsoft Azure Storage provide many ways of storing the data in different formats, which can be structured or unstructured. As with many other cloud storage offerings, Microsoft Azure Storage exposes the HTTP REST API, used by any application and client running on any platform that supports HTTP. We will cover all options for storing data in Microsoft Azure Storage—Table storage (key-value NoSQL database), Blob storage (filesystem for unstructured data), and Queues (integration storage mechanism)—and other options, such as SQL Azure database (a SQL server-based cloud implementation).
- **In-memory stores**: In-memory stores are the fastest data stores that are limited in size, not persistent, and cumbersome to use in a distributed multi-server environment. In-memory stores are used to store temporary and volatile data.

ADO.NET and ADO.NET Entity Framework

.NET Framework has several database access options, and the foundation of most of them is ADO.NET. ADO.NET can be called a foundation for every other data access technology on Microsoft stacks. In a nutshell, **ActiveX Data Objects .NET** (**ADO.NET**) is a collection of classes that implement program interfaces to simplify the process of connecting to data stores without depending on the structure and implementation of a concrete data store and its location. The challenge that it offers is that most developers must write complex data access code (between the application and the database) that requires them to have a good understanding of the database itself, of raw tables, views, stored procedures, the database schema, table definitions and parameters, results, and so on. This is mostly solved by the **Object-relational mapping** (**ORM**) approach. Programmers create a conceptual model of the data and write their data access code against that model, while an additional layer provides a bridge between the entity-relationship model and the actual data store. Entity Framework generates database entities according to database tables and provides the mechanism for basic CRUD operations, managing 1-to-1, 1-to-many, and many-to-many relationships, and the ability to have inheritance relationships between entities among others.

Basically, you have the ability to "talk" about your model not with the database but with the class model you wrote or generated from a database using Entity Framework. This is achieved by the creation of a combination of XML schema files, code generation, and the ADO.NET Entity Framework APIs. The schema files are used to define a conceptual layer, to be used as a map between the data store and the application. The ADO.NET Entity Framework allows you to write the application that uses classes that are generated from the conceptual schema. Entity Framework then takes care of the rest.

Another important component of Entity Framework that is often used by developers is **Language Integrated Query** (**LINQ**). It adds data querying capabilities to .NET languages and extends the language with SQL-like query expressions.

There are three approaches to working with Entity Framework in the project:

- **Database-first**: This approach is used when you already have a database that is going to be used as a data source.
- **Model-first**: This approach is used when you have no database. First, you draw the model in the Visual Designer and then instruct it to create the database for you with all the tables.
- **Code-first**: This approach is used often as it provides a way to write your model in code as classes and instruct Entity Framework to generate the database with objects described in the code.

We will use the first approach.

Creating a data source for a Web API application

We will go through the process of creation of data source that will be hosted in Microsoft Azure. We will use Microsoft Azure SQL databases. Microsoft Azure SQL databases (formerly SQL Azure) is a cloud-based service offering rich data-storage capabilities. It uses a special version of SQL server as a backend so we can easily use that as a data source for Entity Framework.

Creating a Microsoft Azure SQL database

The first step is to create a new Microsoft Azure SQL database. We will use the Create wizard in the Azure Management portal to create a new Microsoft Azure SQL database.

1. Open the Azure Management portal, which can be found at `http://manage.windowsazure.com`. Choose **Custom Create** to review Microsoft Azure SQL database functionality.

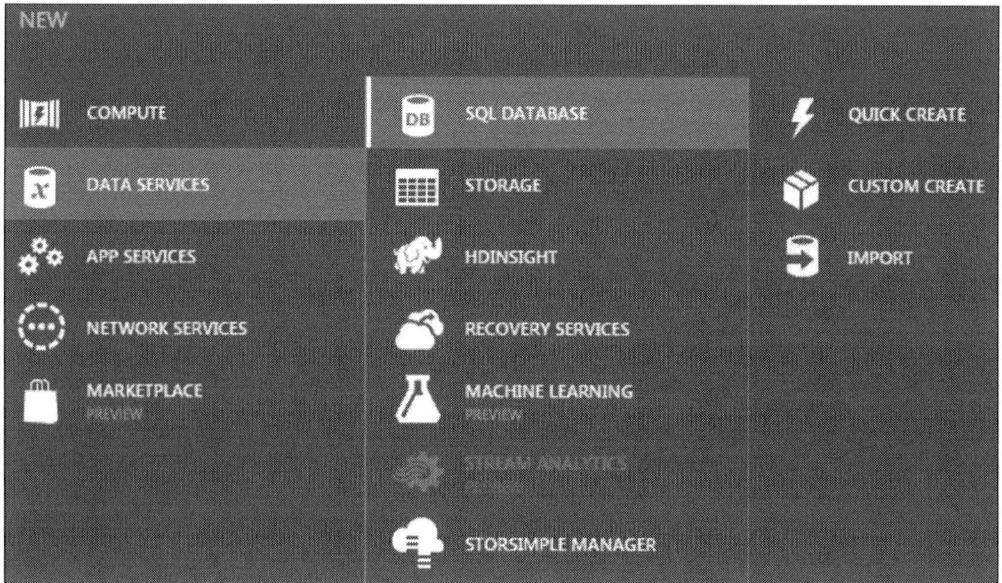

2. Choose the **Custom Create** option to get access to the Advanced wizard.

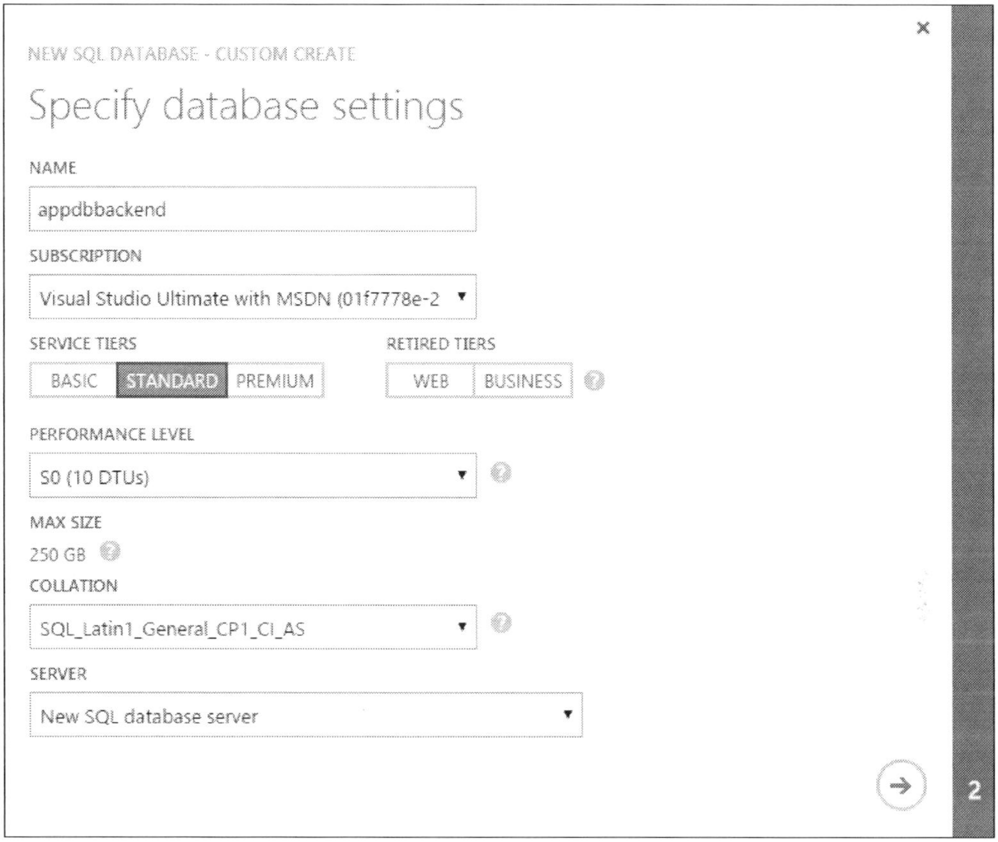

NEW SQL DATABASE - CUSTOM CREATE

Specify database settings

NAME

appdbbackend

SUBSCRIPTION

Visual Studio Ultimate with MSDN (01f7778e-2

SERVICE TIERS

BASIC STANDARD PREMIUM

RETIRED TIERS

WEB BUSINESS

PERFORMANCE LEVEL

S0 (10 DTUs)

MAX SIZE

250 GB

COLLATION

SQL_Latin1_General_CP1_CI_AS

SERVER

New SQL database server

2

To know more about Microsoft Azure SQL database pricing tiers, refer to `http://azure.microsoft.com/en-us/pricing/details/sql-database/#basic-standard-and-premium`.

Options available in the Advanced wizard include:

- **Name**: This is the name that will be included in the connection string. It should be unique as it will be a globally used DNS name.
- **Subscription**: This is the subscription that should be used for your Microsoft Azure SQL database server and database. Placing all your resources inside one.
- **Service Tiers**: You will notice two different sets of services tiers. Retired tiers should not be used as they will be retired in favor of new models. Every service tier is intended to serve a different level of performance.

- **Performance Level**: Performance level is based on a **Database Throughput Unit** (**DTU**) that is a weighted value of database size, disaster recovery capabilities, number of transactions, and other units that are critical for every application using the data. It begins with the basic performance level that is best suited for small projects—databases used for development and testing, infrequently used databases, and so on. Its limits are DB size that is equal to 2 GB, transaction rate, and maximum number of worker threads. Its DTU value is 5. The most powerful performance level is Premium/P3, and its DTU value is 800. Premium/P3 DB size can be up to 500 GB, and as its performance predictability is the best, it can be used for mission-critical applications.
- **Collation**: That is the collation that will be used for Microsoft Azure SQL database as the default option.
- **Server**: Every Microsoft Azure SQL database should be placed on a specific server in the cloud. You can either place it on an existing server or create a new one.

3. Next, provide the account information for the server that will be used for our database. The critical point here is the **Region** field. It should be in the same region where your application resides (if it is cloud-based) or geographically near your location so that latency will be minimized (and as egress traffic is not free, it will not incur any charges in case of cross-data center communication). If you don't want to grant access to the new server from inside Azure, you are free to set it up like that.

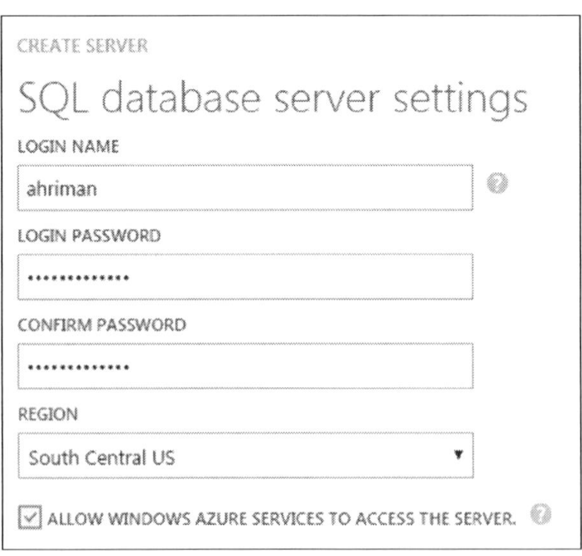

The creation of the Microsoft Azure SQL database instance takes some time (approximately between 1 to 3 minutes).

The service is now ready, so we have a data source that is available whenever and from wherever we need it. It supports most SQL server features as well, so we will use them in this chapter. If you want to, or already have SQL server installed locally, there will not be any difference in the algorithm.

> To know more about Microsoft Azure SQL database and SQL server differences, refer here to `http://azure.microsoft.com/en-us/documentation/articles/data-management-azure-sql-database-and-sql-server-iaas/`.

As Microsoft Azure SQL database is a database-as-a-service, you immediately have the connection string for manipulating the data inside the data source. It can be retrieved from the database homepage or from the dashboard by clicking on **Show connection string**. The second option generates multiple connection strings that are specific for different programming languages, such as PHP.

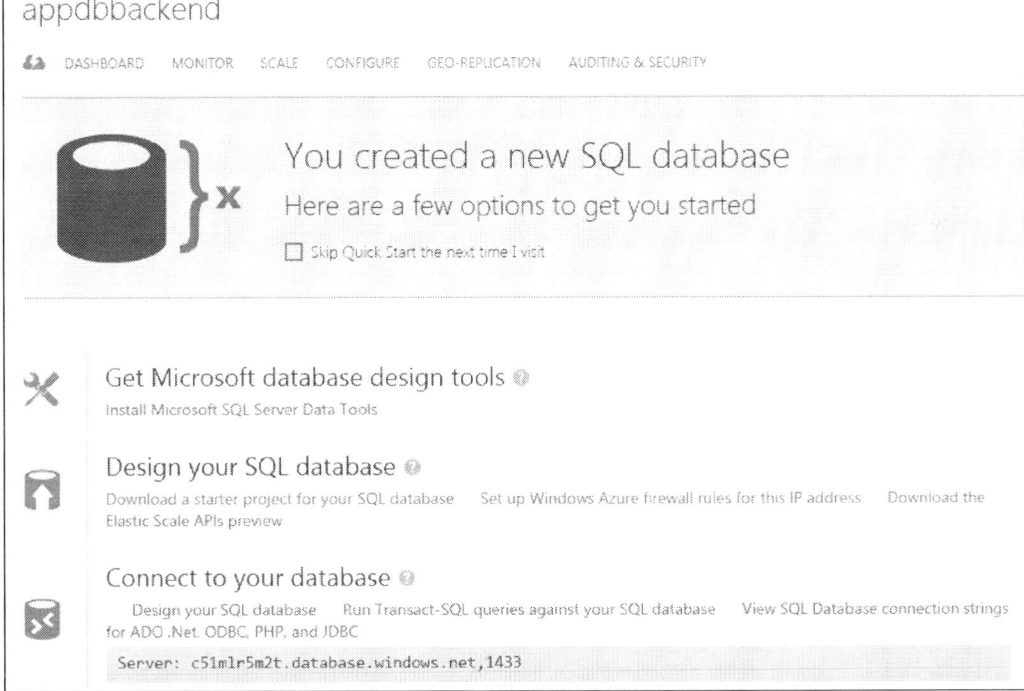

If you use non-.NET technologies in the future, you can leverage the functionality of autogenerating connection strings that can be found on a **Dashboard** page as shown:

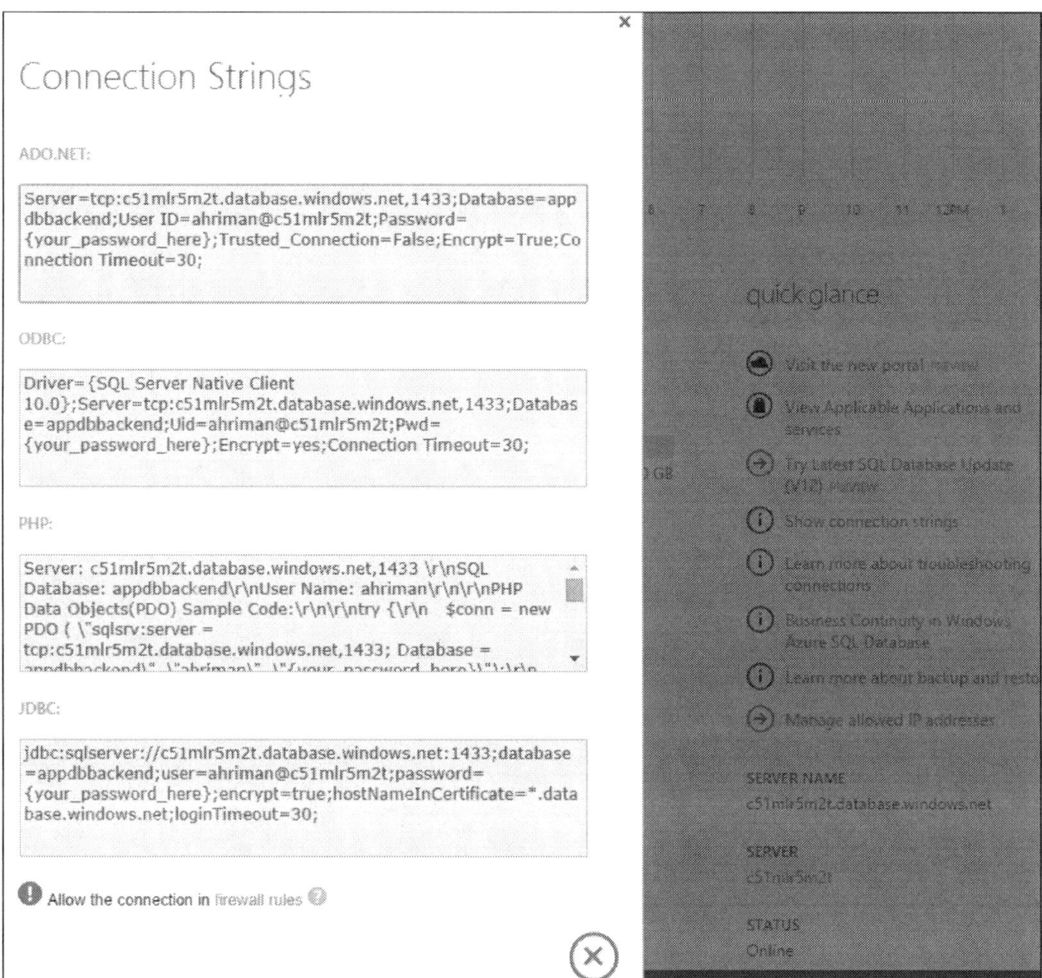

Using the Microsoft Azure SQL database management portal

Microsoft Azure SQL database is a service that is fully compatible with SQL Management Studio and Visual Studio designers, so you can create and manipulate your database the same way you use them for full-fledged SQL Server deployments.

> Starting with SQL server 2008 R2 and SQL server 2008 R2 Express, SQL Server Management Studio can be used to manage and access Microsoft Azure SQL databases. Previous versions of SQL Server Management Studio are not supported.

In our case, we will take another approach that is handy in case if you have neither SQL Management Studio nor Visual Studio installed or have a non-Windows OS Microsoft Azure SQL database management portal.

1. On the Azure Management portal, select your database.
2. On the **Dashboard** page click on **Manage**. You can click on **Open in Visual Studio** as well.

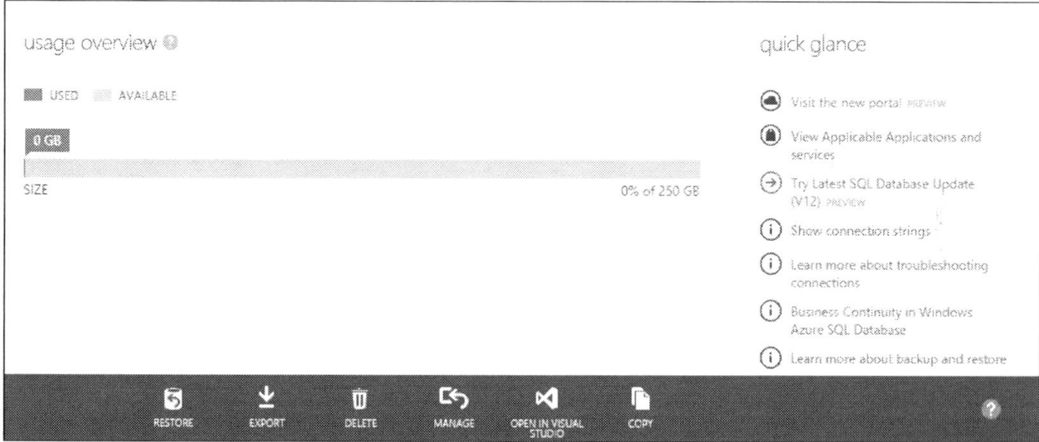

3. Next, provide your credentials on the login page of the Microsoft Azure SQL database portal.

> The Microsoft Azure SQL database management portal has a rich set of capabilities, including designing tables and other objects.

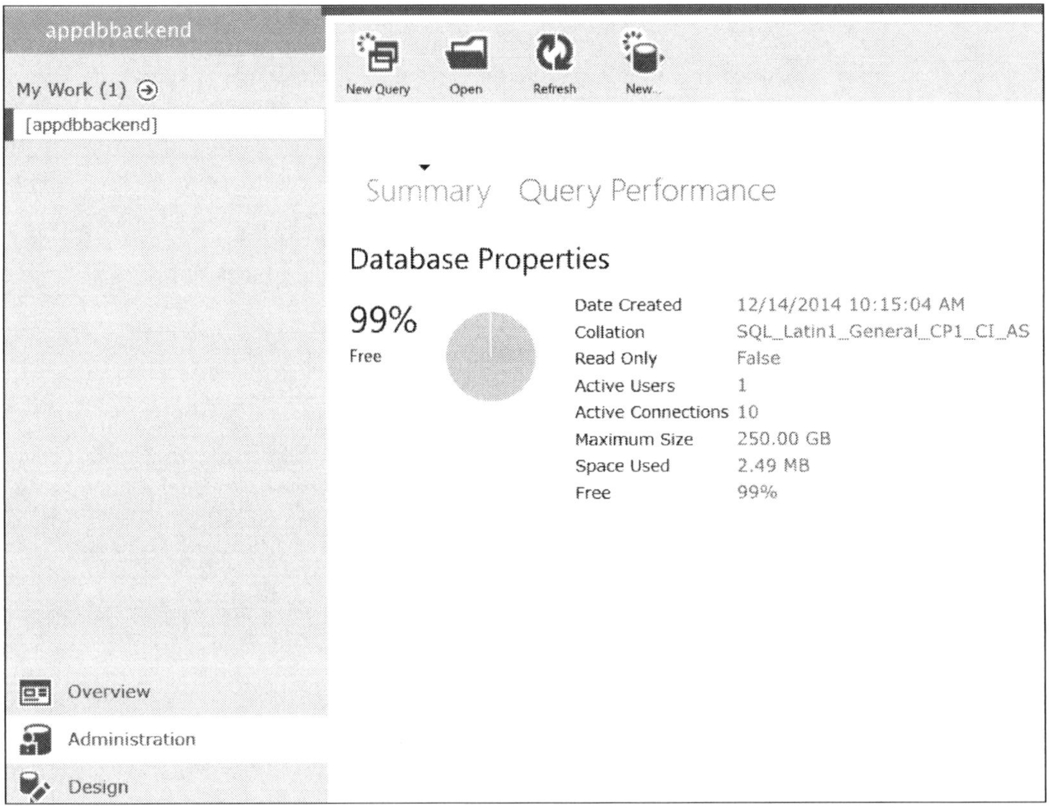

4. Select **Design**.
5. Click on **New Table** to create a new table named `Package`.

6. Using Visual Designer, fill in the needed fields and add columns. Save your work.

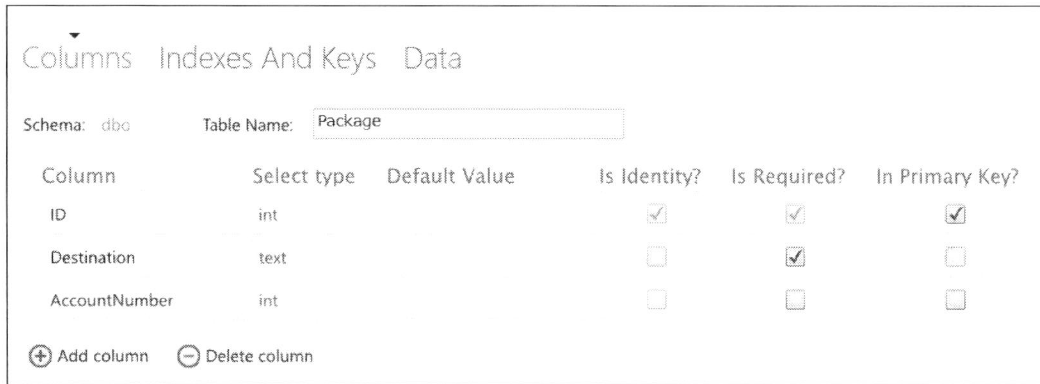

We created a database that we will use as a data source for our Web API project. Do not close the Microsoft Azure SQL database portal for now. Next, we will populate it with test data and add it to the project.

Populating a Microsoft Azure SQL database table with test data

As you already know, Microsoft Azure SQL database is a service that is fully compatible with the SQL Management Studio and Visual Studio designers, so you can populate the database with test data in the same way as for the SQL server. In our case, we are going to use the Microsoft Azure SQL database portal to populate the table `Package` with test data.

1. Click on **Design** and then on **Data**.

2. Using the **Add row** button, populate the table with records.

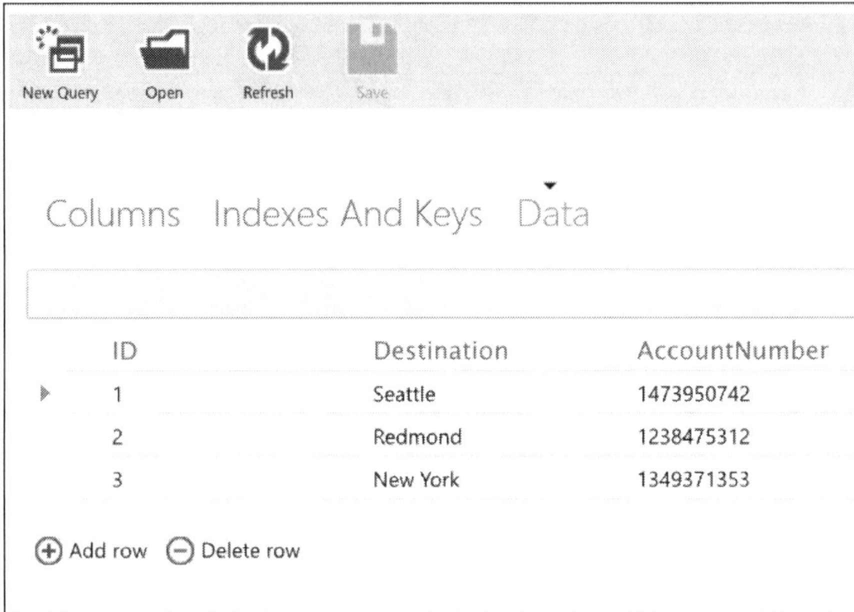

3. Click on **Save**.

Now that the table is created and populated with test data, we can add it to the project.

Adding a Microsoft Azure SQL database to the project

In this section, we will configure our Web API with the Microsoft Azure SQL database created earlier. We will use a Visual Studio 2013 database management tool.

Creating an Entity Data Model

We will continue to use our Contoso application. First, we create a new Entity Data Model from Microsoft Azure SQL database:

1. Open the solution, right-click on the `Models` folder, and click on **Add New Item**; then click on ADO.NET Entity Data Model.
2. Enter the name of the model and click **OK**.

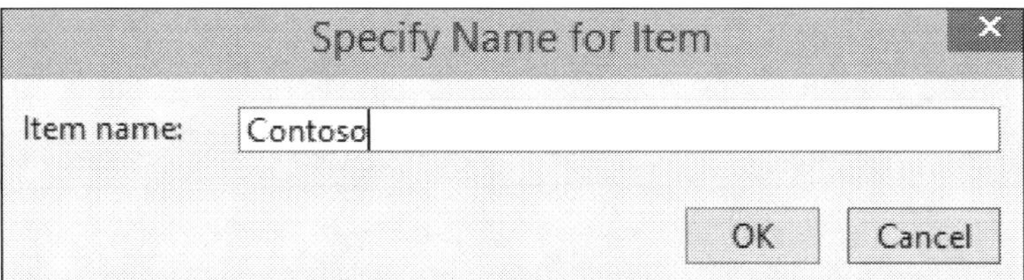

There are four options that can be used to generate the Entity Data Model:

Option	Description
EF Designer from database	Creates a model in the EF Designer based on an existing database.
Empty EF Designer model	Creates an empty model in the EF Designer. You can use the Visual Editor to create the database and then synchronize the local model with the database in the data source.
Empty Code First model	Creates an empty code-first model to create your model using code.
Code First from database	Creates a code-first model based on an existing database.

3. Select the first option—that is, EF Designer from database.
4. Next is the dialog where the connection string to the data source should be selected. By default it can use any installed SQL server locally. We did create an Microsoft Azure SQL database instance and are going to use that.

5. Click on **New Connection**, select Microsoft SQL Server, and enter a value in the field **Server Name** (you can copy-and-paste that from the dashboard on the Azure Management portal). Select SQL server authentication (at the time of this writing, Microsoft Azure SQL database does not support Windows authentication) and enter your credentials. If everything works correctly, you should be able to see your database in the **Select or enter database name** dialog. Be aware that if you are behind the firewall and the ports used by SQL server are closed, it will be block the connection.

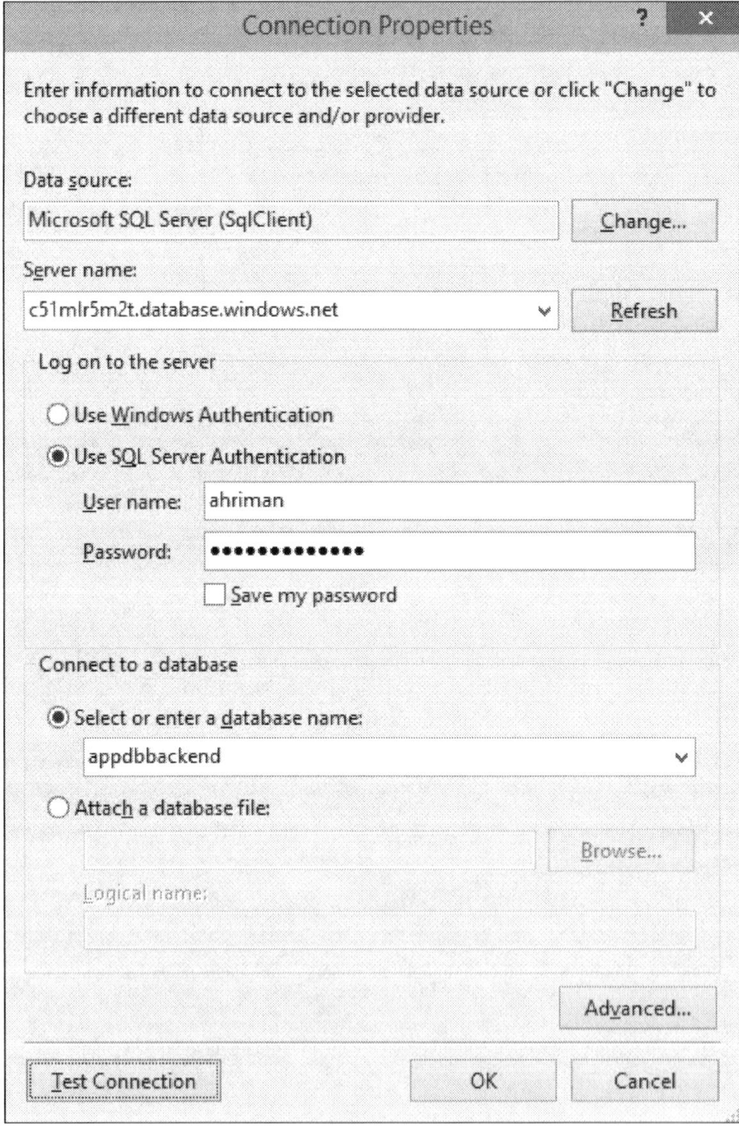

6. In the dialog box that comes up, select **Yes, include the sensitive data in the connection string** (for testing purposes, this is reasonable, but do not select it in production), enter a meaningful value for Entity Data Model, and click on **Next**.

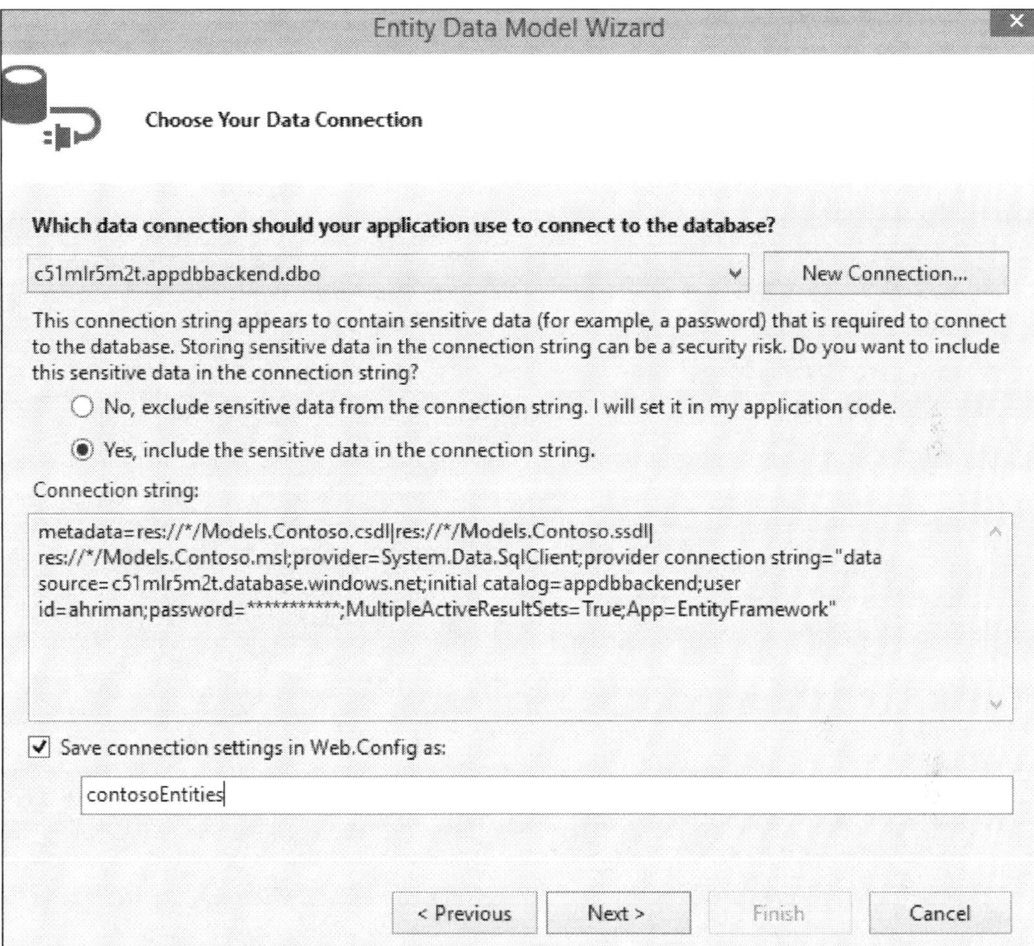

The next dialog asks which version of Entity Framework we are going to use. Select **Entity Framework 6.x**.

The next dialog seems like a designer where you can select entities from a database that should be presented in the application object model. Select a `Package` table, enter a meaningful **Model Namespace** value, and click on **Finish**.

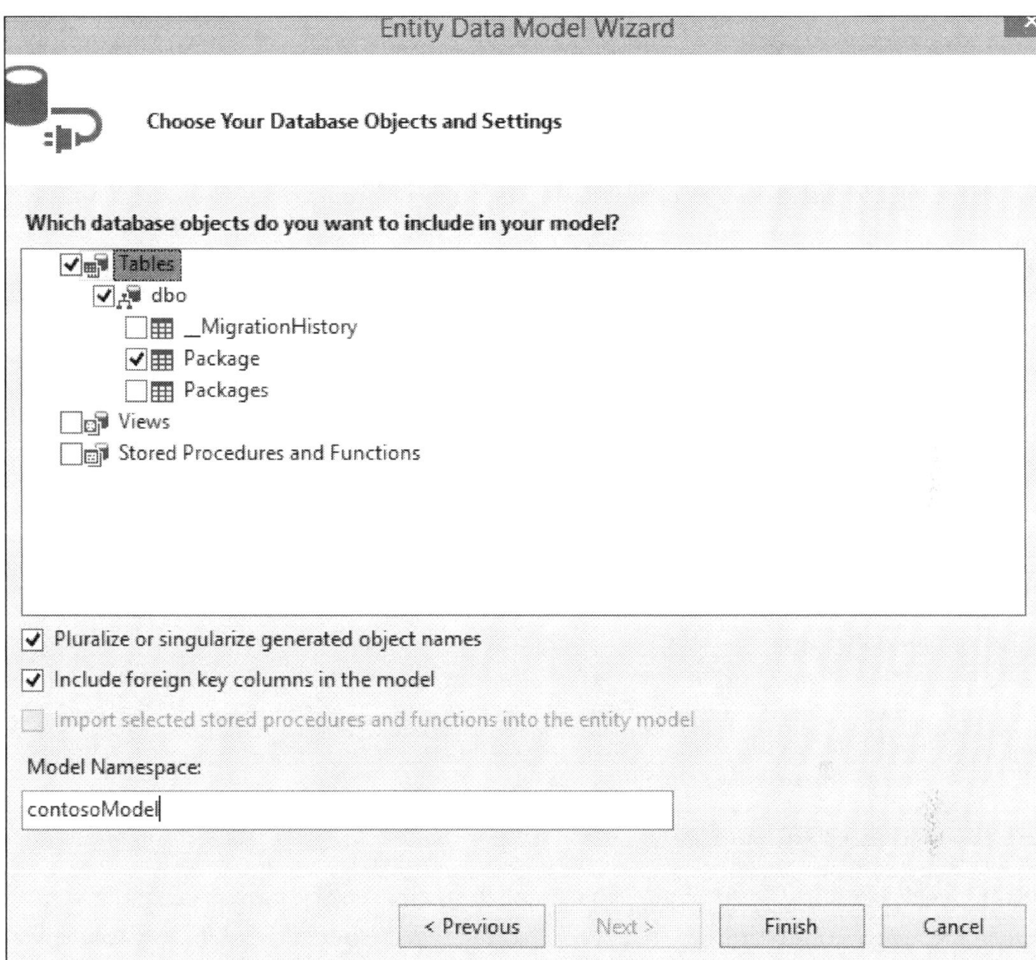

As Entity Framework is an ORM tool, you will have full access to the entities using familiar code and patterns. Let's briefly explore what Entity Framework creates and adds to the project.

If you open Solution Explorer and search for the `Models` folder, you will notice a new file called something like `Model1.edmx`. This file is an XML file that defines the schema for the data model. `Model1.Designer.cs` is the file that contains the mapping objects for the data model. `Model1.Designer.cs` is autogenerated by the `EntityModelCodeGeneratol` tool when you create the Entity Data Model through the wizard. It contains the contexts and entities that are used by Entity Data Model. And, if you open `Model1.edmx` in the XML editor, you will find the three sections that that file consists of:

- **Logical layer**: The logical layer is the layer defined by the **Store Schema Definition Language** (**SSDL**). It defines the structure of the tables in the data model and relations between them.
- **Conceptual layer**: The conceptual layer is defined by the **Conceptual Schema Definition Language** (**CSDL**) and defines .NET object classes. In fact, this is the model that developers use for querying the data model.
- **Mapping layer**: The mapping layer is defined by **Mapping Specification Language** (**MSL**) and connects the entity type definition between the CSDL and the SSDL.

The most important part (from the developer's point of view) to explore is the `contosoEntities` partial class that is the inherited class from `DbContext`. The `DbContext` API provides a productive way of working with the Entity Framework and can be used with the Database First, Model First, and Code First approaches. The `DbContext` class is often referred to as context, and it is the primary class that we will use for interacting with data as objects. `DbContext` manages all the objects during application runtime and provides many useful functionalities, such as change tracking and persisting data to the database, among others.

The class that derives from `DbContext` exposes `DbSet` properties that map object collections to the data source. Once you have a context instantiated, you can use that context for querying, adding (the `Add` or `Attach` methods), updating, and removing (using `Remove`) entities in the context. The context lifetime begins when the instance is created and ends when the instance is disposed of or collected by the garbage collector.

If you are going to use the Code First approach, you will typically need to write the context yourself. If you are working with Entity Framework designer and using the Database First approach, it will be generated for you.

Add to the `PackageController` the following `using` sentences needed to perform the next steps:

```
using Contoso.Services.Models;
using System.Collections.ObjectModel;
using System.Web.Http.Controllers;
using System.Web.Http.Description;
using System.Web.Http.Routing.Constraints;
```

Change `PackageController` according to the following code:

```
public class PackageController : ApiController
    {
        private contosoEntities entities = new contosoEntities();
        public IQueryable<Package> GetPackages()
        {
            return entities.Packages;
        }
        [ResponseType(typeof(Package))]
        public IHttpActionResult GetPackage(int id)
        {
            Package package = entities.Packages.Find(id);
            if (package == null)
            {
                return NotFound();
            } return Ok(package);}

        [ResponseType(typeof(Package))]
        public IHttpActionResult PostPackage(Package package)
        {
            if (!ModelState.IsValid)
            {
                return BadRequest(ModelState);
            }
            entities.Packages.Add(package);
            entities.SaveChanges();
            return CreatedAtRoute("DefaultApi",
              new { id = package.ID }, package);
        }

        [ResponseType(typeof(Package))]
        public IHttpActionResult DeletePackage(int id)
        {
            Package package = entities.Packages.Find(id);
            if (package == null)
```

```
            {
                return NotFound();
            }
            entities.Packages.Remove(package);
            entities.SaveChanges();
            return Ok(package); }
    }
```

We have a full-fledged Web API controller, so we are able to do the tests against a cloud-based data source.

Testing the Web API with Entity Framework and Microsoft Azure SQL database

As we saw in *Chapter 1, Getting Started with the ASP.NET Web API*, testing the Web API is as simple as developing it. Since each action in a Web API controller maps to a resource, we can simply type the URL of the resource to fetch the results from: `http://localhost:49675/api/package/1`.

Earlier, we did the same thing with local data. Now we have the data store that is always online, always accessible from everywhere and from every platform. Isn't it great?

When you create a Web API (or any other) controller using Visual Studio scaffolding, it generates a set of operations called CRUD. We took a look at the `Read` operation. What about the `Create`, `Update`, and `Delete` operations?

They are already in place in the corresponding methods; however, there is no `Update` method (in terms of HTTP REST, the `Update` operation is called `PUT`).

Unlike the `GET` (`Read`) operation, we can't just type the URL of the resource and insert, update, or delete the record. Instead of that, we have two options: code and a tool such as Fiddler or Postman.

Testing an insert operation

As the Web API follows HTTP standards and needs to have a JSON input, the data that you need to insert into the data source should be serialized from the object model we use in the application to the JSON format. Fortunately, with the Web API, the process of serializing/deserializing is automated. We just need to follow the proper process of creating an object of the type needed and passing it to the `PostPackage` method.

The code for the `PostPackage` method is provided here:

```
public IHttpActionResult PostPackage(Package package) {
    if (!ModelState.IsValid) {
        return BadRequest(ModelState); }

    entities.Packages.Add(package);
    entities.SaveChanges();
    return CreatedAtRoute("DefaultApi", new
      { id = package.ID }, package); }
```

It accepts one argument, the instance of the `Package` type. If everything is correct (for example, we don't pass the object with the null value of a non-nullable parameter), it puts the object to the `Packages` collection and invokes the method `SaveChanges` that should be in place as it commits changes to the database.

Let's test this operation manually. For that, you can use a tool such as Fiddler or cURL that can be agile in composing the HTTP query with parameters.

In Fiddler, select the **Composer** pane. Enter the address of the Web API operation and select POST. Enter `Content-Type:application/json` into the flags window as it will indicate that the format of the outcoming message should be treated like a JSON. Populate the **Request Body** field as shown in the following screenshot, and click on the **Execute** button.

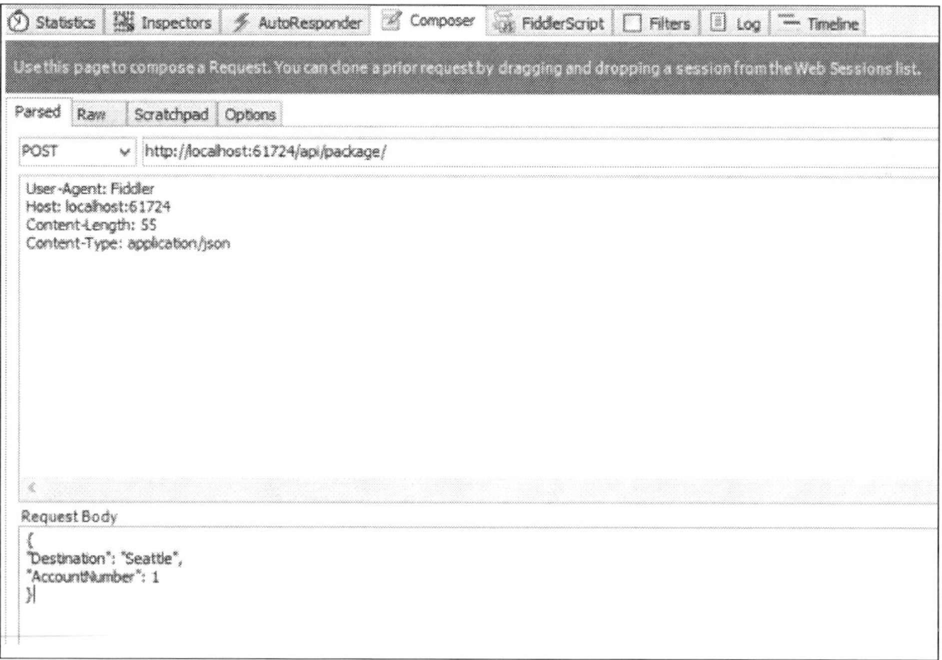

You can invoke the GET operation here by selecting GET instead of POST—the request body data will be ignored in this case—and check whether the record was written successfully.

If you like the command-line interface, you can use a cross-platform tool such as cURL (it can be downloaded from http://curl.haxx.se/download.html). cURL is very handy for GET operations, but for POST it is more complex as you need to be very careful about quotes and double-quotes according to the JSON syntax. Therefore, put your JSON exactly as you want it in a text file, for example like this:

```
{
"Destination": "New York",
"AccountNumber": 1
}
```

Note that there is no ID field in the JSON message. It will be auto-generated on the database side.

Next, pass the file to cURL and invoke the POST operation:

```
curl -v -X POST -H "Content-Type: application/json" -d @package.txt
http://localhost:61724/api/package/
```

The result should indicate that the POST operation was invoked successfully.

```
Adding handle: conn: 0xc943e0
Adding handle: send: 0
Adding handle: recv: 0
Curl_addHandleToPipeline: length: 1
- Conn 0 (0xc943e0) send_pipe: 1, recv_pipe: 0
About to connect() to localhost port 61724 (#0)
  Trying 127.0.0.1...
Connected to localhost (127.0.0.1) port 61724 (#0)
POST /api/package/ HTTP/1.1
User-Agent: curl/7.33.0
Host: localhost:61724
Accept: */*
Content-Type: application/json
Content-Length: 46

upload completely sent off: 46 out of 46 bytes
HTTP/1.1 201 Created
Cache-Control: no-cache
Pragma: no-cache
Content-Type: application/json; charset=utf-8
Expires: -1
Location: http://localhost:61724/api/package/4
Server Microsoft-IIS/8.0 is not blacklisted
Server: Microsoft-IIS/8.0
X-AspNet-Version: 4.0.30319
X-SourceFiles: =?UTF-8?B?YzpcdXNlcnNcYWxiZVxkb2N1bWVudHNcdmlzdWFsIHN0dWRpbyAyMDEzXFByb2plY3RzXF
X-Powered-By: ASP.NET
Date: Mon, 15 Dec 2014 09:58:26 GMT
Content-Length: 51

{"ID":4,"Destination":"New York","AccountNumber":1}* Connection #0 to host localhost left intact
```

You can invoke the `GET` operation here by selecting `GET` instead of `POST`. Check whether the record was written successfully or take a look at the data store on the Microsoft Azure SQL database management portal in the corresponding section.

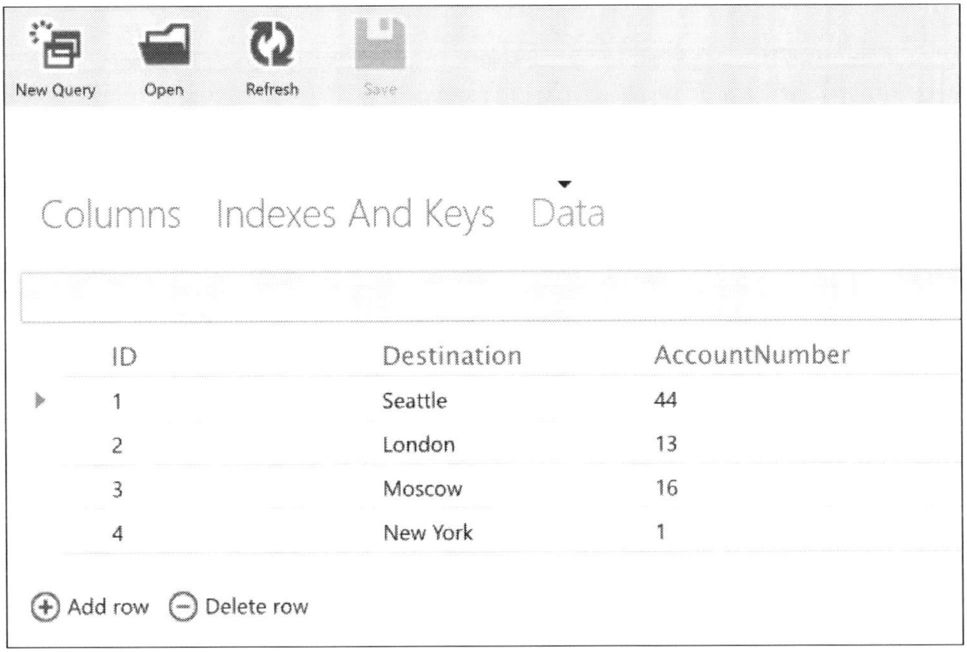

New Query Open Refresh Save

Columns Indexes And Keys Data

ID	Destination	AccountNumber
1	Seattle	44
2	London	13
3	Moscow	16
4	New York	1

Add row Delete row

Summary

This chapter provided an overview of the key layers of every distributed application, data access technologies, and the use of Entity Framework in a Web API application to query and manipulate the data that is stored in the Microsoft Azure SQL database cloud offering. Entity Framework is an efficient way of communicating with data sources both local and cloud-based. It provides a broad range of functionalities that can be used to query, add, update, or delete the entities using familiar syntax, LINQ queries, and a powerful functionality such as change tracking. Microsoft Azure SQL database is a cloud offering that can be used as both a test and production environment for database backend and fits almost any scenario, from a simple page to a mission-critical system, without any administrative effort.

8

Data Services in the Cloud – Microsoft Azure Storage

In the previous chapter, we had an overview of the Entity Framework and Microsoft Azure SQL database as a data source for the Web API application. Despite the fact that a database is a good approach to store and query data, often the more efficient approach is to use something simpler. Microsoft Azure Storage is a REST-based storage-as-a-service, so it can be consumed from every platform that supports HTTP. Microsoft Azure Storage can be both an alternative and a complementary solution to the Microsoft Azure SQL database.

In this chapter we will have an overview of Microsoft Azure Storage and its services: Blobs, Tables, and Queues. We will go through the process of modifying our existing Web API application with the technologies described in the chapter. To do this, we will use Visual Studio 2013.

Microsoft Azure Storage

Microsoft Azure Storage is one of the main components of Microsoft Azure. It offers cloud storage in a scalable and redundant way. It can store petabytes of data of any kind: files, logs, images, videos, and so on. At the same time, Microsoft Azure Storage is flexible and its load balancing system can easily handle traffic of any volume. Microsoft Azure Storage is a powerful option when you need reliable data storage that can be consumed from every platform and is accessible 24/7.

Microsoft Azure Storage provides three options for redundancy for its services:

- **Locally Redundant Storage** (**LRS**): All data in the storage account replicates synchronously to three different storage nodes within the primary region that was chosen when creating the storage account.
- **Geo Redundant Storage** (**GRS**, the default option): All data in the storage account replicates synchronously within the primary region. All data also replicates asynchronously to a secondary region (hundreds of miles away from the primary region), where data again replicates to three different storage nodes.
- **Read Access—Geo Redundant Storage** (**RA-GRS**): This option allows developers to have read-only access to data in the secondary region (as replication to the secondary region is done asynchronously, that data is the eventual consistent version).
- **Zone Redundant Storage** (**ZRS**): This option keeps three replicas of data across two to three facilities. It can keep all three replicas within a single or two different regions.

These options provides a redundancy that is critical to business projects; even if one of the data centers goes offline, the data can be replicated to another region so the data and system state of the system will not be affected. This incurs bandwidth and other costs and is not enabled by default, but it can significantly increase the level of system redundancy and resiliency.

Microsoft Azure Storage consists of four services:

- Storage Tables is used by applications that are designed to store large amounts of data. Data stored in the Tables service is structured but not relational.
- Storage Queues is a common programming abstraction designed for building distributed applications that consist of various components that should communicate with each other by small serialized messages.
- Storage Blobs is the simplest way of storing big chunks of data that are commonly binary files, such as video, music, or image files.
- The Storage Files service exposes Microsoft Azure Storage using the standard SMB 2.1 protocol, so applications using that and running in Azure are able to use filesystem APIs such as `ReadFile` and `WriteFile` or REST API at the same time.

Storage services are grouped by a logical container called account. A Microsoft Azure subscription can have up to 100 storage accounts, each of which can store up to 500 TB of data.

> To know more about the limits, quotas, and constraints of Azure subscriptions and services, refer to `http://azure.microsoft.com/en-us/documentation/articles/azure-subscription-service-limits/`.

Each storage account is secured by two auto-generated 512-bit keys that are used for authentication of requests to the storage account. Whoever has these keys has complete control over the storage account, so these keys should be treated as confidential information just like your private passwords. Each of the keys can be regenerated if compromised.

As mentioned earlier, Microsoft Azure Storage is based on REST so that its functionality can be consumed from every platform that supports HTTP. For convenience, developers can use Azure Storage SDK and libraries that provide a way to communicate with the storage leveraging the .NET object model. As shown in the following diagram, it has a parent object that is represented as a storage account: the `CloudStorageAccount` class. Next, there is a set of `CloudServiceClient` classes, where `Service` is equal to the service name; this is an entry point into the service within the storage account selected. And there are sets of classes that are specific to the service. For example, `CloudQueue` is the object that provides the functionality of enqueing, dequeing messages into a queue selected, and so on. The same goes for `CloudBlobContainer`, which represents Blob containers, and `CloudBlob`, which represents Blob objects. Both of these have functionalities specific to the Blobs.

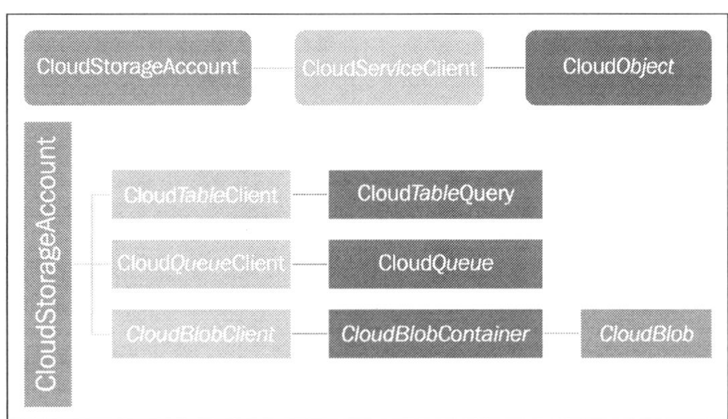

Let's have an overview of each service and then add Storage support to the Web API application.

The Microsoft Azure Storage Blobs service

The Azure Storage Blobs service (where **Blob** stands for **Binary Large Object**) allows us to store any kind of binary content into Azure documents, videos, images, databases backups, and so on.

Basically, Blobs are files like those you store on your hard drive. There are two types of Blobs: block Blobs and page Blobs. The maximum size of a block Blob is 200 Gb, and those up to a size of 64 Mb can be uploaded in one operation. If a block Blob is of a larger size, it can be split into multiple blocks that will be uploaded in parallel and committed after that. Azure can tie them together and expose them as a file. Page Blobs can be up to 1 Tb in size and represent a collection of 512-byte pages. You can write or update a specific page, and that is the main difference between block Blobs and page Blobs. The primary use of page Blobs is for **Virtual Hard Drives (VHDs)** that are used everywhere in Azure as a backend for virtual machines or data storage.

As the Blob service is REST-based, each file placed into Blob storage gets a unique URL. As shown in the preceding diagram, it follows a strict syntax. First, the base URL for accessing Blobs or containers, `http://storageaccountname.blob.core.windows.net/`, is used. Then, container and Blob names are added. This is exactly like a filesystem, except it is on the cloud.

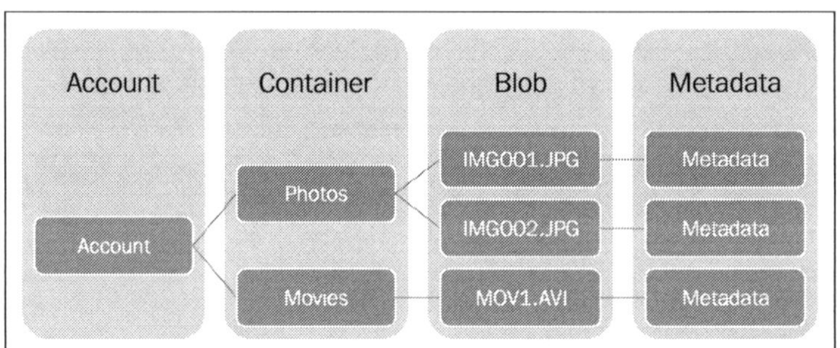

Security

Azure Storage has a simple access control model. By default, the Storage account has a single key that is used to control access and only the owner of the storage account may access data within that account. The developer has the following options for permitting access if there is a need to do that:

- **Container-level permissions** (only Blob service): The developer can set a container's permissions to permit the access to the container and Blobs within.

- **Shared access signature**: Resources can be exposed via shared access signatures. This provides developers with a way to dynamically create signatures by specifying the interval for which data is available and the set of permissions that a client will have; for example, read-write access to the Blob for one hour. It should be regenerated when expired or it will be revoked automatically.
- **Stored access policy**: Stored access policy can be used to manage shared access signatures and provides an advanced access management functionality.

The Microsoft Azure Storage Queues service

Microsoft Azure Storage Queues is a ready-to-use REST-based service that provides reliable, persistent messaging within and between services. The Storage Queues service provides a FIFO message delivery system and is also addressable with URL; so, every queue receives a URL resembling `http://storageaccountname.queue.core.windows.net/queue`.

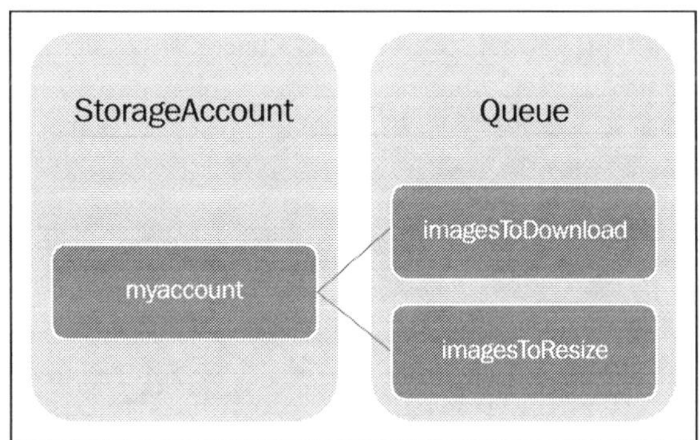

To find out about differences between Service Bus Queues and Storage Queues, refer to `https://msdn.microsoft.com/en-us/library/azure/hh767287.aspx`.

Typically, the use of the Storage Queues service follows the work ticket pattern—a message that is placed by a producer contains a task that has to be completed by a consumer. Take, for example, a website with an image gallery that contains thumbnails as well. It has a frontend with the upload form and backend that processes images. When a user uploads an image, it is placed into a Blob in the Storage Blobs service. Then, the frontend gets a link to that Blob and generates a message whose body consists of this link. The queue can't hold a large message, such as an image, and sending the link instead provides the solution to that limitation as well as reducing the copy overhead. The backend receives the message, extracts the link from it, gets the Blob with the image, processes it (generating the thumbnail), places it into another Blob, gets the link to the processed Blob, and sends the message to another queue that is going to the database.

Previously, we mentioned the message that we place into the queue. What exactly is a message, if we are talking about Azure Storage Queue? Basically, a message is an entity that can be sent into the queue. Microsoft Azure Storage Queues messages are entities that can be serialized as XML or as a base64 text. Each message can be up to 64 Kb in size. 64 Kb is not the maximum payload you can use for the message. Actually, the overhead of the base64 encoding leads to a maximum payload of just 48 Kb, so it should be taken into account when designing a system. This means that queue messages are not a proper way of transferring large amounts of data; they are about describing what a worker has to do and giving a link to the data if needed.

There are several options to receive messages from a queue: a client can peek at messages to see what's in the queue and get messages. When peeking at messages, you do not own the returned messages exclusively; this means that the message is not actually retrieved. While getting messages, you own the message for a specified time. You can also read more than one message per request, but no more than 32 messages.

One of the most important questions about using Azure Storage Queues is the concurrency. The situation when concurrency becomes a concern in the Storage Queues is when multiple receivers retrieve messages. When the receiver retrieves a message, the response he has consists of the message and a pop receipt value that should be used to delete the message. In the Azure Storage Queue service, the message is not automatically deleted but becomes invisible for other clients for the time interval specified. The client should delete the message before the `TimeNextVisible` element of the response that is calculated based on the value of the time interval.

Azure Queues do not support either optimistic or pessimistic concurrency, so the client processing retrieved messages should ensure the idempotency of the processing. Update operations use the "last writer wins" strategy.

Another important issue is the poison message problem. Basically, a poison message is a message that contains information that the client cannot successfully process. It can be a malformed message, a lack of client computing resources, or any other reason that leads to the situation when the execution time exceeds certain limits.

The first solution for the poison messages issue is to send a message to the sender using another queue. In this case, we see that message as another kind of result. Another way is to create a special dead letter queue for poison messages where we will send all messages that cannot be successfully processed. Then, we review the list of all the failing messages and decide what to do with each of them.

One of the differences between Azure Storage Queues and Service Bus Queues is that Service Bus Queues provides automatic dead-lettering.

So, what makes Azure Storage Queues a perfect scalability mechanism? As mentioned earlier, the primary reason for using queues is to connect separated components of the distributed system. While simply calling a web service from a client, you rely on both sides; if one is down, there is no communication. It is also hard to scale up and down the system depending on amount of work. If you implement a queue mechanism, you have a third side that plays the role of a buffer and broker. If the web service is down, the client can still send requests that are placed in the queue while it is waiting for the web server to come back online. Queues are also the effective component of an automatic scalability strategy. Based on the number of messages within the queue, the system can change the number of backend workers, increasing it if the volume of messages is high or decreasing it if there are none or not many of them. This adds to the scalability and flexibility of the Microsoft Azure platform itself, and you have a powerful yet simple queue mechanism.

One of the strategies of scaling queues is to create multiple queues and spray messages to them randomly. The main limitation of that strategy is that a single storage account has a limit of operations per second. To find out about best practices for maximizing scalability of Queue-based solutions, refer to `https://msdn.microsoft.com/en-us/library/azure/hh697709.aspx`.

The Microsoft Azure Storage Tables service

The Microsoft Azure Storage Table service is a non-relational, key-value-pair storage system that gives us the opportunity to store large amounts of unstructured data in tables. The Microsoft Azure Table service is optimized in the way that the data is very simple and fast to retrieve or insert (in a NoSQL way). We will cover the very basics of the Microsoft Azure Table service. As this service is REST-based, every entity that is going to be saved into the table gets a unique URL. As shown earlier, it follows a strict syntax. First, the base URL starts with `http://storageaccountname.table.core.windows.net/`. Then, the table name is added.

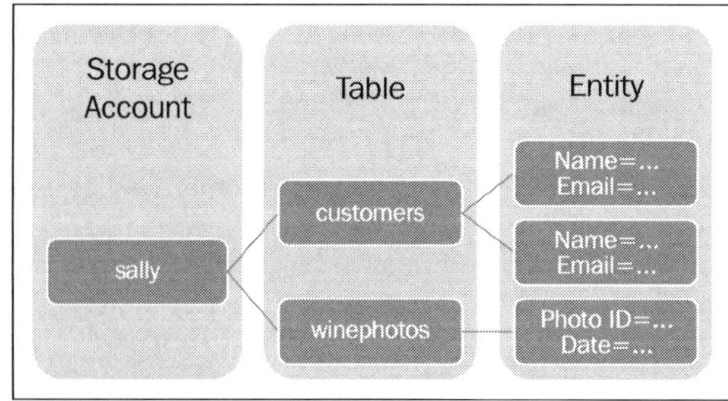

Tables and entities

In the Microsoft Azure Tables service, the term "Table" is used to describe a group of stored entities. An entity is a row of data, and a row is a set of properties. Tables do not have (or need) the same schema, so we can have an entity that stores information about different categories of products, for example.

Entities can have up to 252 properties. The size of all of the properties and values is below 1 Mb, and they can be one of these supported data types: `Byte array`, `Boolean`, `DateTime`, `Double`, `GUID`, `Int32`, `Int64`, and `String`.

Each entity has three essential properties: `PartitionKey`, `RowKey`, and `TimeStamp`. These properties are used not only to group entities within a table but also to increase (or decrease, in the case of incorrect use) the scalability and efficiency of access to the table. The `PartitionKey` is used for grouping entities within a specific partition, and the `RowKey` is a unique identifier of the entity within that partition. The combination of both in a relational world could have an analogy of a primary key. `PartitionKey` and `RowKey` values are indexed, creating a clustered index and enabling fast look-ups. At the same time, the Table service does not have any secondary indexes.

> The lack of secondary indexes is the important reason behind the need for getting the design correct upfront. It is difficult to change it later. Relational database performance issues can often be addressed by adding indexes, but this is not an option with the Table service. `PartitionKey` and `RowKey` values are crucial components of the Table design. If their choice is not right or optimal, it can significantly decrease the overall performance. On the other hand, if chosen correctly, they will improve performance.
>
> Patterns that can be used in addressing all these issues and questions can be found in the Storage Table design guide at `http://azure.microsoft.com/en-gb/documentation/articles/storage-table-design-guide/`.

The `Timestamp` property is the property that is set by a system and has the value of the last time the entity was created or modified. This property can be used to detect whether the entity value changes within a specific time period (using `ETag`).

You can store up to 200 Tb of data in one table if you want as 200 Tb is the upper limit of data size that you can store inside one storage account.

Using Microsoft Azure Storage in the Web API application

In the previous chapter, we performed a data storage in the Microsoft Azure SQL database or relational cloud-hosted data storage. In this chapter we will create a data source that will be hosted in Microsoft Azure. We will use Azure Storage Tables, continuing to use the application we did in the previous chapter.

Creating storage accounts

There are three ways you can create a new storage account in Azure:

- **PowerShell**: You can download needed commandlets from the `http://azure.microsoft.com/en-us/` website and use a new Azure Storage Account.
- **Old management portal**: You can create a new storage account using the old management portal that can be found on `http://manage.windowsazure.com`. This is the portal we will use.
- **RESTful API** (**Azure Management API**): You can invoke REST API programmatically to create a new storage account.

The first step is to create a new Microsoft Azure Storage account:

1. Open the Azure Management portal, which can be found at `http://manage.windowsazure.com`.
2. On the left-hand side of the page, select **Storage** and **Quick Create**.

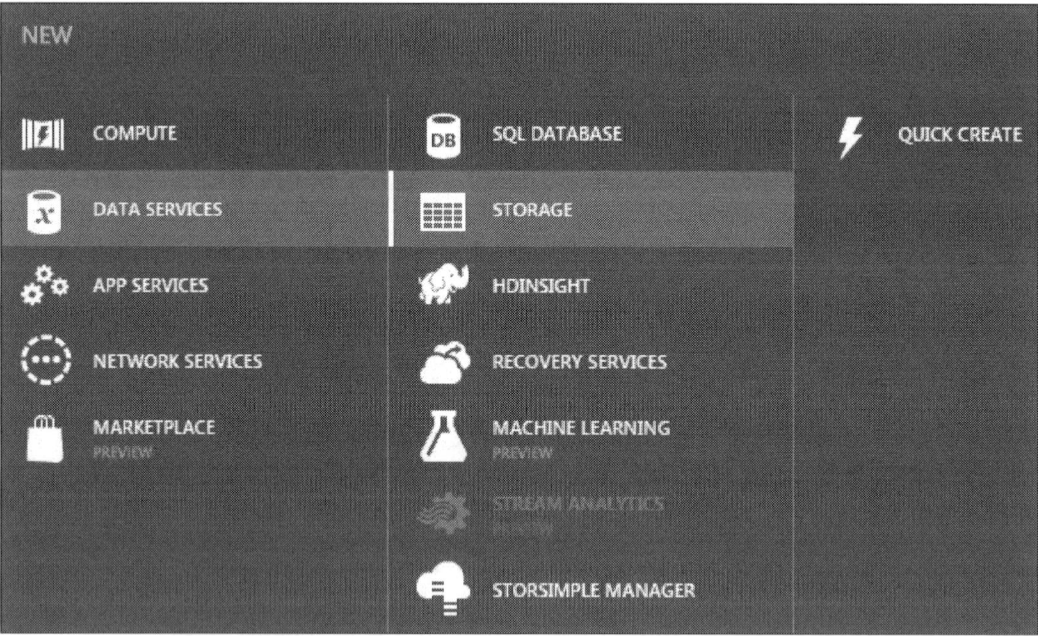

3. Enter the information into the fields. There is only one mandatory empty field, URL; you can fill it in and leave the others with their default values.

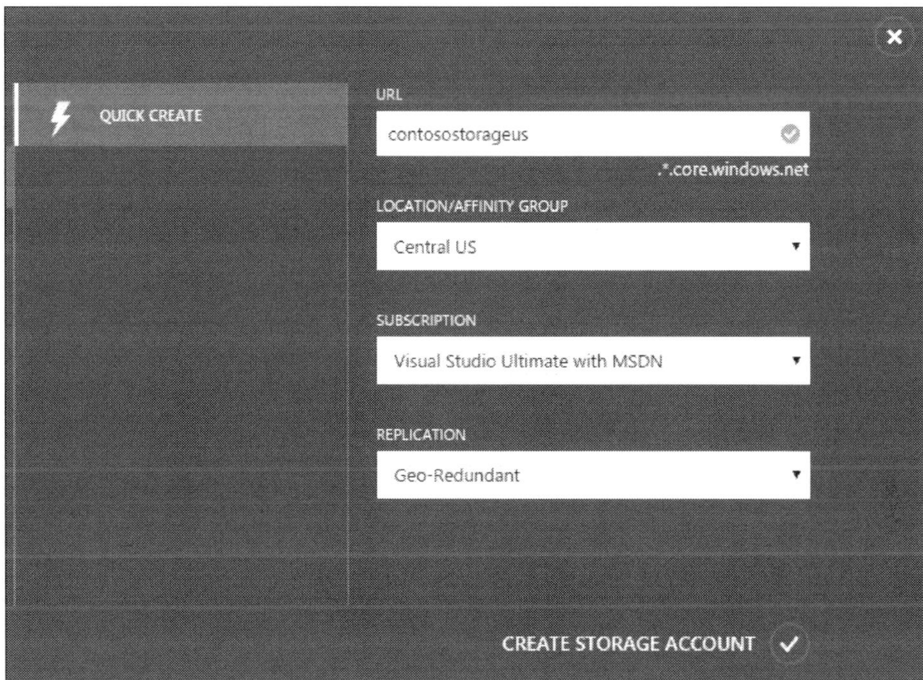

Options available in this wizard include:

- **URL**: This is the name that will be included in the base URL. It should be unique as it will be a globally used DNS name.
- **Location**: This is where the account will be located. It can be in the specific region that is a logical container for grouping resources inside the specific data center, thus decreasing the latency between them. Placing the storage account in the same region with the application will minimize the latency.
- **Subscription**: This is the subscription that should be used for the account.
- **Replication**: Redundancy mode should be used for the account. In our case, it will be Geo-Redundant so every entity will be replicated into two data centers.

4. Click on **Create Storage Account** at the bottom.
5. To access your storage account, you need to use 512-bit storage access keys generated for you by Microsoft Azure.

6. Select the storage account you want to manage.
7. At the bottom of the page click on **Manage Access Keys**.

8. You can use a primary key for your own account as the account administrator and give your co-administrator a secondary one so that you will always be able to manage the storage account and regenerate the secondary one if needed.

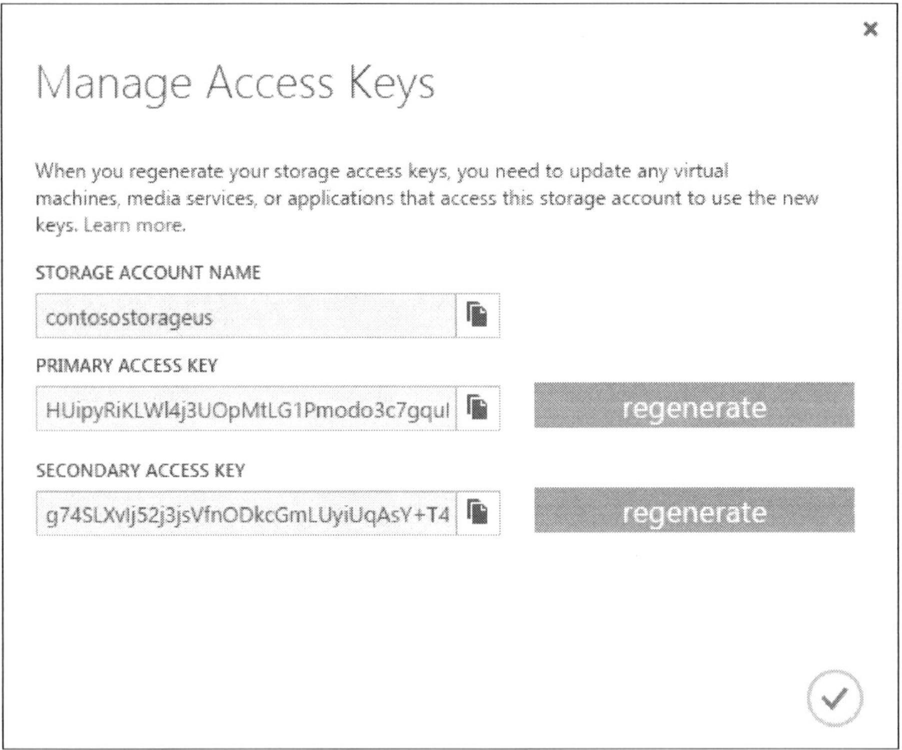

9. For now, get a copy of the primary key by clicking on the copy icon.

We did create a Microsoft Azure Storage account and got the key to manage it. The next step is to add storage support to the Web API application.

Adding storage support to the Web API application

There are a few ways to add Storage support to the application. The first one is to add needed libraries and dependencies manually. The second one is to use the NuGet package manager; we will use the package manager console, but it also has a GUI that can be used the same way.

1. Click on **Tools** and select **NuGet Package Manager**. Select **Package Manager Console**. This will load the Package Manager Console.

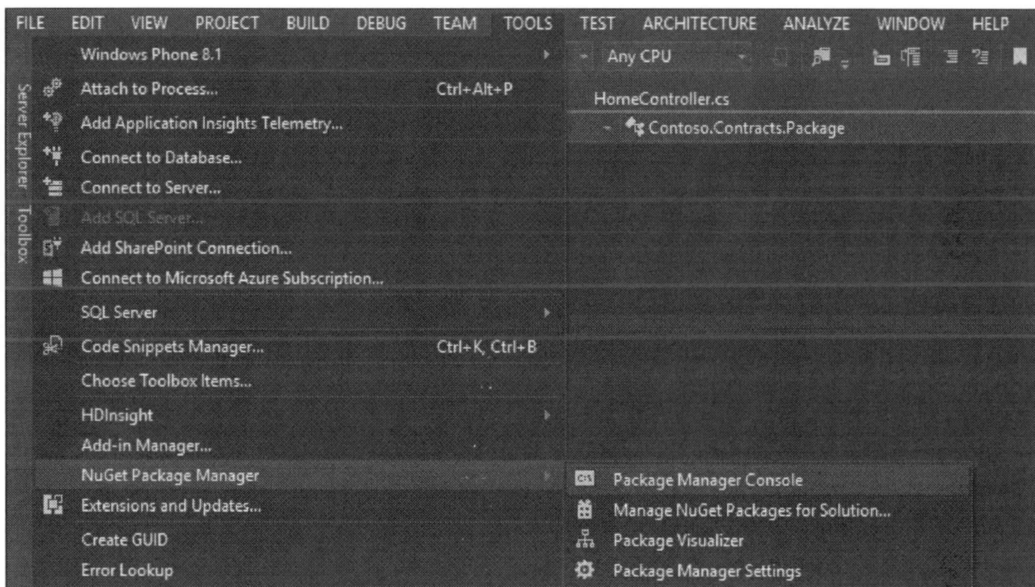

2. Execute the command for installing the needed dependencies and references:

   ```
   Install-Package WindowsAzure.Storage
   ```

3. Open the `PackageController.cs` file and add the following `using` statements:

   ```
   using Microsoft.WindowsAzure.Storage;
   using Microsoft.WindowsAzure.Storage.Auth;
   using Microsoft.WindowsAzure.Storage.Table;
   ```

4. Add the method `InitializeStorageAccount`. This method will return `CloudStorageAccount` for further use:

   ```
   private CloudStorageAccount InitializeStorageAccount()
   {
       string accountName = "";
   ```

```
        string accountKey = "";
        StorageCredentials creds =
          new StorageCredentials(accountName, accountKey);
        CloudStorageAccount account =
          new CloudStorageAccount(creds, useHttps: true);
        return account;
    }
```

Modify the preceding code and change the placeholders for `accountName` and `accountKey` to match your own storage account values.

In this code we used `accountName` and `accountKey` to create an instance of the `StorageCredential` class that is then used as a base for creating an instance of the `CloudStorageAccount` class that represents the storage account in the object model of the application. This is the main entry point into the cloud storage and it provides the functionality for Blobs, Queues, and Tables. We also use the additional argument `useHttps`. Storage has a REST-based API, so every call we make should be encrypted over the wire.

There are many other ways of creating the `CloudStorageAccount` object—for example, using the `CloudStorageAccount.Parse` static method. You can also store the credentials in the configuration file:

1. Open the `Package.cs` file and change it so that the class is inherited from `TableEntity`, not from `Entity`. `TableEntity` is a base class that provides such properties as `PartitionKey`, `RowKey`, and `Timestamp`:

   ```
   public class Package : TableEntity
   ```

2. Add the `using` directives:

   ```
   using Microsoft.WindowsAzure.Storage.Table;
   using System.Diagnostics;
   ```

3. Add the method `SavePackageToTheTable(Package package)` to the end of `PackageController`:

   ```
   private void SavePackageToTheTable(Package package)
   {
       try
       {
           CloudTableClient client =
             InitializeStorageAccount()
             .CreateCloudTableClient();
           CloudTable table =
             client.GetTableReference("packages");
   ```

```
            table.CreateIfNotExists();

            TableOperation insertOperation =
              TableOperation.Insert (package);
            table.Execute(insertOperation);

            Debug.WriteLine("Insert operation is done.");

        }
        catch (Exception ex)
        {
            Debug.WriteLine(ex);
        }

    }
```

4. Change the content of the `PostPackage` method as follows:

```
public void PostPackage(Package p)
{
    SavePackageToTheTable(p);
}
```

After the instance of `CloudStorageAccount` (we did invoke the `InitializeStorageAccount`) is returned, the code uses it to create the instance of `CloudTableClient`, which is used to interact with the Tables service. Then, by using the `GetTableReference` method of the `CloudTableClient`, the code creates a `CloudTable` object that represents a specific table. Note that the `GetTableReference` method is not safe; if there is no table in the storage and you try to invoke any operation, you receive the server error `TableNotFound`. It can easily be mitigated by the use of the `CreateIfNotExist` method of the `CloudTable` object. `CreateIfNotExist` can be called multiple times; when there is no table, it creates one, but if a table can be found it performs just a check.

Next, the code creates a `TableOperation` object that is a logical representation of a table operation. In our case, we use it as an insert, so we use the Insert method. The `Execute` method allows us to execute the `TableOperation` object. When this object is called, the `OData` command is generated and sent to the REST API. There are multiple operations that can be used with `TableOperations`: `Delete`, `Replace`, and `Merge`, among others.

Let's test this operation manually. For this, you can use a tool such as Fiddler (available at `http://www.telerik.com/fiddler`) or cURL.

In Fiddler, select the **Composer** pane. Enter the address of the Web API POST operation, and select **POST**. Enter `Content-Type:application/json` into the flags window as it will indicate that the format of the outcoming message should be treated like a JSON. Fill the **Request Body** field as shown in the following screenshot and click on the **Execute** button. You can use any online GUID generator to create the value for the **AccountNumber** field.

You should see the line **Insert operation is done** within a Debug window in Visual Studio. Note that, even if you pass the JSON payload, it is correctly serialized into the object model used in the application.

Click on the **Execute** button again to see whether the error appears.

```
Request Information
RequestID:8313ec39-0002-012b-7888-79a9dd000000
RequestDate:Mon, 29 Dec 2014 18:11:30 GMT
StatusMessage:Conflict
ErrorCode:EntityAlreadyExists
```

To know more about the Tables service error code values and their descriptions, refer to `http://msdn.microsoft.com/en-us/library/azure/dd179438.aspx`.

The error code is obvious; a unique entity with the `PartitionKey` and `RowKey` is already in the table. Our method is actually not idempotent; the method `Insert` will throw an error when there is a duplicate entity in the table. To fix this, change the `Insert` method to `InsertOrReplace`.

```
TableOperation insertOperation = TableOperation.
InsertOrReplace(package);
```

Click on the **Execute** button again to ensure that everything works fine.

Viewing data from the table

We successfully added the Package entity to the table. There are many ways of viewing data from the table. We will take a look at querying the table via code and using Visual Studio Server Explorer Azure integration. Data can be programmatically queried from the table by using various options.

You can use `TableOperation`, passing `PartitionKey` and `RowKey` values:

```
try
{
    CloudTableClient client =
      InitializeStorageAccount().CreateCloudTableClient();
    CloudTable table = client.GetTableReference("packages");
    TableOperation retrieveOperation =
      TableOperation.Retrieve<Package>("ny", "wa");
```

```
        TableResult query = table.Execute(retrieveOperation);
        if (query.Result != null)
        {
            Debug.WriteLine("Package: {0}",
              ((Package)query.Result).Destination);
        }
        else
        {
            Console.WriteLine("The packages from that
              region were not found."); }     }
            catch (Exception ex)
            {
                Console.WriteLine(ex); }
```

The code calls the `Retrieve` method, passing `PartitionKey` and `RowKey` values. A much more advanced way of querying is the use of filters, basically a mechanism that allows limiting the set of data returned by a query. Change the content of the `GetPackages` method to the following code:

```
    CloudTableClient client =
      InitializeStorageAccount().CreateCloudTableClient();
        CloudTable table = client.GetTableReference("packages");
        TableQuery<Package> query = new TableQuery<Package>().Where(
        TableQuery.GenerateFilterCondition
          ("PartitionKey", QueryComparisons.Equal, "ny"));
        var packages = table.ExecuteQuery(query);
        foreach (Package package in packages)
        {
            Debug.WriteLine("Package. AccountNumber: {0},
              Destination: {1}, Origin: {2}",
              package.AccountNumber, package.Destination,
              package.Origin);
        }
        return packages.AsQueryable<Package>();
    }
```

This code generates a `TableQuery` object using LINQ-like syntax and filters. Filters are a powerful mechanism that can be used with any supported data type. This code generates a filter condition that is applied when iterating through records in the table. In our case, only records with the `PartitionKey` value that is equal to `ny` will be returned. In Fiddler, select **GET** and click on the **Execute** button.

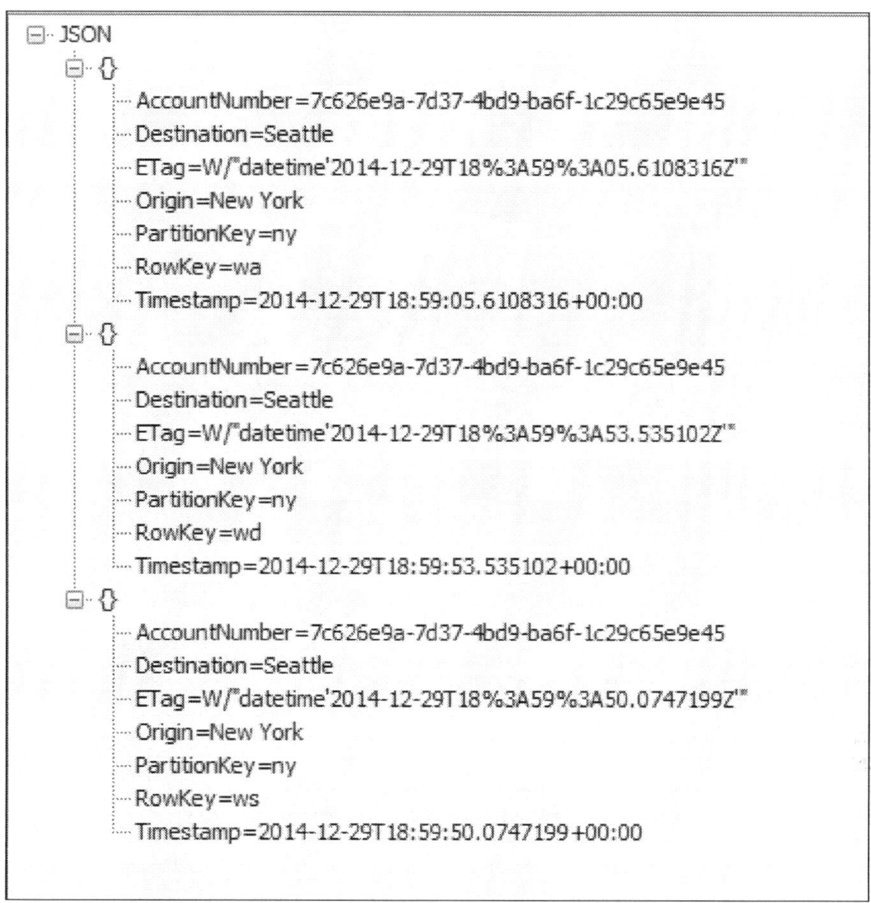

Filters can be combined:

```
TableQuery.CombineFilters(
  TableQuery.GenerateFilterCondition("PartitionKey",
  QueryComparisons.Equal, "ny"),
TableOperators.Or,
                     TableQuery.GenerateFilterCondition("PartitionKey",
  QueryComparisons.Equal, "se")
```

The result of the execution has an IEnumerable type, so you can use LINQ operators.

We just queried the table via the code. Let's now take a look at the Visual Studio built-in functionality to do the same:

1. In Visual Studio, press *Ctrl* + *Alt* + *S* to open Server Explorer. The latest versions of Visual Studio are integrated with Microsoft Azure, so you can administer some of the services. Click on the **Azure** branch to open it.

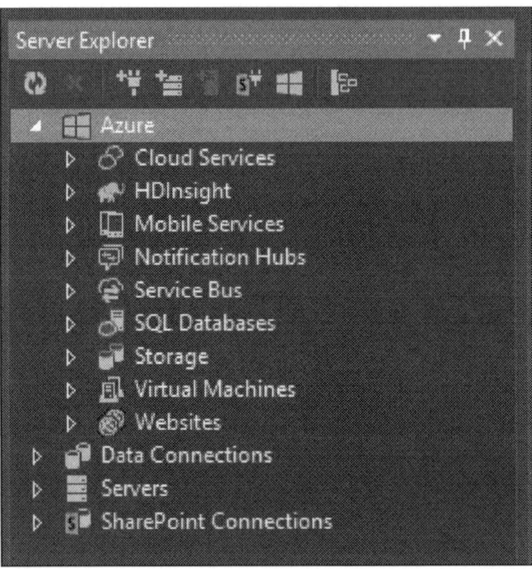

2. Click on the **Storage** branch to open it. If you did not log in already, the login page will appear. It will take a few seconds to load your resources.

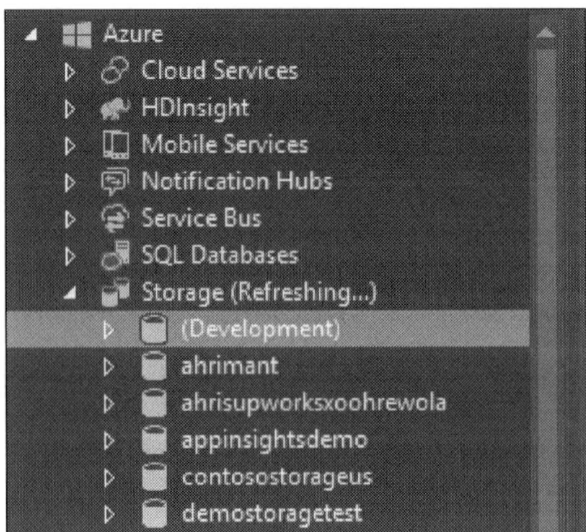

3. Click on the needed storage account to load its resources. Select the **Tables** branch.

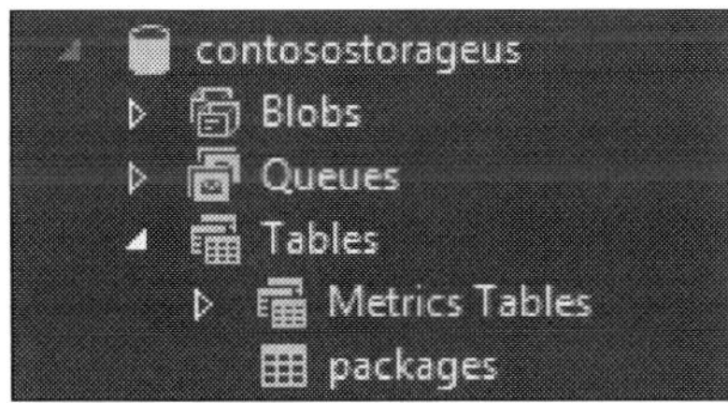

4. Now you have access to the tables stored in the storage account. There are Metrics Tables that are important in the process of diagnosing any issues with the storage account and user tables. Click on the **packages** table to see its content.

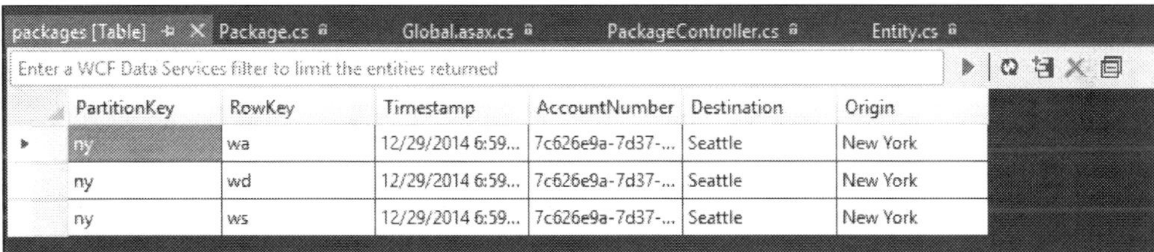

5. The visual interface has basic functionality; you can add, delete, and change entities. You can also execute WCF Data Services filters. For your convenience, there is an integrated visual tool that helps to generate a filter value.

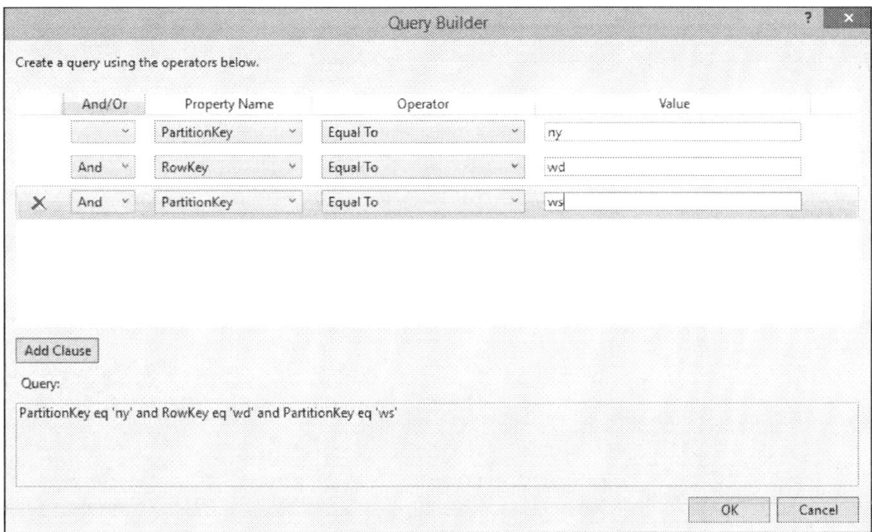

Summary

This chapter provided an overview of the Microsoft Azure Storage services—Tables, Queues, and Blobs—and the use of the Tables service for storing data within the cloud storage using API and Visual Studio Server Explorer. Microsoft Azure Storage is one of the main components of Microsoft Azure, offering cloud storage in a scalable and redundant way. Being a REST-based service, Microsoft Azure Storage functionality is agile and can be consumed from any platform that supports HTTP.

In the next chapter, we will continue the exploration of data options in Microsoft Azure and will look at DocumentDB—the NoSQL document database—and Microsoft Azure Marketplace using MongoLab MongoDB as an example.

9

Data Services in the Cloud – NoSQL in Microsoft Azure

In *Chapter 7, Data Services in the Cloud – an Overview of ADO.NET and Entity Framework*, we got an overview of Entity Framework and Microsoft Azure SQL Azure databases as a data source for the Web API application. In *Chapter 8, Data Services in the Cloud – Microsoft Azure Storage*, we discussed Microsoft Azure Storage service that contains Tables, Blobs, and Queues that solve different tasks of storing the data within the reliable scalable cloud storage system, and use storage service for storing our data. In this chapter, we will discuss NoSQL and one of the options that is supported in Microsoft Azure—DocumentDB.

NoSQL technologies are extremely important in the modern world, as they are created to address problems such as effective work across many servers and workloads such as JSON documents that are not typical for relational systems. NoSQL encompasses many storage technologies that provide high scalability, different data types and formats.

Microsoft Azure supports many NoSQL technologies; some of them (such as MongoDB) are supported through Microsoft Azure Marketplace as a third-party offering by Microsoft partners, and some such as a DocumentDB, are Microsoft owned offerings.

In this chapter, we will go through the overview of NoSQL versus SQL, Microsoft Azure Marketplace that is an entry point into third-party offers (such as MongoDB and MySQL) marketplace, and Microsoft DocumentDB—a NoSQL database Microsoft developed. Next, we will go through the process of modifying our existing Web API application with the DocumentDB. To do this, we will use Visual Studio 2013.

Understanding NoSQL

Each database management system uses its own database model to manage the structure of the data kept. The choice of the database management system can have serious consequences for the database application—how the data will be stored, which structures will be used, how the application should build its database access layer, among others.

The most popular database model is the relational model (introduced in 1970s) due to its maturity; it is powerful and flexible and has a logical mathematical model that is easy to understand because of the familiar way of connecting entities with simple relations (that is, a `Person` table connected with the `Company` table).

However, there have been issues that were never addressed by the relational model, and if application demands that there should not be a strict structured data or it should be scaled in a more flexible way, then developers may assess the NoSQL model.

The NoSQL model is getting rid of some SQL limits and constraints. NoSQL databases use unstructured approach and offer many ways to work with the data in specific scenarios (for example, document or key-value storage). That schema-less approach gives the virtually unlimited process of working with entities or, on the other hand, simple process that can be extremely efficient when using key-values entities. These entities can be represented as familiar data objects or JSON, as in the case of DocumentDB. A developer can work with NoSQL data according to the ways that are provided by the implementations—each solution provides its own query mechanism.

Another significant detail about databases that becomes important in distributed systems is how a database management system handles reliable transaction processing.

There are two popular standards that can be summarized by the acronyms **Atomicity, Consistency, Isolation, Durability** (**ACID**) and **Basically Available, Soft State, Eventual Consistency** (**BASE**). There is also the **Consistency, Availability, Partition tolerance** (**CAP**) theorem that states that it is impossible for a distributed system to have all three characteristics that CAP consists of. Understanding these terms is crucial in designing database management solution.

Let's review each of these in short.

The CAP theorem explains that there are three system requirements for the successful design and implementation of any application that is going to be deployed in the distributed environment. The main problem that CAP states is that implementing all three is impossible:

- **Consistency**: Data should be consistent across all database nodes

- **Availability**: The system should be available when needed
- **Partition Tolerance**: The system should be working and responding even in case of temporary system failure or other type of interruption—failure of one or more nodes should not cause the system to stop responding

ACID says that database transactions should be:

- **Atomic**: If any part of the transaction fails, then the entire transaction should be rolled back. A transaction is considered successful only after all tasks have been performed (all or none rule).
- **Consistent**: The transaction must not make the database inconsistent in any way.
- **Isolated**: The transactions should not interfere with each other.
- **Durable**: Results of successfully completed transactions should be persistent even in case of system failure.

These characteristics often cannot be attained in large systems. If attained in a scenario such as online shopping, then when there is one user interaction with the buying process, then, some sections of the database should be locked until the user is finished. In this case, the "I" characteristic is sometimes violated by tolerating the possibility of some transactions interfering with each other. What gives the possibility of serving many clients instead of blocking or slowing down the processing pipeline because of one client.

The BASE-compliant database is using a different set of expectations (for example, it does not require the consistency after every transaction and expects the system to eventually be in the consistent state, which means that it tolerates stale data or responses that are not absolutely accurate):

- **Basically available**: The system should guarantee the availability of the data stored. Still, there is a possibility that the response can fail to obtain the needed data or the inconsistent data.
- **Soft state**: As the system state is changing even when no one is interacting with it (due to the eventual consistency), it can be described as a soft state.
- **Eventual consistency**: The system will eventually become consistent. Serving the requests and inputs, the system will continue to propagate the data without checking the consistency of every transaction.

The CAP theorem and the ACID and BASE standards play a big role in the decision making process when designing the architecture. For example, a system that works satisfactorily in real-time system can be BASE compliant. Historical data can be modeled using ACID.

Now, let's close the NoSQL and relational models overview with one last difference. Last but not least, we will discuss scalability. Both NoSQL and relational models are easy to scale vertically by increasing server resources, but in a distributed system, that is, only a part of the solution. NoSQL systems usually have easier ways to being scaled horizontally by creating clusters of multiple machines.

So, the choice of the database management software heavily depends on the scenario and the nature of the data. There is no common methodology that aims to provide the exact guidance on when and where to use one or another system.

An overview of Microsoft Azure NoSQL technologies

It is known that data storage technologies can be either relational that use SQL or nonrelational. As we already got the overview of one of the most used relational data storage methods, let's review what options are supported in Microsoft Azure:

- **Document-oriented stores**: Document-oriented databases are one of the main NoSQL databases types, and are used for storing vast amounts of semi-structured data (like JSON objects). Implementations are very different in terms of functionality and formats. An example of data could be a scanned document that needs to be processed. Microsoft has a service called DocumentDB which is integrated into Microsoft Azure.
- **Key-value stores**: Key-value databases use the associative array as a fundamental data model. In this model, data is stored as a collection of key-value pairs. The key-value model is one of the simplest data models and often is used as a base for richer models. The examples of those are Riak, Cassandra and Microsoft Azure storage tables.
- **Column stores**: Column databases store data as sections of columns of data for a particular key (instead of storing them as rows). Column stores offer very high performance and highly scalable architecture what make them a perfect candidates for use in big computations. One example is Hbase that is supported in Microsoft Azure.
- **Graph stores**: Graph stores are based on nodes and edges for the relationships and the storage of the data. One example is Neo4j that is supported in Microsoft Azure.

We will get an overview of Microsoft DocumentDB that is Microsoft developed document service.

Microsoft DocumentDB

Microsoft DocumentDB is a fully managed service by Microsoft, and is reliable, highly scalable, and capable of storing terabytes of data storage technology. The user does not need to install and manage the infrastructure for this, and the service is multi-tenant by default with the clear conceptions of scalability described in terms of capacity units, which are a specific amount of storage and reserved throughput, so the user always knows and is sure that he will receive the performance he expects. There are large Microsoft projects that use DocumentDB, for example, MSN portal. DocumentDB is a simple, fast, and reliable storage technology that can be leveraged to build applications.

The Microsoft DocumentDB object model

Every DocumentDB database contains a collection of JSON documents, but these JSON documents have nothing in common with documents such as Microsoft Office documents. The DocumentDB document is a stringified JSON object and as JSON has its roots in JavaScript, it is very easy for JavaScript or any other developer to use DocumentDB. The choice of JSON is obvious as JavaScript is a very popular way to transmit and store information on the Internet.

Collections are the containers for the JSON documents and also units of scale, transactions, and query. If you want to scale the DocumentDB database, it should be performed by increasing or distributing storage across the collections.

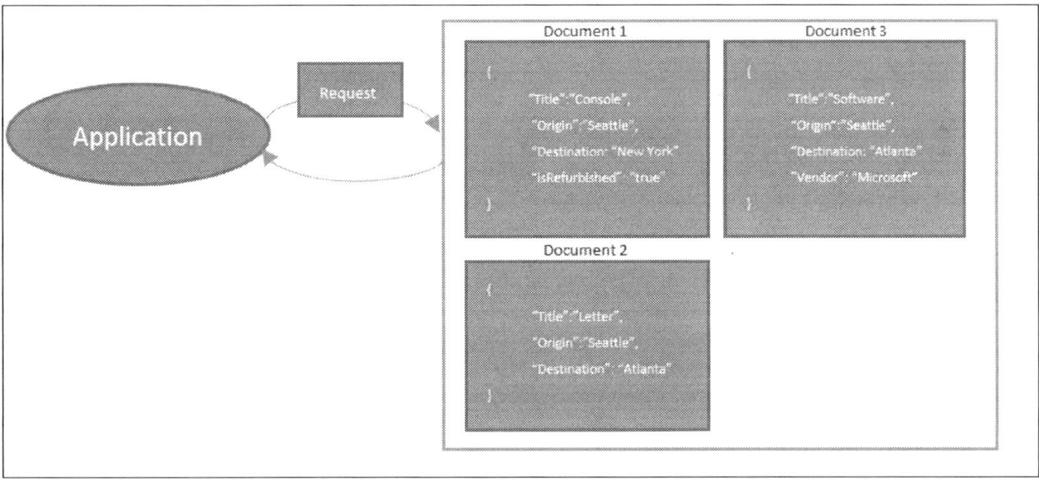

As for the data itself, instead of storing it in a row in a table, it is stored within a separate JSON document. For example, **Document 1** contains the title, origin, destination, and the isRefurbished field information for a product named **Console**. Here, we can see another difference between DocumentDB and a relational store—relational tables have a fixed schema, and each row contains a value for all of the columns, which is, for example, not true for DocumentDB. **Document 2** does not have the isRefurbished element at all and **Document 3** does have the Vendor element. DocumentDB has no fixed schema. Another advantage of DocumentDB having its roots in the NoSQL nature is that DocumentDB was designed to support vast amounts of data in a single database. In this sense, DocumentDB uses an approach of storing the collections on different servers, and that is the reason why DocumentDB is a very scalable and reliable solution. However, there is a limitation—while this approach uses distribution of collections on different servers, each query should target only one collection. Its consequence is that often accessed data will be placed in the same collection. Each collection is replicated multiple times, so if a single server experiences any problem, it will be mitigated by routing queries to another copy.

This replication has its own downside as there is no guarantee that if you choose to read the data from any available replica it will be up-to-date and consistent with the latest updates if any. As an answer to this question, DocumentDB provides three consistency levels:

- **Strong**: This is the slowest level, but it is guaranteed that there will always be correct data.
- **Bounded staleness**: This provides a guarantee that the application will receive changes in the order there were made. There is a possibility that the data will be out of date.
- **Eventual**: The fastest access level bounded with the highest possibility of getting the out-of-date data.

There are indices as well—every JSON element in every document is indexed so the access time is very small.

For accessing the data within the collections, calls to the RESTful interface should be made—DocumentDB has its own SQL-based query language that can be leveraged inside these calls as a queries. Another feature of DocumentDB is JavaScript support directly inside the core. This means that if you want to have a stored procedure or trigger, it can be written in JavaScript that will be wrapped and executed for you by the DocumentDB engine.

In the next section, we will create the DocumentDB database account and use it as a data storage in the Web API application.

DocumentDB in a Web API application

To use DocumentDB, you should create a DocumentDB database account. At the time of writing this, DocumentDB is in preview and one can create the database account only on the Microsoft Azure preview management portal.

Creating the DocumentDB database account

As said, to create a DocumentDB database account, you should log in to the Microsoft Azure preview management portal. Perform the following steps:

1. Open the Azure preview management portal that can be found at `http://portal.azure.com`.
2. Navigate to **New** | **DocumentDB**:

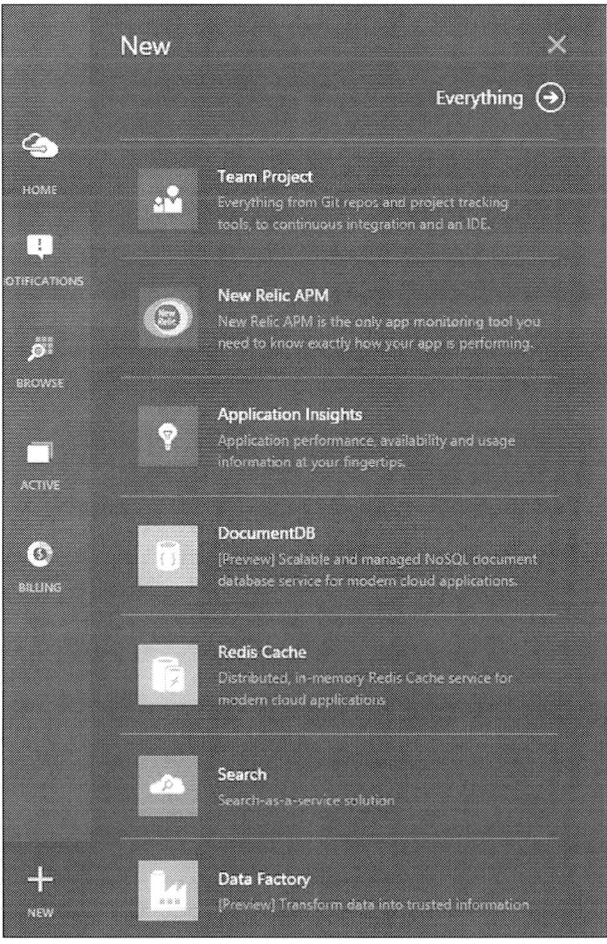

3. In the **New DocumentDB** wizard, specify the settings:

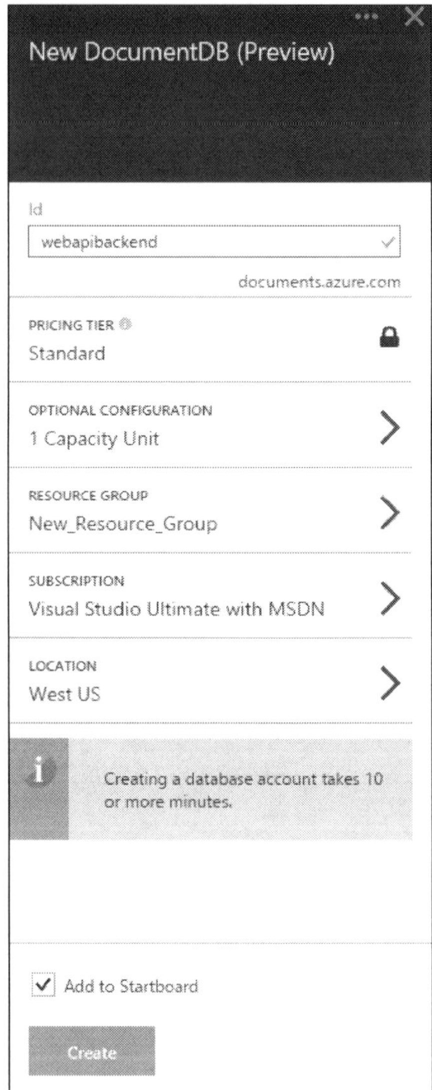

The options available in that wizard include:

- **Id**: This is the name that will be included into the base URL. It should be unique as it will be a globally used DNS name.
- **Pricing Tier**: This is what will be used to bill the account.
- **Resource Group**: These are used to manage all resources in the application together as a logical group.

- **Location**: That is the location where the account will be located. It can be located in a specific region or in an affinity group that is a logical container for grouping resources inside the specific datacenter thus decreasing the latency among them.
- **Subscription**: This is the subscription that should be used for the account.

This information will be needed further and is critical for the optimization purposes (for example, locating the database account in a region that is far away from the application will cause latency) so fill it cautiously.

4. Click on **Create** at the bottom.
5. To access your storage account, you need to use storage access keys generated for you by Microsoft Azure.
6. Select the DocumentDB account created.
7. Click on **Keys**:

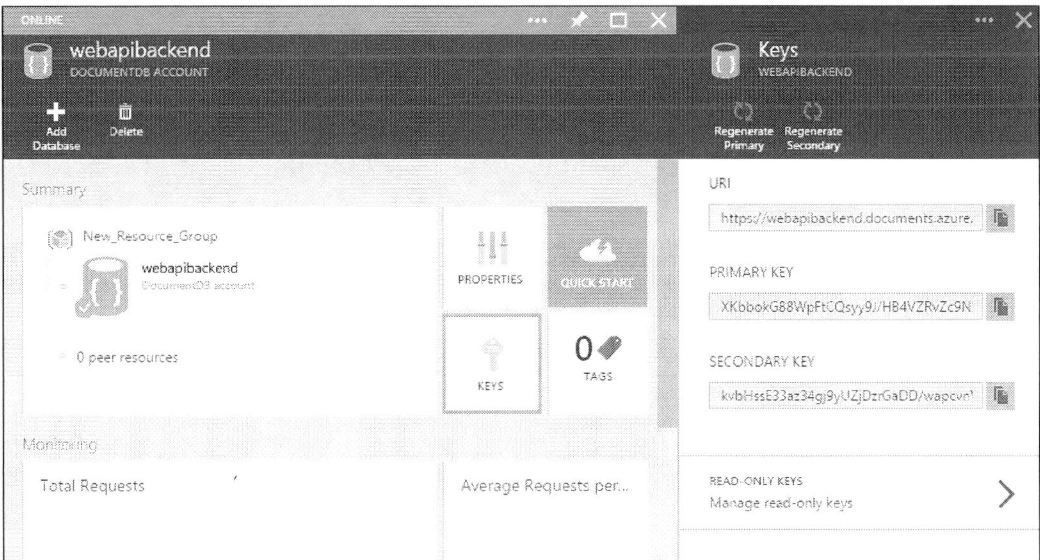

8. You can use a primary key for your own account as the account administrator and give your co-administrator a secondary key, so you will always be able to manage the storage account and regenerate the secondary key if needed.
9. For now, get a copy of the primary key by clicking on the Copy icon.

We created a DocumentDB database account and got the key to manage it. The next step is to add the DocumentDB support to the Web API application.

Using DocumentDB in the Web API application

Open the Contoso project. To use DocumentDB in the application, libraries should be installed. There is a NuGet package that we will install:

1. Click on **Tools** and select **NuGet Package Manager**. Select **Package Manager Console**. This will load the Package Manager Console.

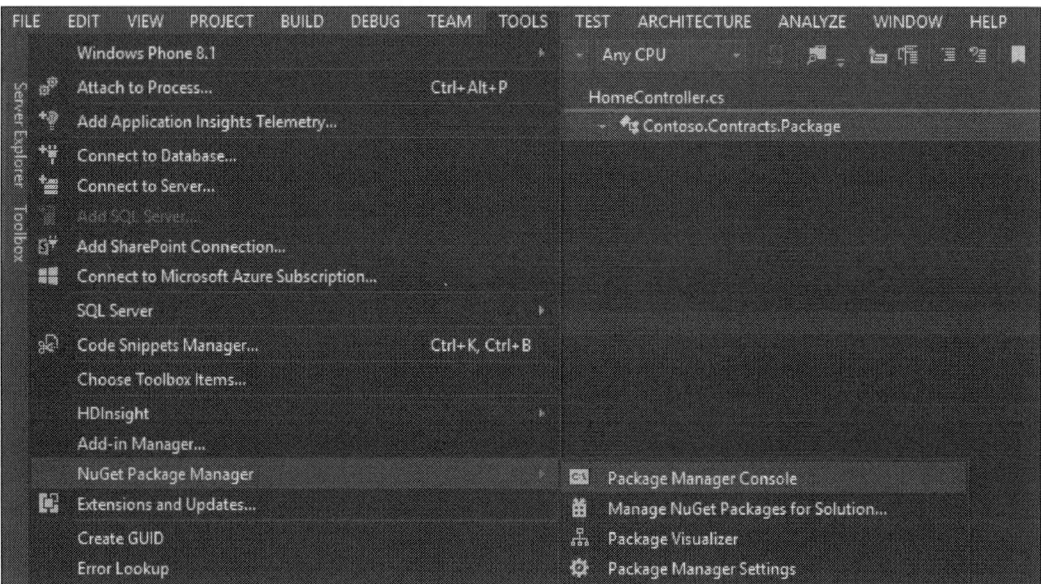

2. Execute the command to install the needed dependencies and references. The command listed here will install the DocumentDB dependencies and client library so that we are able to work with the DocumentDB database:

```
Install-Package Microsoft.Azure.Documents.Client -Pre
```

3. Open the `Web.config` file and add the following statements to the `appSettings` section:

```
<add key="EndPointUrl" value=" https://webapibackend.documents.
azure.com:443/"/>
<add key="AuthorizationKey" value=" XKbbokG88WpFtCQsyy9J/
HB4VZRvZc9NYm4V/"/>
<add key="DatabaseId" value="ContosoBackend"/>
<add key="CollectionId" value="Packages"/>
```

4. Change placeholders according to the Azure preview management portal.

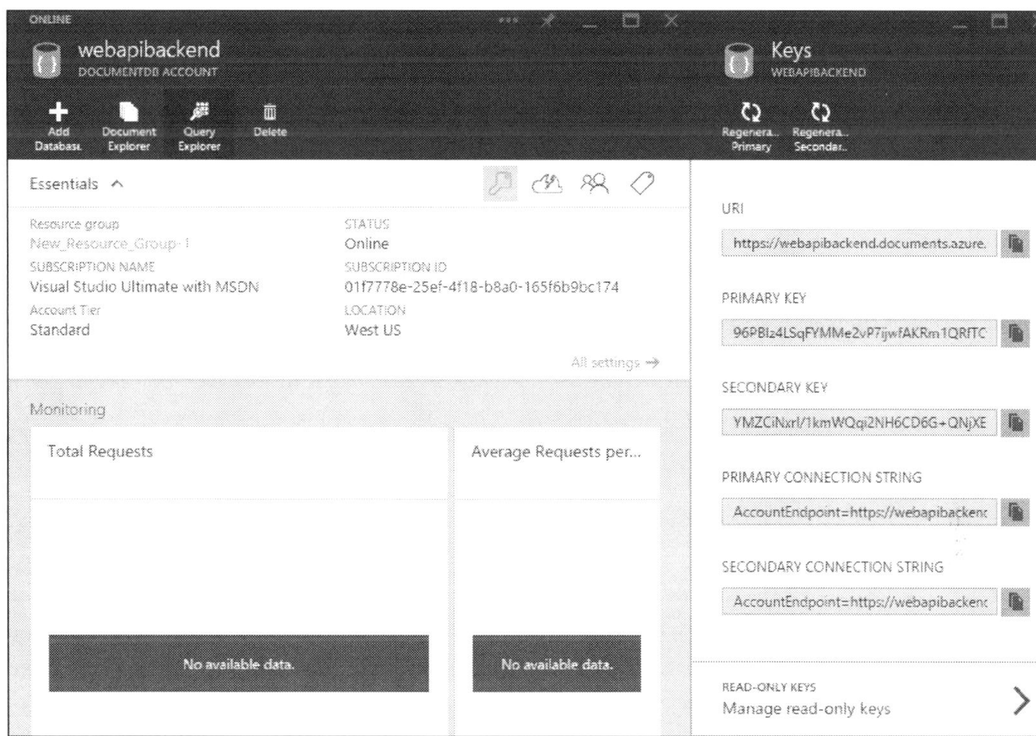

5. Create a `PackageRepository.cs` file that will be used for basic CRUD with DocumentDB.
6. Open the `PackageRepository.cs` file and add the following `using` statements:

```
using System;
using System.Collections.Generic;
using System.Configuration;
using System.Linq;
using System.Threading.Tasks;
using Contoso.Transport.Service.Models;
using Microsoft.Azure.Documents;
using Microsoft.Azure.Documents.Client;
using Microsoft.Azure.Documents.Linq;
```

7. Add the following code to the beginning of the class `PackageRepository`:

```
private static Database _database;
private static DocumentCollection _collection;
private static DocumentClient _client;

private static string _databaseId;
private static string _collectionId;
private static string _endpoint;
private static string _authKey;
```

These fields will be used for initializing the database, collection, and document by values added to the configuration file.

8. Client and collection properties will be used to initialize static fields:

```
protected static DocumentClient Client
        {
            get
            {
               Uri endpointUri = new Uri(_endpoint);
               _client = new DocumentClient(endpointUri,
                  _authKey);
               return _client;
            }
        }

        protected static DocumentCollection Collection
        {
            get { return _collection; }
        }
```

9. Add the methods `InitCollection` and `InitDatabase`. They will be used for initialization of database and collection, accordingly:

```
private static async Task InitCollection(string databaseLink)
private static async Task InitCollection(string databaseLink)
        {
            var collections = Client.CreateDocumentCollection
              Query(databaseLink).Where(c => c.Id ==
              _collectionId).ToArray();

            if (collections.Any())
            {
                _collection = collections.First();
            }
            else
```

```
            {
                _collection = await
                  Client.CreateDocumentCollectionAsync
                  (databaseLink, new DocumentCollection
                  { Id = _collectionId });
            }
        }

        private static async Task InitDatabase()
        {
            var query = Client.CreateDatabaseQuery().Where
              (d => d.Id == _databaseId);

            var databases = query.ToArray();
            if (databases.Any())
            {
                _database = databases.First();
            }
            else
            {
                _database = await Client.CreateDatabaseAsync
                  (new Database { Id = _databaseId });
            }
        }
```

10. Add the `Initialize` method. This method will call all the methods we have defined earlier and initialize the system to work with the DocumentDB:

```
private void Initialize()
    {
        _databaseId = ConfigurationManager.AppSettings
          ["DatabaseId"];
        _collectionId = ConfigurationManager.
          AppSettings["CollectionId"];
        _endpoint = ConfigurationManager.
          AppSettings["EndPointUrl"];
        _authKey = ConfigurationManager.
          AppSettings["AuthorizationKey"];
        InitDatabase().Wait();
        InitCollection(_database.SelfLink).Wait();
    }
```

11. Add the call of the `Initialize` method to the class constructor:

```
        public PackageRepository()
        {
            Initialize();
        }
```

12. Now it is time to add the CRUD functionality to our repository—the connection to the DocumentDB can be established. Add the following method to the `PackageRepository` class:

```
public Task<List<Package>> ExtractPackageAsync()
    {
        return Task<List<Package>>.Run(() =>
          Client.CreateDocumentQuery<Package>
          (Collection.DocumentsLink)
          .ToList());
    }


public Task<Package> ExtractPackageAsync(string id)
    {
        return Task<Package>.Run(() =>
          Client.CreateDocumentQuery<Package>
          (Collection.DocumentsLink)
          .Where(p => p.Id.Equals(id))
          .AsEnumerable()
          .FirstOrDefault());
    }

public Task<ResourceResponse<Document>>
  CreatePackageAsync(Package package)
    {
        return Client.CreateDocumentAsync
          (Collection.DocumentsLink, package);
    }

public Task<ResourceResponse<Document>>
  DeletePackageAsync(string id)
    {
        var doc = Client.CreateDocumentQuery<Document>
          (Collection.DocumentsLink)
          .Where(d => d.Id == id)
          .AsEnumerable()
          .FirstOrDefault();

        return Client.DeleteDocumentAsync(doc.SelfLink);
    }
```

Note that methods are asynchronous and use the LINQ that is a set of features that provides a way to query the data with the use of a syntax like C#. This is the big advantage of DocumentDB—once you establish the connection and retrieve the needed objects, you are able to use the LINQ functionality.

Let's define the `PackageController` class.

13. Add the Web API CRUD functionality to the `PackageController.cs` file. As we are using a repository, the actions follow a simple syntax and just call the repository methods:

```
public class PackageController : ApiController
    {

        private PackageRepository _repository;

        public PackageController()
        {
            _repository = new PackageRepository();
        }

        // GET: api/Package
        [HttpGet]
        public async Task<IHttpActionResult> Get()
        {
            var packages = await _repository.
ExtractPackageAsync();
            return Ok(packages);
        }

        // GET: api/Package/1
        [HttpGet]
        public async Task<IHttpActionResult> Get(string id)
        {
            var packages = await _repository.
              ExtractPackageAsync(id);
            return Ok(packages);
        }
        // POST: api/Package
        [ResponseType(typeof(Package))]
        [HttpPost]
        public async Task<IHttpActionResult>
          PostPackage(Package package)
        {
            if (!ModelState.IsValid)
            {
                return BadRequest(ModelState);
            }

            var response = await _repository.
```

```
                    CreatePackageAsync(package);
                return Ok(response.Resource);
            }

        public async Task<IHttpActionResult> DeletePackage(string id)
            {
                var response = await _repository.
                    DeletePackageAsync(id);
                return Ok();
            }
    }
```

14. Add the following `using` directive to the `PackageController` class:

    ```
    using Newtonsoft.Json;
    ```

15. The last change we should make is the correction of the `Package` class itself. Add the `string Id` field to the code. Add the `JsonProperty` attribute:

    ```
    [JsonProperty(PropertyName = "id")]
            public string Id { get; set; }
    ```

We created the repository with the basic CRUD functionality, Web API controller, and everything needed to establish the connection to the DocumentDB database account.

Testing the Web API with the DocumentDB database account

Let's test the operation manually. As previously shown, it can be done with the help of Fiddler or cURL.

In Fiddler, select the **Composer** pane. Enter the address of the Web API operation and select **POST**. Enter `Content-Type` as `application/son` into the flags window as it will indicate that the format of the outcoming message should be treated like JSON. Fill **Request Body** as shown in the image and press the **Execute** button.

Note the new `Id` field that is used as a unique identifier of the document:

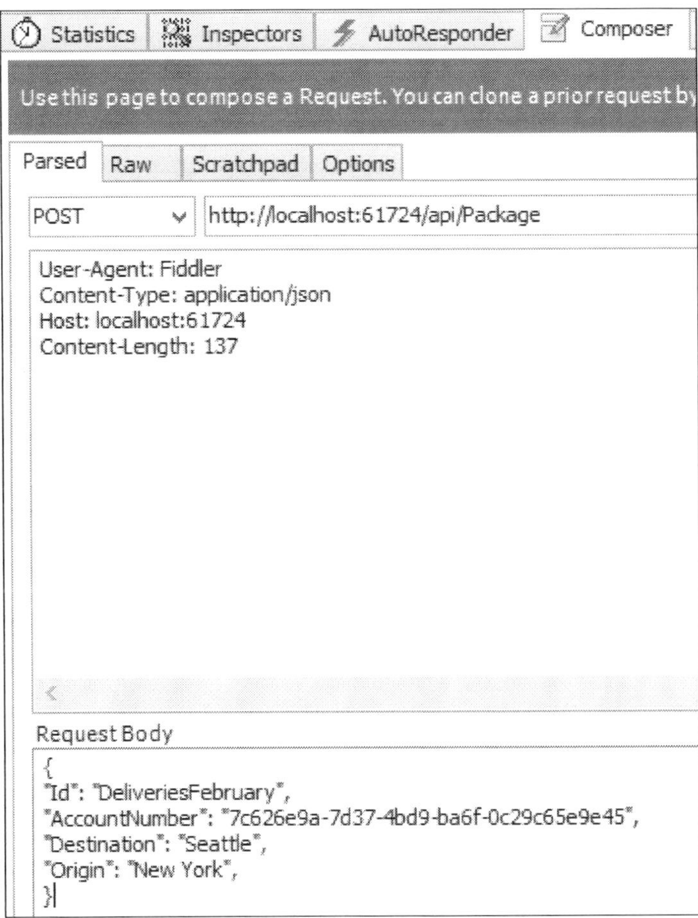

You should see the line `Insert operation is done` within a **Debug** window in Visual Studio.

We successfully added the `Package` entity information in the form of a DocumentDB document. There are many ways of viewing data from the table. We will take a look at querying the document via code and using the Microsoft Azure preview management portal DocumentDB explorer.

As we have already implemented the functionality to read the data from the document, use Fiddler to call the `Get` action of the `Package` controller.

When action is executed and information retrieved, you will able to view the payload you received.

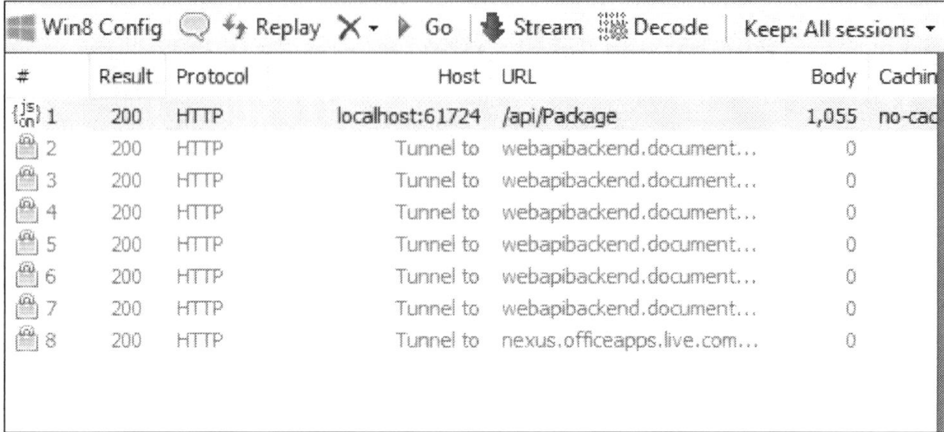

Click on the record in the Fiddler explorer window to view the result.

We did query to the document within the DocumentDB collection via the code. Let's take a look at the Microsoft Azure preview management portal functionality to do the same. If you want to use the desktop client, there is DocumentDB Studio on GitHub.

On the preview management portal, press on your DocumentDB database account. Next, click on the **Document Explorer** tile to load it. With the help of the explorer, you can do the basic functionality—view, edit, and add documents.

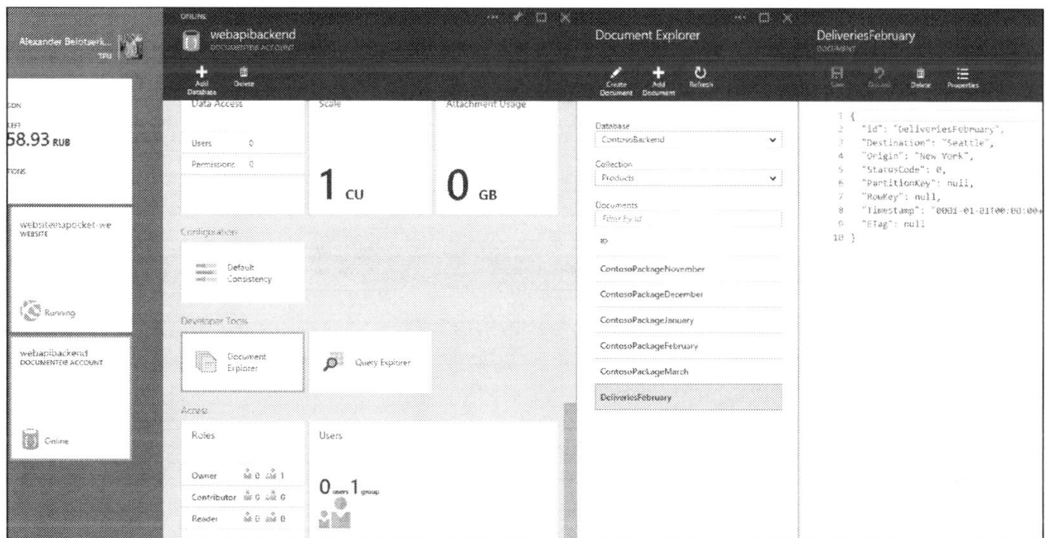

Using Fiddler, call the `Delete` action of the `Package` controller to delete the document from the DocumentDB storage.

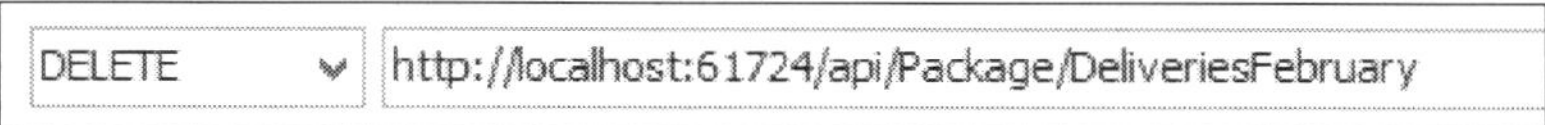

Here, we saw an overview of the DocumentDB service and integrating it into the application. In the next section, we will go through the process of creating an account for MongoDB using Microsoft Azure Marketplace.

Microsoft Azure Marketplace

Microsoft Azure is a platform that has many integrated managed services, including data storage services, and many more that are supported through a partner channel that is called Microsoft Azure Marketplace preview. Basically, it is the marketplace where you can create an account for any partner-provided offering and purchase it if you think that it suits your needs. Among the NoSQL choices that are available through the Microsoft Azure Marketplace are:

- MongoDB services provided by MongoLab
- Redis Cloud store based on Redis
- RavenHQ store based on RavenDB

Almost all offerings that are available for purchase through Microsoft Azure Marketplace are managed by partners, and it should be taken into account that any issues are to be resolved by these partners' technical support, but not by Microsoft Azure.

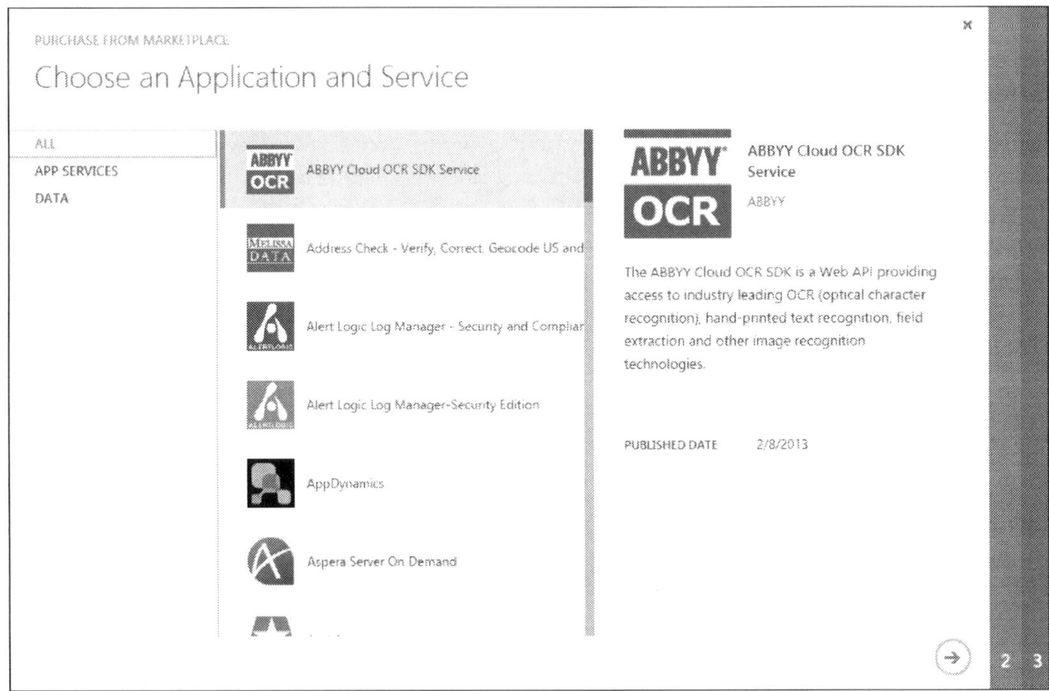

You are also free to install and run any NoSQL software in Microsoft Azure virtual machines creating your own environment that can be set up as needed. Offerings available as services through Microsoft Azure Store are almost fully managed by partners, so you will not have to spend time creating a scalable and reliable database infrastructure. At the same time, you would have the same degree of control in setting a database up as you have when using virtual machines.

MongoLab MongoDB on Microsoft Azure

The Microsoft Azure Marketplace is the place where independent software vendors can offer their solutions to Azure customers. It enables Microsoft Azure developers to use software from third-party vendors like MongoDB, MySQL, and RavenHQ among others. The software is used on a subscription basis.

Creating a MongoLab MongoDB subscription

The first step is to create a new MongoLab MongoDB subscription:

1. Open the Azure management portal that can be found at `http://manage.windowsazure.com`.
2. On the left-hand side of the page, select **Marketplace**.

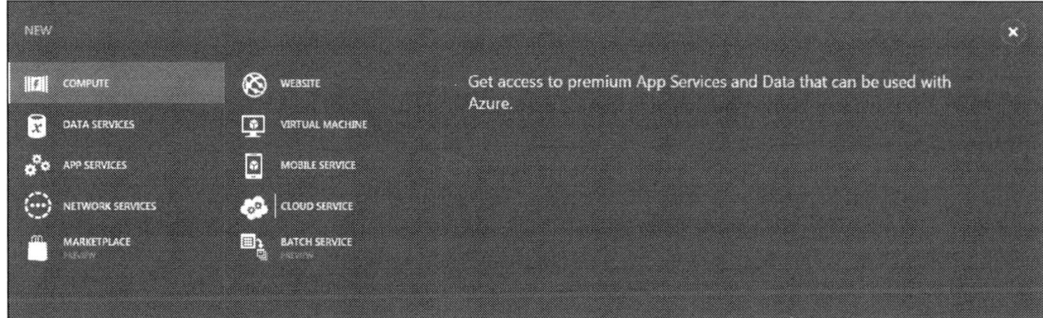

3. Select **MongoLab** in the **App Services** branch.

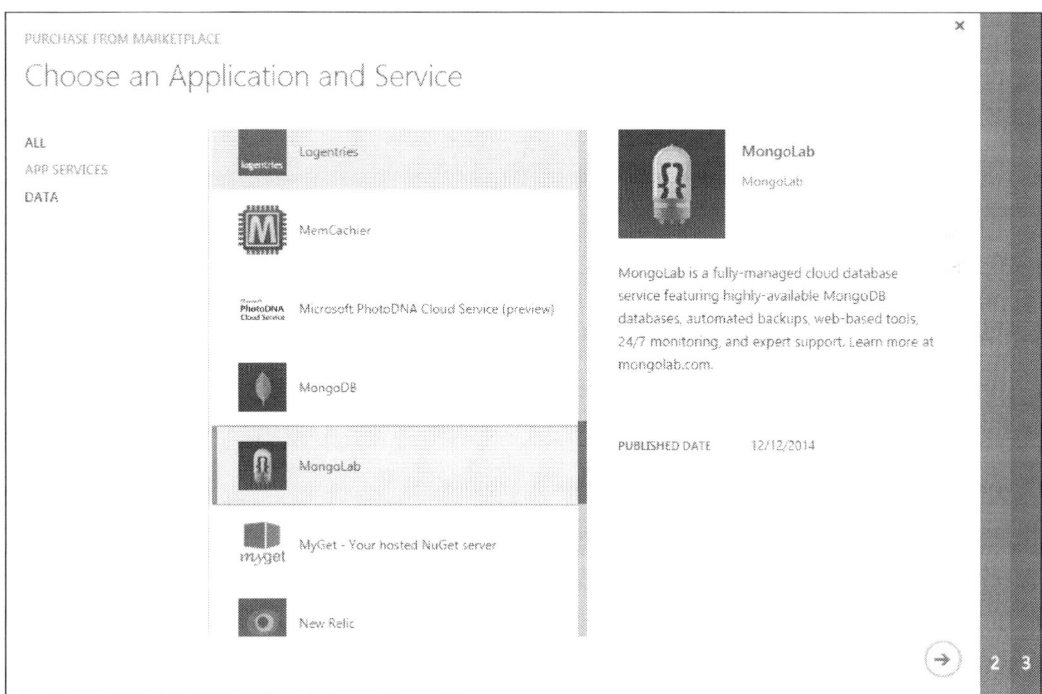

4. On the next page, you can personalize the subscription. Starting from the plan (the price is shown in the local currency) the set of which is unique for every vendor, you can set a promotion code if you have it, subscription, name and region. Select the **Sandbox** plan – it is free to use and test.

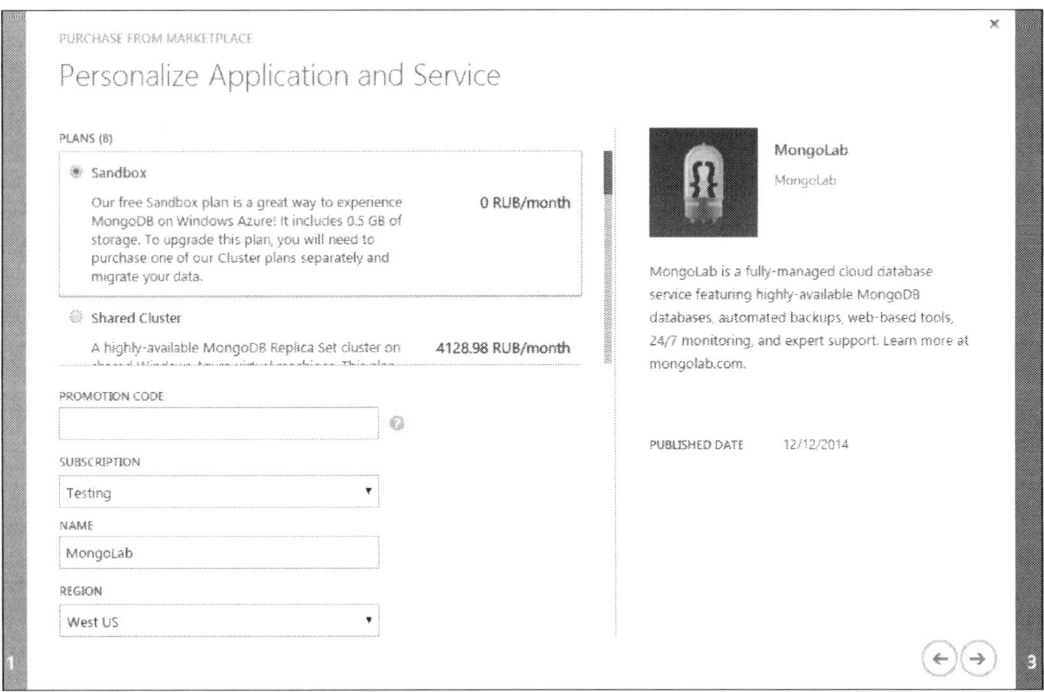

5. Review the information on the next page and press the **Purchase** button.

The last step is to get the connection information for the created MongoDB database. It can be done by going to the Marketplace pane on the left-hand side of the Microsoft Azure portal and pressing the **Connection info** button.

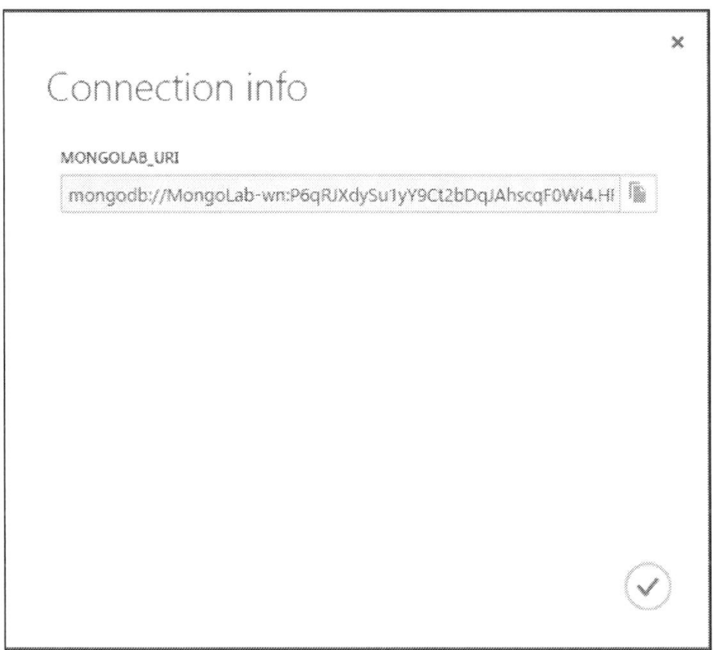

If you change the connection string for your current data source in the application configuration to that one, it will be used further. As it is MongoDB-as-a-service, it provides an opportunity to change some settings by pressing the **Manage** button; however, the most difficult tasks—infrastructure-related and scalability—are performed by a vendor.

Summary

This chapter provided an overview of the Microsoft Azure Marketplace and Microsoft Azure DocumentDB, and their use to create an account for MongoDB as a service and the use of Microsoft Azure DocumentDB to store data as a JSON document in the cloud using the API and document explorer.

Index

A

B

C

I

K

L

M

N

O

P

Q

R

S

T

U

V

W

Z

Thank you for buying

Building Web Services with Microsoft Azure

About Packt Publishing

Packt, pronounced 'packed', published its first book, *Mastering phpMyAdmin for Effective MySQL Management*, in April 2004, and subsequently continued to specialize in publishing highly focused books on specific technologies and solutions.

Our books and publications share the experiences of your fellow IT professionals in adapting and customizing today's systems, applications, and frameworks. Our solution-based books give you the knowledge and power to customize the software and technologies you're using to get the job done. Packt books are more specific and less general than the IT books you have seen in the past. Our unique business model allows us to bring you more focused information, giving you more of what you need to know, and less of what you don't.

Packt is a modern yet unique publishing company that focuses on producing quality, cutting-edge books for communities of developers, administrators, and newbies alike. For more information, please visit our website at `www.packtpub.com`.

About Packt Enterprise

In 2010, Packt launched two new brands, Packt Enterprise and Packt Open Source, in order to continue its focus on specialization. This book is part of the Packt Enterprise brand, home to books published on enterprise software – software created by major vendors, including (but not limited to) IBM, Microsoft, and Oracle, often for use in other corporations. Its titles will offer information relevant to a range of users of this software, including administrators, developers, architects, and end users.

Writing for Packt

We welcome all inquiries from people who are interested in authoring. Book proposals should be sent to `author@packtpub.com`. If your book idea is still at an early stage and you would like to discuss it first before writing a formal book proposal, then please contact us; one of our commissioning editors will get in touch with you.

We're not just looking for published authors; if you have strong technical skills but no writing experience, our experienced editors can help you develop a writing career, or simply get some additional reward for your expertise.

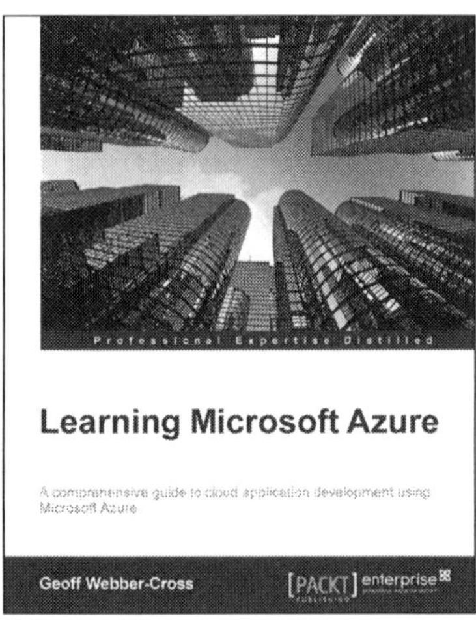

Learning Microsoft Azure

ISBN: 978-1-78217-337-3 Paperback: 430 pages

A comprehensive guide to cloud application development using Microsoft Azure

1. Build, deploy, and host scalable applications in the cloud using Windows Azure.
2. Enhance your mobile applications to receive notifications via the notifications Hub.
3. Features a full enterprise Azure case study with detailed examples and explanations.

Microsoft Azure Development Cookbook

Second Edition

ISBN: 978-1-78217-032-7 Paperback: 422 pages

Over 70 advanced recipes for developing scalable services with the Microsoft Azure platform

1. Understand, create, and use the hosting services of Azure for processing and storage.
2. Explore different approaches to implement scalable systems by using Azure services.
3. Pick the appropriate automation strategy and minimize management efforts.

Please check **www.PacktPub.com** for information on our titles

Automating Microsoft Azure with PowerShell

ISBN: 978-1-78439-887-3 Paperback: 156 pages

Automate Microsoft Azure tasks using Windows PowerShell to take full control of your Microsoft Azure deployments

1. Deploy and manage virtual machines, virtual networks, and an online database for application provisioning, maintenance, and high availability of your data.
2. Upload your movies, data, and disk images to the cloud with just a single line of PowerShell code.
3. A pragmatic guide full of hands-on examples on managing Microsoft Azure using PowerShell.

Learning Windows Azure Mobile Services for Windows 8 and Windows Phone 8

ISBN: 978-1-78217-192-8 Paperback: 124 pages

A short, fast and focused guide to enhance your Windows 8 applications by leveraging the power of Windows Azure Mobile Services

1. Dive deep into Azure Mobile Services with a practical XAML-based case study game.
2. Enhance your applications with Push Notifications and Notifications Hub.
3. Follow step-by-step instructions for result-oriented examples.

42878169R00179

Made in the USA
Lexington, KY
11 July 2015